THE
DREAM BIBLE

THE
DREAM BIBLE

THE DEFINITIVE GUIDE TO
EVERY DREAM SYMBOL UNDER THE MOON

Brenda Mallon

A GODSFIELD BOOK

First published in Great Britain in 2003
by Godsfield Press Ltd,
Laurel House, Station Approach, Alresford,
Hampshire SO24 9JH, UK

10 9 8 7 6 5 4 3 2 1

Designed and produced for Godsfield Press by
The Bridgewater Book Company

Illustrators: Kim Glass and Ivan Hissey
Picture researcher: Lynda Marshall

Printed and bound in China

ISBN 1-84181-190-4

Contents

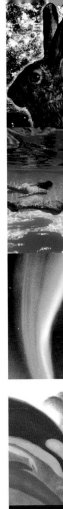

Introduction: Why We Dream

Dreams are real life, too

Every night we dream of images that puzzle and amaze us. For two to three hours a night, we journey in a landscape where the rules of everyday life are waived. Anything and everything is possible: people fly, fish walk, and loved ones who have left us return and speak to us once more.

It is no accident that we spend a third of our lives in sleep and that much of this is in dream sleep. This is a major part of our lives and it is clear that sleep is not just about giving the body much-needed time to relax, rest, and repair, but about providing us with the opportunity to dream.

The Dream Bible will show you why dream dramas take place and why it is important to learn the language of your dreams. You will discover how to delve for the deeper meanings they contain, to discover your inner wisdom.

DREAMING HAS MANY PURPOSES:

- *To clarify problems*
- *To reveal true feelings about others*
- *To take pressure off when times are tough*
- *To give insight into our motivation*
- *To let us experiment with different actions*
- *To act as a catharsis*
- *To develop creativity*
- *To rehearse future success*

EARLIEST DREAM BOOKS

Dreams have fascinated people for millennia. Among the earliest "books" are dream dictionaries dating from four thousand years ago. The Epic of Gilgamesh, from the seventh century B.C.E., contains a remarkable sequence of dreams reflecting universal themes, such as death and conflict, that we too meet in our own millennium. So, when we study our dreams, we continue an ancient tradition.

Throughout history, dreams have been used in the diagnosis of illness, in problem solving, and as warnings. Many great thinkers, including the scientist Albert Einstein, the author Robert Louis Stevenson, and the artists Salvador Dali and William Blake, have all been inspired by dreams.

When we fall asleep, we cross the threshold between our waking world and the world of our unconscious, that part of ourselves that is so often unacknowledged. We go to the places that we may try to avoid during daylight hours. In that dream darkness we may meet monsters and magicians, creatures who whisper to us, and strangers who threaten us. Whatever we meet, it comes to bring insight and well-being. However, we often have to walk through deep shadows before we can reach the light, and we may have to fall apart before we experience true wholeness.

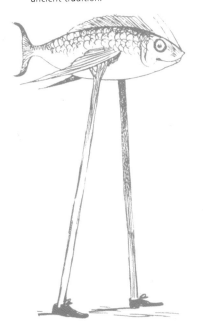

LEFT *The creatures that populate the world of our dreams may be strange and disturbing.*

THE BODY-MIND CONNECTION

We dream to promote well-being in body as well as in spirit. The condition of your body influences your dreams in many subtle ways. Research shows that people who suffer from migraines or asthma have certain types of dreams prior to an attack. If they understand their dreams, this gives them time to take their medication to alleviate the

severity of the attacks. The Ancient Greeks called such dreams *prodromic*, which means "to run before," indicating that the dreams come before any overt signs of illness. Therefore, your dreams can act as an early-warning system, once you learn their language.

The Greek philosopher Hippocrates, the father of modern medicine, saw the diagnostic potential of dreams. He recognized that dreams could show physical and psychological unease long before there were obvious physical symptoms to alert the dreamer. Oncology specialist Bernie Siegel, author of *Love, Medicine, and Miracles*, emphasizes the importance of dreams in his work with certain cancer patients for whom earlier treatment has been unsuccessful. These dreams inform, advise, and heal the spirit even when all hope seems gone.

If you record your dreams, you will discover patterns that alert you to possible stress and ill health, as well as indicators that you are successfully caring for yourself.

LEARNING THE LANGUAGE OF DREAMS

In dreamscapes where dreams hold sway we have to learn another language. It is a language of image, symbol, myth, and metaphor. When dreaming, we become the stuff of our dreams: We are the burning house, we are the flying angel, we are the broken machine, and we are the driver of the fire truck. Each part of the dream represents a part of life: Relationships, anxieties, and successes.

Language is used dramatically in dreams and includes a common vocabulary. This vocabulary comes in the form of universal themes, such as dreams of falling, of being chased, of teeth falling out, and many others, which we will explore later in this book. In learning the language of dreams, we can discover how knowledge of the collective unconscious and of archetypes (see page 17) can help our

spiritual, emotional, and intuitive growth.

The brain and the mind still hold deep mysteries and no one knows all the powers that lie there. We do know that nightmares are wake-up calls to look at what is happening in our lives and that the saying "to sleep on it" reflects the common-sense awareness that dreams help us solve problems. *The Dream Bible* will help you become your own expert translator of your dream language.

RIGHT *Universal themes, such as falling, form part of the dramatic vocabulary of our dreams.*

WHEREVER HUMANS HAVE BEEN, we have always used symbols. It seems that we cannot do without them; they appear to be hardwired into our minds and bodies. Symbols have a power beyond words, carrying a multitude of meanings that speak to the soul, the mind, and the emotions. Symbols challenge us to go beyond what stares us in the face, to go beyond the obvious. Symbols are

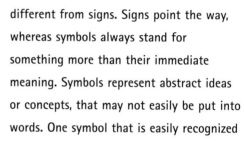

different from signs. Signs point the way, whereas symbols always stand for something more than their immediate meaning. Symbols represent abstract ideas or concepts, that may not easily be put into words. One symbol that is easily recognized is the dove, the symbol of peace. A symbol of protection throughout much of the world is the Christian cross.

In dreams a symbol always shares some quality with an object. This quality may be in the form of the shape, color, emotional tone, function, or setting.

The language of the unconscious is the language of symbols. Used in therapy and in self-help, symbols help us heal and develop the potential to become our true, authentic selves. Symbols express an inner reality of which we are often unaware, although humankind has been in touch with this reality since earliest times.

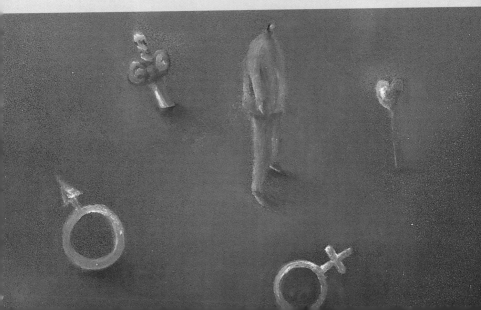

Dream Wisdom

Chinese Dream Diviners

ONE OF THE EARLIEST CHINESE BOOKS about dreaming was written in 600 B.C.E. It was called *Shi Ching*, meaning "Book of Songs," and was devoted to explaining the meaning of a variety of dreams. Later books provided a list of the common categories of dreams that we can still recognize in our own dreams today: For example, people, animals, objects, rites and rituals, gods and goddesses, flowers, plants and trees, and feelings and emotions.

In Chinese culture, a dream diviner would listen to the dreamer's description of a dream and provide a meaning.

Dream diviners would offer an interpretation of the dream using symbols that applied to a particular category. Dream divination still takes place in cities such as Hong Kong.

DIFFERENT TYPES OF DREAMS FROM CHINESE TRADITION THAT ARE SIMILAR TO UNIVERSAL DREAM THEMES:

Direct dreams—*easily understood and plain in their meaning*

Symbolic dreams—*could be interpreted through the mythic and cultural symbols they include*

Incubated dreams—*provide the answers to sincerely asked questions*

Opposition dreams—*the opposite of the way the dreamer thinks or behaves when awake*

Thought dreams—*reflect the dreamer's waking thoughts*

Seasonal or environmental dreams—*a response to a change in season or an environmental event*

Medical dreams—*show disorders or disease in the body or mind*

Dreams and Initiation Rites

IN MANY SPIRITUAL TRADITIONS, dreams are or have been taken as signs that a new beginning or initiation is about to take place.

In the Taoist religion, dreams indicated when an initiate was ready to become a priest. Part of the ritual involved the initiate taking drugs to destroy inner negative forces known as *corpse-demons*. The drugs brought on vivid dreams, including dreams that the initiate's parents were dead, that a grave had been destroyed, that his house had burnt down, and that he was suffering mutilating punishments. These nightmares signified the destruction of his former life and indicated that he was ready to take on his new role as a Taoist priest.

RIGHT *The intense ritual of initiation ceremonies can bring about vivid dreams.*

In many shamanistic systems, when the initiate and the priest share the same dream on the same night, it is a sign that the initiation can proceed. In the Ancient Egyptian cult of the goddess Isis, when the priest and the initiate dreamed of the goddess simultaneously, it was regarded as a sign that the initiation ritual could begin.

Initiation rites often include cutting or changing the hair, and this may feature in dreams at times of initiation.

Symbola

IN HIS BOOK, *The Art of Looking Sideways*, Alan Fletcher describes how, when two people in Ancient Greece made a contract, they broke something in half (such as a plate), so that each party could be identified by having the matching piece. These broken pieces were called *symbola*, from the word *symballien*, meaning "to join together." Thus, *symbol* came to mean one thing that represented another, always standing for something more.

Think about a coin. The metal may not have much intrinsic value, yet with a head of state stamped on it and a value attached to it, it can buy us what we need. The dollar bill, made of paper, symbolizes the financial power of the U.S. Treasury and allows us to trade. Symbols in dreams carry the same potential: They represent something unseen and allow us to perceive that which is invisible.

A SYMBOL:

The visible appearance of an invisible meaning.

ALAN FLETCHER: THE ART OF LOOKING SIDEWAYS

Dispelling Dreams

THE IROQUOIS TRIBE of North America had a highly developed "religion of dreaming," as the Jesuit missionary priests described it. To these Native Americans, dreams were wishes of the soul that had to be listened to and acted upon. Dreams had to be played out, danced out, or, in some other way, brought into waking life. Otherwise, the unfortunate aspect of the dream would become a reality.

If a warrior dreamed that he had been afraid and had run away from an enemy in his dream, he would ask his tribesmen to recreate the event by acting out the scenario, while he went into hiding for a short time. This cathartic process allowed the dreamer to dispel the dream fear and insured that the whole community understood his feelings. By enacting the dream in a safe way, unconscious fears were exorcized.

RIGHT *The reenactment of a dream allows the dreamer to dispel its negative effects.*

This reenactment technique can be used to dispel negative emotions that linger after a disturbing dream. You could also make drawings or choose objects to represent dream characters, then replay the dream with your preferred outcome. For instance, you could bring in another person to help you or to create a diversion so you could escape. The process of reenactment empowers you and dispels dream fears.

Lucid Dreams

MORPHEUS, A SHAPESHIFTING GOD, is called the father of sleep. He leads us to the land of dreams, where we find dreams that inspire us. *To inspire* means "to breathe life into," and in its original use it meant that the spirit of life came as you took your first breath. In inspirational dreams, you find new ways of living, fresh ideas that may lead to you making radical changes in your life. Many of these inspirational dreams involve lucid dreaming.

In lucid dreams, we know we are dreaming while we are having the dream; we don't have to wait until we wake up to remember it. A significant factor in lucid dreaming is that you can change the content of the dream while you are dreaming. Anything is possible. You can experiment with new lovers or try exciting sports that you would never attempt in waking life and, as you do so, know that at any point you can change anything you do not like.

Lucid dreams demonstrate the wonderful breadth of our creativity. In lucid dreams we can fly, venture into space, solve problems, heal ourselves and others, and create the world that we want to live in. In lucid dreams, we can dissolve boundaries and move into higher states of consciousness.

Archetypes

THE FAMOUS PSYCHOANALYST CARL JUNG introduced the term *archetypes*. These are images that come from the deepest part of our unconscious minds and bring us symbols that occur in all cultures throughout history. They often appear in those numinous dreams (see page 29) that have the power to change our lives. The following archetypes may appear in your dreams:

PERSONA

This is the mask that we wear to play different roles in different social situations. In dreams, we may feel hurt because we have been criticized or rejected and feel that we are not understood. We have to take care not to confuse our roles with the person we are beneath that mask.

THE SHADOW

This is the aspect of our nature that we may prefer to keep hidden. It is the aggressive, malevolent side that causes pain and discord. The shadow often appears in dreams as a dark, threatening figure or may be a faceless intruder if the dreamer has not yet acknowledged the darker side of their nature.

ANIMUS/ANIMA

In our dreams, we meet our archetypal opposites. For women, this means that we are faced with our masculine energy, called *animus*. For men, the *anima* represents the female energy. Each of us has a masculine and a feminine dimension and part of our life journey is to accept both sides of ourselves so we can become balanced individuals.

Healing Dreams

HIPPOCRATES RECOGNIZED THAT dreams can communicate physical and psychological unease of which the dreamer is unaware when awake. He knew that dreams could help in the healing process.

Each year I run a workshop for people who are involved in the cancer journey. They may be caregivers, health professionals, or people who have or have had cancer. One year a woman called Irene came to my workshop. The only dreams she could recall were utterly dark and filled with terrible despair. She confided that, two years previously, her husband had died of cancer and then, to her utter dismay, her nineteen-year-old son had committed suicide. Irene was bereft and could barely get through each day. She was encouraged to draw her dreams and we talked about them in the group.

Irene returned to my workshop a year later. She said, "I had to come back because I know now that the dreams helped to save me. I wanted to show you this dream." Irene displayed her drawing of a glorious rainbow. She was on the left-hand side and at the bottom of the rainbow on the right-hand side were two figures: Her husband and son. "I can reach them in dreams now. We haven't talked yet, but we will." She was reconnected by that symbolic bridge between earth and heaven, and this time she wept with joy because she had found a means of coming to terms with her bereavement and had regained the will to go on living.

Psychic Dreams

DREAMS THAT FORETELL EVENTS have been recorded all over the world. Anthropologists have shown that belief in a supernatural means of perception in dreams is universal among primitive peoples. The Ancient Greeks saw dreams as portals into the future and a popular Roman belief was that dreams were messages sent by gods or spirits.

The Romans recorded numerous predictive dreams, including the dream of the murder of Julius Caesar. Caesar's wife Calpurnia dreamed that the roof of the house had fallen in and that Caesar had been stabbed and lay dying in her arms. On waking, she warned her husband. He tried to postpone the meeting at the Senate but was persuaded to allow it to go ahead by one of the conspirators. Hours later he was stabbed.

Today, we also have predictive dreams, as I know from my own dreams and from the hundreds of people who have told me about their personal dream experiences.

I feel that some dreams are like mystical experiences. Numerous times, I feel that I'm leaving my body—I feel very free and light. In this type of dream, I meet people, and find myself in places that I've never seen, although they frequently feel familiar. It is in this sort of dream that I see future or past events.

SALLY, QUOTED IN **VENUS DREAMING: A GUIDE TO WOMEN'S DREAMS AND NIGHTMARES**

THERE IS DEEP YEARNING TO UNDERSTAND what our dreams mean. For thousands of years, people have recorded dreams and developed different ways of making sense of them.

Today, many psychotherapists like myself use dreams to discover the root of anxiety and to find inner strengths to overcome difficulties. Therapists and dream specialists can help uncover meanings, but it is for the dreamer to make sense of the dream. One technique is to build up your ability to see connections between the symbolic images they

reveal and your waking life. This is what the philosopher Aristotle was referring to when he said that the art of dream interpretation requires the ability "to see resemblances." In learning the language of dreams, you will learn to trust your own interpretations increasingly. As you build up your own "dream database," you will have a unique reference to help in dream analysis.

Written by the Ancient Greek dream diviner, Artemidorus, the *Onierocritica* describes dreams that were a response to the day's debris—a sorting-out of the trivial events—and dreams that startled the soul. Those puzzling dreams that involve thought and reflection he called *allegorikon*. He pointed out that dreams should be seen in the context of the dreamer's life, emotional state, situation, and character.

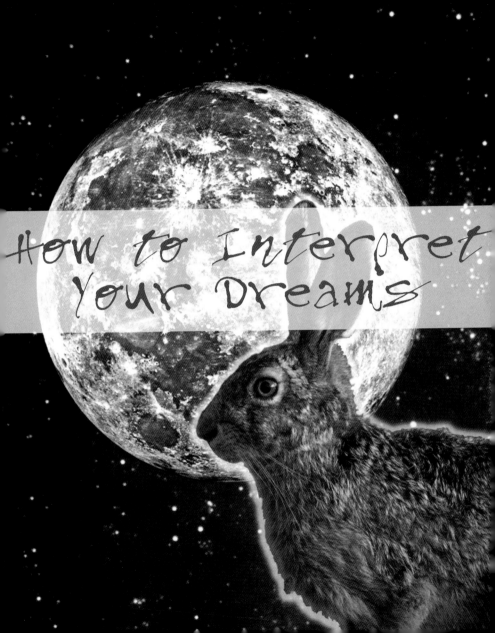

How to Interpret Your Dreams

Recording Your Dreams

YOUR DREAM JOURNAL can be a sketchpad, a bound book, or a ring binder—it's up to you. I find it useful to transfer my dream notes into a more permanent record, where I include more details of the dream. On the right-hand page I record the dream, and on the left-hand page I write any connections I make to help me interpret it.

- Keep a notebook by your bed and enter the day's date.
- Record your dream on waking.
- Draw any images that were particularly strong or unusual.
- Don't censor your dreams; write down the details even if they appear foolish or irrelevant.
- Write down any names or snatches of conversation.
- Record key words if you are in a hurry.
- Don't try to understand the dream while you are writing it up.
- Give your dream a title.

RECALLING DREAMS

- If you have difficulty recalling dreams, write down your mood on waking and any fragments of your dreams you can remember.
- Write yourself a note before you go to sleep: "Tonight I'll remember a dream."
- Try to remember a dream at a time that is out of your usual routine.

ABOVE *Understanding your dreams will lead you toward inner wisdom.*

YOU ARE YOUR OWN BEST EXPERT

The person who best understands the meaning of your dream is you. You dreamed it and you hold the key to it because your dream is about your life. A dream therapist like myself may help illuminate the meaning, but you are the one who can unlock the wisdom in the dream. Use the questions in the panel below to guide you to make the connections. Answer these questions honestly—don't censor your first responses—and then look back at what you have written. When you look at the overall picture, what do you see?

Try not to bring any preconceptions to your interpretation of your dream as this could prevent you from arriving at its real meaning.

CONNECTIONS

- *What is the emotional feeling in the dream? Anxiety, pleasure, horror?*
- *What was your mood when you woke up? Unhappy, relieved, frustrated?*
- *What was the dream setting? Where you live now, a previous home, another country?*
- *Who acted in your dream drama? Your family, colleagues, friends?*
- *If you were in the dream, how were you behaving? Assertive, aggressive, passive?*
- *What about the color? Bright or dark tones? Brilliant Technicolor or subdued?*
- *Can you identify the trigger for the dream? A TV program, a conversation?*
- *What do you think the dream is telling you?*

Interpretation Techniques

THESE TECHNIQUES will help you work on your dreams so that you can readily understand and interpret them.

EMPTY-CHAIR METHOD

Gestalt therapy is based on the theory that in order to find the "whole picture," the *gestalt* of our selves, we need to discover the repressed and unconscious areas of the mind. Psychotherapist Fritz Perls found that dreams embodied rejected and repressed parts of ourselves. He believed that each element of the dream is part of the dreamer and that by looking at the significance of each we can realize the whole meaning of the dream. Thus, in a dream of a car, a highway, and a robber, there is some aspect of the dreamer that is symbolized by each element. This method is highly effective at unraveling the significance of all parts of the dream so that those repressed parts of ourselves can be recovered.

Set up a dialogue and learn from the responses you give yourself.

- Place an empty chair opposite yours.
- Imagine the dream element is sitting on the empty chair.
- Ask questions and imagine the replies:

Why are you bothering me?

What do you want?

Where are you from?

What can I do to stop you from pestering me in my dreams?

The replies you give are the key. They will reveal underlying concerns that may not be apparent in waking life. If it is possible to do so, you should tape record your replies and listen to the whole recording when you have finished.

DREAM INCUBATION

Dream incubation, from the Latin *incubatio*, which means "sleeping in a sanctuary," was practiced by many ancient cultures. The sanctuary might be a special cave, a shrine, a temple, or any designated power site. There, the earth gods or healing gods would be summoned to bring guidance. Purification rituals and meditation also took place and the person would sleep in a designated spot.

YOUR PERSONAL RITUAL

To practice dream incubation at home, you need to relax and prepare for a dream that responds to your question or request.

- Take a cleansing shower or bath and visualize washing away the cares of the day.

- Put on clean night clothes.
- Lie down and think about what you want from your dream. Be specific.
- Write down your request or question.
- As you fall asleep, think about the request or question.
- Next morning, write out your dream and see how it relates to your request.

BELOW *Followers of dream incubation slept in shrines, where the gods would influence their dreams.*

The Forgotten Language of Dreams

DREAMS CONTAIN METAPHORS and symbols that we use every day of our lives. The word *metaphor* comes from the Greek *meta*, meaning "over," and *pherein*, which means "to carry," so a metaphor carries one thing over to another. Examples of metaphorical expressions are "Her eyes were sparkling stars" or "He was a lion, strong and fearless." When you analyze your dreams, look for metaphors, because these strengthen images.

NAMES

"I met a man. I saw that his name was Wright and that he was applying for a job in my company." It's not too hard to work out the connection between "Wright" and "Mr. Right." This dreamer was hoping to meet Mr. Right, her ideal partner, when she had this dream.

RIGHT *The visual images that appear in our dreams may represent metaphorical expressions.*

PUNS

Puns add humor. For example, Ann Faraday, in her book *The Dream Game*, describes a woman who was having a problem with excessive alcohol intake. In a dream she comes across a puppy who "nips." The dreamer recognized that her alcohol "nips" were causing her pain.

HOMONYMS

Homonyms, words that sound the same but which have different meanings, give useful clues to dream meanings. Dreaming of a *pail* may really refer to being *pale* or unwell.

Recurring Dreams

RECURRING DREAMS ARE COMMON and reveal patterns in our lives. They deal with the personal unconscious, our unique experience of the world, and can help to make us aware of what hinders or motivates us.

When you have a notebook with two or three months of dreams recorded, read through it. See what recurring themes there are and look for patterns, such as dreams at times of stress. Women might see what they dream at the time of their period. Pick out special images in your dreams, both those you like and those you dislike. You'll be startled at the number of dreams you have forgotten all about, so reading your own dream journal can be like reading an adventure story.

Build up your own "dream database." For instance, write the heading "Animals" and make a note of any that have appeared in your dreams. Note when they appeared and any

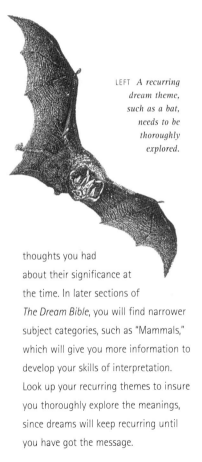

LEFT *A recurring dream theme, such as a bat, needs to be thoroughly explored.*

thoughts you had about their significance at the time. In later sections of *The Dream Bible*, you will find narrower subject categories, such as "Mammals," which will give you more information to develop your skills of interpretation. Look up your recurring themes to insure you thoroughly explore the meanings, since dreams will keep recurring until you have got the message.

The Need ~~for~~ Nightmares

NIGHTMARES, whether single or recurring, are wake-up calls. They urge us to pay attention to something that is causing us distress. They alert us to potential problems and help us face issues that we avoid when awake. They may appear as a result of post-traumatic stress as our psyche struggles to come to terms with disastrous events.

Whatever the nightmare theme, try the "face and conquer" technique used by the Senoi people of Malaysia. When awake, imagine that you turn and face the threat. Tell it what you want it to do or explain how it makes you feel. This gives you the opportunity to address your fears directly and helps dispel the anxiety. Also, speak from the point of view of the threat. What does it feel like if you swap roles and tell the nightmare from the threat's point of view? If you still cannot make sense of the nightmare after you have spent time on it, then let it go. Be patient, because some dreams are part of a longer process and other dreams will come along to help you solve the puzzle. Some dream meanings take a long time to crystallize.

LEFT *Nightmares urge us to pay attention to events that have caused distress.*

Numinous or "Big" Dreams

SOME DREAMS ARE SO VIVID and so powerful that they almost take your breath away. You wake up with a sense of awe, aware that something profound has happened. These are the dreams you never forget.

Psychoanalyst Carl Jung called such dreams *numinous* because they felt sacred and had an element of command about them. The dreamer often feels impelled to act after such a dream. Jung said, such dreams are "the richest jewels in the treasure house of the soul." You will find examples of such dreams throughout *The Dream Bible*.

Here are some pointers to help you recognize your own numinous, transformational dreams:

- They bring greater awareness to you, in an unforgettable way.
- They are out of the ordinary league of your dreams.
- They prompt you to look at your life from a fresh perspective.

ABOVE *Numinous dreams connect you with infinity and fill you with awe.*

- They reassure you in times of great stress or crisis.
- They give you the confidence to go on when you falter.
- They arouse and stimulate you to greater effort.
- They allow you to come to terms with death and loss.
- They bring greater spiritual awareness, inspiring a search for the meaning about what it is to be alive.
- They help you to recognize your vast potential.

YOUR BODY IS YOUR HOME and its place in dreams is highly significant. Dreams in which eyes, arms, heart, and brain appear may be directly connected to your physical condition. Is the dream symbolic, or does it connect to other areas? The heart symbolizes emotions, whereas the mouth is linked to communication, kissing, and eating.

Your dreams help you keep in good health and alert you to danger. In

3

my book *Dreams, Counseling and Healing*, I wrote about a woman who dreamed that her head had been X-rayed, showing a black hole at the base of her skull. The dream had such an impact that she saw a doctor and insisted on being X-rayed. On her X-ray, there was a black circle—a tumor that was successfully removed later.

Dreams can also offer remedies, indicate prognosis, help in the healing process, and reveal a pregnancy, giving us an additional source of medical information and support.

When personal illness strikes, dreams may show us a journey. We travel across empty plains, facing danger and touching the depths of despair, yet we travel on. Such "hero journeys," as mythologist Joseph Campbell calls them, are part of our personal growth. Carl Jung describes this as *individuation*. Our dreams help us reach the heights of our emotional, physical, and spiritual selves.

Starting with the Body

Starting with the Body

All elongated objects, such as sticks, tree trunks, and umbrellas (the opening of these last being comparable to an erection) may stand for the male organ ... In men's dreams, a necktie often appears as a symbol for the penis ...

SIGMUND FREUD: THE INTERPRETATION OF DREAMS

However simplistic Freud's view may seem now, the psychoanalyst did draw attention to the power of sexual symbolism in dreams. Today, we see the power of sexual symbols to market products all around us and, because the survival of all life depends on sexual intercourse, it is of vital importance and so we dream about it.

You may be surprised by your dreams about sex, but remember that all things are possible in this uncensored world. Don't be alarmed if you dream of making love with someone of the same or opposite sex, or of swapping partners. This may simply mean that your dreaming self is exploring all aspects of sexuality.

Part of the cycle of creation involves the fertilization of an egg and then birth: Thus eggs in dreams are highly significant. At the Christian Easter, decorated eggs represent new life, carrying through from an earlier pagan tradition.

I dream in Technicolor, with sound, smell, taste, everything. Some people have told me they dream in black and white, or silently. This has amazed me. My dreams are like being there.

BEVERLEY, PARTICIPANT AT A DREAM WORKSHOP

ABOVE *Sexual symbolism is an important and wholly natural element of our dreams. An erect umbrella may represent the penis.*

In some dreams, you may find that a human body is amalgamated with that of another creature. For example, you may dream of someone with the head of an eagle and the body of a man. Think about the qualities associated with the bird in your dream. An eagle's head may represent power and strength, whereas the head of an owl may be linked with wisdom.

Spirit healers may also bring bodily healing in dreams. There are many examples of people who have gone to bed feeling unwell and, having experienced a dream in which someone came to them and touched the afflicted part or brought rays of light to heal the whole body, woke up feeling well again. The healing power of dreams is as old as humanity.

Head AT THE TOP OF THE BODY, the head gives us our "head start." The brain (see page 37) is of crucial importance because the head, together with the heart, controls our whole system.

The head is a symbol of wisdom, knowledge, vigilance, learning, and power. Throughout history, heads were collected as trophies—either human heads, which the Celts collected, or heads from animals, such as bears, lions, and foxes. Such trophies symbolize power over others. If you have a dream featuring a head, consider how it relates to positive or negative aspects of control and judgment as well as cognitive, or thinking, ability.

Monster heads and grinning gargoyles carved on roofs and pillars were created both as protection for the building and to intimidate would-be attackers. Early Celts also carved stone heads as magical protectors.

Many migraine sufferers have dreams preceding an attack. Typical themes include being struck on the head and being shot in the head.

CONNECTIONS

◉ Being "head-hunted"

◉ "Head honcho"

◉ "Head of the household"

◉ "Headmaster" or
   "Headmistress"

◉ Out of control:
   "Head case"
   "Out of his head"

◉ "Head over heels in love"

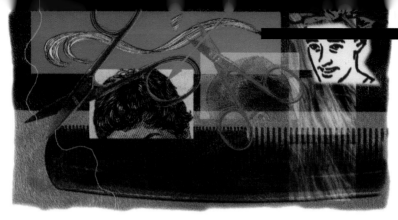

Hair

AS A SYMBOL, HAIR REPRESENTS ENERGY and fertility, natural growth, and crowning glory. Priests of many religions once shaved off the hair on their heads as a sign that they had renounced earthly desires. In statues of the Buddha, the topknot of hair symbolizes wisdom and light. One of the five symbols of faith for Sikhs is *kesh*, or "uncut hair." In the Hindu tradition, hair is a symbol of the soul because it grows out of the head, the place of consciousness. It grows again after it is cut and continues to grow after death.

Shaven heads also represent strength, mimicking the shaved heads of new army recruits or some right-wing extremists. A Masai mother shaves her warrior son's head at adolescence as he undertakes the rite of passage that takes him from boyhood to manhood.

Shaving the face is a Western rite; this can be seen in the gift of the first shaving kit from father to son. In sitting *shiva* (mourning) during the seven days following a death, Jewish men do not shave.

CONNECTIONS

- Could your dream of a visit to a hairdresser indicate a desire for a change of image?
- If you dream that you are losing your hair, you could be worried about a loss of authority.

SKULL THE SKULL IS A METAPHOR FOR DEATH and is used in paintings as a symbol for time passing and mortality. Pirates and buccaneers carried the "skull and crossbones" flag to strike fear into the hearts of their victims and the symbol is still found on bottles that contain poison. The motorcycle club, the Hell's Angels, also uses the skull and crossbones.

As the skull forms the housing for the brain and support for the face, eyes, and mouth, it has always been given high symbolic value. In ancestor worship, human mummified heads represent veneration. Norse warriors kept the skulls of their slain victims and turned them into drinking cups. Skulls in piles indicate genocide or can represent the Holocaust.

Jesus was crucified on a hill called Golgotha, which means "place of the skull." Foul deeds are indicated when a skull is lying on the ground, since murderers often bury their victims in shallow graves and the skeleton is readily exposed.

In the dream I see a skull quite clearly: Clean, shining, and white. I see from the shape of the cheekbones that it is that of a Chinese person. The skull is a great gift and I know that to receive it is a great privilege.

The dreamer, who was a Buddhist, felt that the dream represented new understanding. She associated it with the festival of Ching Ming, when the Chinese go to the graves of their ancestors, take the bones out of their urns, and clean, polish, and replace them.

CONNECTION

If you dream of a skull, think about any anxieties about death that you might have had, for instance, brushes with death in an accident.

CONNECTIONS

◈ *If you dream of injury to your brain,*
  is there a physical cause?

◈ *Are you being "brainy" or clever at*
  the moment, or do you need to be?

◈ *Do you have a "lot on your mind,"*
  which is causing you stress?

Brain

THE BRAIN IS NOT A SOLID MASS. It is a series of fluid-filled corridors, a maze of connections. The brain and the heart are the two most important organs in the body. To dream of your brain indicates that you need to think about the message of the dream. Does the dream relate to physical injury? Are you suffering from headaches that you need to have treated by a physician?

A "brainstorm" symbolizes a flash of inspiration that can strike at any time.

Inca excavations have unearthed many skulls with holes in them. "Brain surgeons" drilled holes into the craniums of people who had suffered head injuries in battles or who had neurological illnesses. This process was called *trephination* or *trepanning* and was believed to reduce pressure on the brain. These excavated skulls showed that healing had taken place and the patients had survived their ordeal.

Face

EXPRESSIONS ON FACES IN DREAMS CAN TELL YOU A GREAT DEAL, even when no words are spoken. If a person has no face, with no features of eyes, nose, and mouth, it may mean that they are "faceless" or inscrutable. We sometimes describe people who hide behind their work roles as "faceless bureaucrats." Does this represent someone in your life?

Look at the connections with language. Do you have to "face up" to a difficult issue? Sometimes we say that someone is "bare faced," meaning that they are shameless and unconcerned about activities that would make others feel guilty.

If you see one person with two faces, or a face that changes dramatically, in a dream it could indicate "two-faced" actions or behavior. On one level, the person appears to do one thing, then does the opposite and so cannot be trusted. This duality can be applied to everyone, so think about whether it applies to your dream character—or to you in your waking life.

CONNECTION

If you dream of a faceless individual, perhaps there is someone in your life who is unwilling to allow you to get to know the "real person."

Cheek

ROSY CHEEKS OFTEN REFLECT GOOD HEALTH, and the reddened cheeks of a clown symbolize humor and slapstick comedy. Sunken cheeks indicate poor nourishment and sadness. We also see people with cheeks drawn in after war or a state of siege. If cheeks are emphasized in a dream, consider how they relate to your health.

If some one is "cheeky" in your dream, are they being rude and impudent? If cheeks are emphasized it might refer to this kind of behavior. To "give cheek" is to be insolent. It also connects to "bare-faced cheek," which is to be so assured and arrogant that you don't take other people's views into account.

If cheeks and jaw are significant, this may refer to being "cheek by jowl" with someone: Being too intimate in an underhanded way, which will cause trouble for a third party.

"Cheek" may also refer to the buttocks, so look out for any double meaning in your dream.

CONNECTIONS

- *If the cheeks are red, have you blushed or felt embarrassed recently?*
- *Has someone been insulting while covering it with a smile so that they appear cheeky rather than aggressive?*

Nose WE BREATHE AND TAKE IN AROMAS through the nose. Our sense of smell tells us whether our environment is sweet or putrid and helps us identify food that is unfit for consumption. "Having a nose" for news indicates the ability to sniff out interesting stories and ground-breaking coups.

Consider the shape and size of the nose in your dream. Can you make any connections to people you know? Sometimes, wine masters have a well-developed "nose" that aids their ability to identify the quality and subtleties of wine. There is also the notion that a man with a large nose has a large penis.

If your nose is injured in a dream, does it reflect a waking physical difficulty such as hay fever or rhinitis? Or could it symbolize that you are acting out of pique, "cutting off your nose to spite your face," that is, hurting yourself by being proud and unyielding?

CONNECTIONS

◉ *To be "nosy" or "to poke your nose into someone else's business" indicates interference.*

◉ *"To smell a rat" is to have a hunch that something is wrong.*

◉ *"Led by the nose" is to be under the control of someone else, like a bull that is led by a ring through its nose.*

Mouth

MOUTHS ALLOW US TO SPEAK, EAT, WHISTLE, and kiss. Sometimes the mouth can betray us with a slip of the tongue or, in the case of Judas Iscariot, when he kissed the cheek of Jesus Christ he sealed his fate—Jesus was crucified and Judas, in his shame, committed suicide.

In some cultures, a woman's mouth is covered by a veil because the mouth is equated with the symbol *vagina dentate*, or "vagina with teeth." The labia of the vagina are also referred to as "lips." Generally, there are many sexual connections and mouth/vulva symbolism is found worldwide. This sexual aspect is highlighted in the attention drawn to lips by lipstick, which even Queen Cleopatra used.

CONNECTIONS

◉ *Blue lips indicate problems with blood circulation and may symbolize death.*

◉ *Is someone "mouthing off" in your dream, giving vent to anger by shouting?*

Teeth IF YOU DREAM ABOUT YOUR TEETH

or a visit to the dentist, it may be simply that you are anxious about the condition of your teeth. This may be a dream warning to have a dental check-up. However, many dreams about losing teeth come at a time of change, such as when leaving home for the first time or when a relationship or an attachment has ended.

Wisdom teeth, the last of our four molars, erupt when we are older and have more knowledge. If you dream of these teeth, do you need to "wise up" and be more intelligent about a particular situation? Or does the dream reflect emerging knowledge, such as the following example?

In the dream, I became aware that my teeth were beginning to loosen, crack, and fall from my mouth. I reached into the back of my mouth and painlessly extracted molars with jagged-edged roots. I experienced no fear, but was so intrigued that I told my mother. She said that she had had exactly the same dream during the first few weeks of each of her pregnancies and joked that I must be pregnant. What she didn't know was that I was indeed about seven weeks pregnant.

CONNECTION

⊙ *Do you need help in developing your "bite," namely your assertive side?*

Tongue

AS WELL AS HELPING US TO TALK AND EAT, tongues reveal the state of our health. In Western and Chinese medicine, they are examined to aid diagnosis when someone is ill. If you dream of a tongue, it would be worth checking your own in a mirror to see if it looks healthy.

There are many connections between the tongue and sexuality. In medieval times, the tongue symbolized the penis and a stuck-out tongue was the equivalent of showing the middle finger (see page 51). Devils and insatiable beasts were often depicted with their tongues sticking out in a lewd fashion to continue this phallic connection.

Think about how your tongue connects to your power of speech and what you truly want to say. In an ancient Hindu story, those who tell lies are sent to hell, where their tongues grow enormously long. If you dream that your tongue is very long, perhaps you're not being truthful in your waking life.

CONNECTIONS

◎ *"Tongue-tied" means that you are unable to get your words out. Are you having difficulty communicating?*

◎ *"Do you need to "hold your tongue" in a disagreement?*

◎ *Do you want to give someone a "tongue lashing"?*

Eyes

IN MYTHOLOGY, the eye is sacred because it symbolizes vision and wisdom. The "eye of God" is all-seeing and all-knowing. Both the eye of God and the eye also relate to transcendent heavenly wisdom and spiritual illumination.

The third eye symbolizes your intuitive, psychic ability and an element of "second sight," being able to see what others cannot. This could relate to seeing into the future. If this is so, it may protect you from "the evil eye," which reputedly brings misfortune.

Dreaming of eyes relates to your ability to see. The size, shape, color, and other details of the eyes will influence the meaning for you. Eyes wide open indicate awareness, whereas closed eyes may indicate a desire not to see or a fear that what you see will upset or frighten you.

CONNECTIONS

◎ *Seeing "eye to eye"—Are you getting along well with someone?*

◎ *"An eye for an eye"—Are you feeling vengeful?*

◎ *"Eye sore"—Is something offending you at the moment?*

◎ *Does "eye" symbolize "I" the person? In dreams, "my eye is hurting" may indicate "I am hurting."*

◎ *Eyeglasses will aid sight if they are the correct prescription, but otherwise they distort vision. Do the eyeglasses in your dream help or hinder?*

Ears

THE ABILITY TO RECEIVE NEW INFORMATION FROM OTHERS, and also to listen to your own inner voice may be represented when ears are emphasized in dreams. Secrets are also whispered into ears, and if this happens in your dream you may be anxious that people are whispering about you behind your back.

In mythology, the ear is linked to divine inspiration. Gods whispered in ears as dreamers slept and told of events that would come to pass.

Deafness in dreams may symbolize problems with communication. "To turn a deaf ear" is to choose deliberately not to hear what may be unpleasant to you. You may need to think about any situations you have been avoiding and give them some attention.

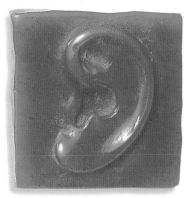

CONNECTIONS

◉ *Hearing aids—Are you concerned about your hearing or do you need to listen to others more attentively?*

◉ *Earrings—These symbolize decoration and ornamentation. Do you feel the need to add some glitter to brighten yourself up?*

◉ *"In one ear and out the other"—Are you having problems with your memory? Could it be linked to stress? We are often forgetful when stressed.*

Throat

THE THROAT IS LINKED TO VOCAL cords and the ability to speak. It also connects the body to the head, linking feeling with thoughts. Sometimes, when we have trouble expressing emotions, we feel a constriction in our throat. If you dream of problems in the throat area it may reflect difficulty in saying what you feel. In this dream, you can see intense anxiety:

It's dark. There are two versions of me—one standing in a lake and the other standing on my shoulders. The water is rising quickly but I can't move. As the water reaches my chin the "me" standing on my shoulders starts talking; then, a knife appears in the "me's" hands. I reach down and

slice the throat of the "me" standing in the water. Both versions of "me" fall into the water. The first "me" is bleeding profusely and the second is drowning. Then I wake up.

The double suicide in the water symbolizes the dreamer's emotional life. This young woman feels "out of her depth" and at risk. She is also stuck. She "can't move." Who is she? Which of these two "me's" is really her? Why is there so much self-harm? As with many dreams of the body, you can learn a lot by looking at the different elements of the content and relating it to events in your life at the time of the dream.

CONNECTION

◎ *Are you feeling "choked up" about anything? It could indicate that you are finding it impossible to make your feelings known to others.*

Breast

THE BREAST PROVIDES OUR FIRST sustenance and symbolizes love, affection, intimacy, and nurturing. Breasts are linked to sexuality and are a source of attraction. However, size isn't everything, as this dream told to me by a thirty-year-old man indicates:

I am in the lounge with my friend Jane, who is very attractive. Suddenly, her breasts begin to inflate until they are the size of basketballs. I am completely turned off. Then they deflate, and she is attractive again. This happens several times.

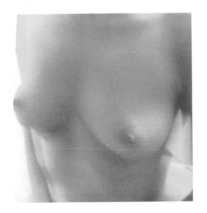

Cynthia Pearson, who runs dream groups in America, reported the dream of a woman who had had reconstructive surgery following a mastectomy. In the dream, she was cradling her reconstructed breast, which was wearing a baby's bonnet, and she was singing to it. This act of symbolic nurturing emphasizes the willingness to accept her new breast in a positive way.

Starting with the Body

CONNECTIONS

◎ *"In the bosom of the family"—Being at the heart or center of the family.*

◎ *"Make a clean breast of it"—To tell the complete truth after a period of delay or lying.*

Back THE BACK MAY REPRESENT WHAT CANNOT be seen or what is behind us. What is happening behind your back in your dream? Have you turned your back on anything?

The spine runs down the back and supports the body, symbolizing strength. Having "backbone" represents courage. Being "spineless" has the opposite meaning.

Dreams of being stabbed in the back may indicate feelings of betrayal. Harry Bosma, who suffered from chronic fatigue syndrome, had violent dreams in which this happened. He felt that the back-stabbing symbolized his sense that his body had turned against him.

CONNECTIONS

- *To "back off"—Do you need to remove yourself from a difficult situation to give yourself time to think? Do you want someone else to "back off" and give you more space?*

- *"Back up"—Do you want more support at the moment? Is there a situation at home or at work in which you need public approval?*

- *Do you need to go back to any unfinished business from the past?*

Nails

LIKE THE TALONS OF BIRDS AND THE CLAWS OF ANIMALS, our nails have many practical uses and can also be used as weapons. The length of the nails, their condition, and their cleanliness will give you clues about the significance of your dream.

In magical rituals, nail clippings from a victim were used in potions to bring harm. Sometimes, images of the target were painted on walls or made as effigies or wax figures. By injuring the image, it was believed that you damaged the person or animal it represented.

When they appear in dreams, nails may also refer to metal nails used in buildings. Nails may symbolize binding because they are used to join materials together. In the Christian tradition, nails symbolize Christ's agony and passion when he was nailed to the cross and crucified.

"Nailing your colors to the mast" indicates that you have decided on your position and have made a public display so that there can be no doubt about what you believe. Does your dream refer to a recent decision that you have made?

CONNECTIONS

◎ *Are you being "nailed down" at the moment, and made to give an explanation?*

◎ *Are you "hitting the nail on the head," getting to a definite conclusion?*

Arms

OUR ARMS AND HANDS ALLOW US TO HOLD ON, to move around, and to swim. They enable us to use tools in ways that other animals cannot. In dreams featuring arms, look at the muscle tone or any other significant feature, such as tattoos. Two arms raised in the air may represent submission, "hands up," or jubilation, as when a winning goal is kicked and the crowd reacts.

Arms may refer to weapons and carrying arms may indicate an aggressive stance. A "call to arms" means bringing people together in preparation for war, whereas a "coat of arms" is a heraldic emblem of the family.

CONNECTIONS

- "Keep at arm's length"—To keep at a distance, to keep others from being too familiar.
- "Up in arms"—To be angry, ready to fight.
- "Arms" may really signify "alms"—charitable donations of money or goods.

Hands

WHEN YOU DREAM OF HANDS, see which hand is used predominantly. The left hand is associated with bad luck, weakness, and, in the extreme, evil. The left hand is not used in greeting, shaking hands, or to signify honor, as in saluting. *Sinister* comes from the Latin word meaning "left-hand path." This describes the use of magic for evil purposes.

However, in the West, it is on the left hand that a wedding ring is worn. The ring finger, particularly of the left hand, was known in fifteenth-century England as the *doctor's finger*, because physicians used it to mix, taste, and anoint their medicines. Also, there is the belief that the vein from the ring finger runs straight to the heart, hence the positioning of the wedding ring. This finger is still connected symbolically with the phallus, as it was in the Roman era. Then, male prostitutes used to signal potential customers by raising that finger in the air. In medieval times, the Church called it *digitus infamus* or *senus*, "the obscene finger."

An itchy hand is linked to money: Left to receive money, right to give it out.

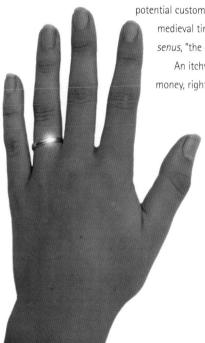

CONNECTIONS

◎ *"Hands on" means that someone is gaining practical experience.*

◎ *"Handout" is a payment where nothing is expected in return.*

◎ *"Hand-me-down" is an item that has been passed on.*

◎ *"Helping hand" means to help someone out.*

Legs

LEGS AND FEET CONNECT US TO THE EARTH, and keep us upright. They carry the rest of our body and allow us to move around. When you dream of legs, consider their condition and what they are doing. If your legs have "given way," does this mean that you cannot carry on, that you feel you can no longer support yourself?

One-legged gods were seen as phallic symbols. In Quabbalism, the ancient Jewish mystical tradition, legs represent firmness and power, which links to the idea of standing up for yourself. Your legs lift you up, which may symbolically represent raising your status. Are you getting a "leg up" to help you on your way?

I dreamed that my legs were chopped off just above my knees in an accident.

Is any part of the leg emphasized—thigh, knee, calf, or shin? If so, does the dream draw attention to waking problems, such as tendon strain?

CONNECTIONS

- *"Not a leg to stand on" means that there is no reason or defense for your position.*
- *"Kicking out"—Are you feeling angry?*
- *"Legless"—Are you out of control, like a person who is drunk?*

Feet

FEET ARE WHAT WE STAND ON. They ground us and support our whole body. How are your feet? Are they in good condition, ready to take the next step? In reflexology, the foot reveals connections to mind and body. If you dream of your feet being massaged or treated in some way, it may indicate that you could benefit from reflexology or podiatry.

To dream of feet takes us to our foundation. Think about what grounds you. The footprints you leave show the path you have taken and allow others to track you. "Footing the bill" means that you pay the price for whatever service you have received.

Kissing or washing feet signifies humility, service, and devotion. Stamping your feet indicates anger, while "voting with your feet" means walking away from something that you don't like.

Heels may link to the vulnerable point of the body—the Achilles' heel. The god Achilles was supposed to be invincible except for a place on his heel. There is also the homonym "heal," so if you dream of heels, does it refer to recovery after ill health or a difficult time emotionally?

CONNECTIONS

- *Are you getting "cold feet" about a project, losing your enthusiasm?*
- *Are you getting a "foot in the door," being accepted on a new venture?*

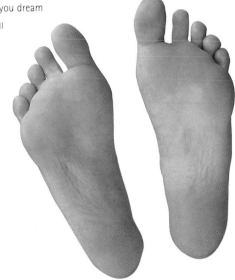

Stomach

THE STOMACH IS WHERE FOOD IS PROCESSED, where we feel satiated and nourished. After dreams in which a stomach appears, ask yourself how well you are being nourished at the moment. The stomach is also an important indicator of emotional and physical health. When we are nervous and apprehensive, we feel churned up and have difficulty digesting food or we get a stomachache because we feel sick with worry. People with gastric disorders or ulcers sometimes dream of parts of the stomach bursting or of spoiled, indigestible food.

The navel is at the center of the belly and the former place of contact between mother and child, so it is held as a highly significant spot in the body. Decorating the navel as belly dancers do with jewels or tattoos, or piercing the belly button to draw attention to it, affirms this significance.

The stomach is regarded as the seat of the emotions, and we often feel nauseous when we are emotionally excited or stressed.

CONNECTIONS

◈ *Being unable to "stomach" something means that someone can't think of or accept it.*

◈ *"Fire in the belly" is an almost irresistible desire to follow a course of action.*

Liver

THE LIVER CREATES BILE, STORES GLYCOGEN, detoxifies the system, and helps the metabolism process nutrients. If liver disease is present, the color of the skin may be affected, so a pale-skinned person takes on a jaundiced, or yellow, appearance. If you dream of your liver, consider the health implications. If you are physically fit, could it refer to emotional issues?

Bile, which is bitter, relates to "biliousness"—irritability and peevishness. In medieval times, "black bile" was thought to cause melancholy and depression, while "yellow bile" produced anger.

For the Greek philosopher Plato, the liver was an extremely important organ. He described it as the part of the body that receives messages and acts as a mirror:

The gods created in the belly an organ like a mirror, whose surface was sensitive to or sufficiently attuned to the mind to receive its messages and then had the power to project these rational messages as irrational messages into dreams.

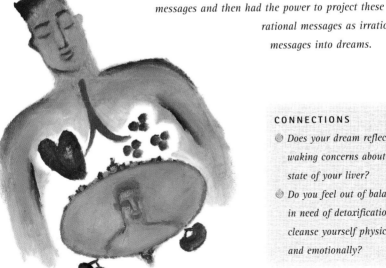

CONNECTIONS

- *Does your dream reflect waking concerns about the state of your liver?*
- *Do you feel out of balance, in need of detoxification to cleanse yourself physically and emotionally?*

Heart AS A MAJOR ORGAN

IN THE BODY, the heart is not only a ceaseless engine, it is the symbolic center of our emotions. If you dream of a heart, first consider any possible physical events that could have prompted the dream, then look at emotional aspects.

Dreams in which the chest is being targeted by an assailant, or when the dreamer is being shot in the heart, have been recorded by people with cardiac problems. Chest pains at night may prompt the dreams, the pain being symbolized by some form of attack or accident. Other common features of these dreams are blood, pressure on the chest, the left arm being injured, and a sense of urgency or fear.

The emotional connections to the heart are endless. The "Sacred Heart of Jesus" is of great significance to Catholics, as is the bleeding heart, which symbolizes suffering for belief. The heart also symbolizes romantic love and courage.

CONNECTIONS

◎ *"Don't let your heart rule your head"—Are your intense feelings leading you to take dangerous risks?*

◎ *"My heart was in my mouth"—This symbolizes fear and anxiety.*

Lungs

THE LUNGS ARE THE BODY'S "BREATHING SPACE." They are the bellows of the body, which stoke up energy, enabling us to breathe and act. Do you give yourself enough breathing space?

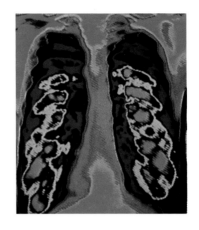

A heavy smoker dreamed that she saw her lungs and that they were black. The dream imagery influenced her decision to quit smoking, and, whether it was a warning about impending disease or not, its beneficial impact helped the dreamer. When you have a chest infection, pneumonia, or bronchitis, you may have water-filled dreams. These symbolize the build-up of fluid or mucus in the lungs.

Breath has been linked with the "soul" or "spirit" since time immemorial, because the breath is the visible life force. We know that once a person has drawn their last breath, their life on earth has ceased.

For the Chinese, the lungs are the seat of righteousness and the source of our inner thoughts.

CONNECTION

☺ *Parks in cities, such as Hyde Park in London and Central Park in New York, are often called the "lungs of the city" because they give space for people to breathe, away from the noise and pollution of heavy traffic. Does your dream reflect concern about green spaces and environmental issues?*

Skin

SKIN GIVES PROTECTION FROM THE OUTSIDE WORLD. When there is a break, a cut, or a wound, it can be painful and let in infection. Before it can heal, a wound must be cleaned. Have you been injured psychologically? Have your defenses been breached?

A scab is formed once the skin is broken and is part of the healing process. If you are picking at a scab in a dream, it may mean that you are interfering, that you won't leave things alone so that they can heal. Scars may also be left once the skin has healed. If you dream of a scar, does it relate to a mark on your body or is it a reminder of an emotional injury?

A caul is a remnant of the amniotic sac that some babies are born with. In many traditions, this is seen as being very lucky and is believed to protect the person from drowning. If you dream of a membrane-like veil or mask, does it relate to a lack of vision or a lack of clarity, or does it offer some form of protection?

An African tribe, the Santals, believe that the soul leaves the body as a lizard and that touching the dried skin of a lizard or snake will protect them from illness.

CONNECTIONS

- *To escape by "the skin of your teeth" means to narrowly avoid a damaging event. Have you narrowly avoided disaster recently?*
- *A "skinflint" is miserly. Have you been less than generous with friends or have they been mean with you?*

Womb

The oldest oracle in Greece, sacred to the great mother of earth, sea, and sky, was named Delphi, from delphos, meaning "womb."

BARBARA WALKER

THE UTERUS, OR WOMB, IS THE SOURCE OF CREATIVITY. Symbolically, it is the source of all life. It may suggest fertility and pregnancy, as well as creating a new life for the dreamer.

After Jillie had undergone a hysterectomy, she had a dream in which a man and a woman attacked her and kicked her to the floor. While she lay on the floor, she saw a pattern of tiles and then awoke, saying to herself, "I've got to look at the pattern." She had a strong sense that she needed to find a new pattern in her life and change old patterns. She saw the man and woman as her female and male side being angry about the operation, regarding it as a sign that her body had let her down. After surgery, many women dream of being assaulted. This symbolizes the feeling of being invaded and bruised by the experience.

CONNECTIONS

◎ *"A bun in the oven" is a saying that describes a pregnancy. The oven represents the uterus or womb.*

◎ *"Rented womb" describes surrogacy, where a woman agrees to carry an embryo for another woman who is unable to conceive or carry a baby herself.*

Vagina

SEXUALITY, REPRODUCTION, and hidden potential are symbolized in dreams of the vagina. As the vagina is concealed within the body, it is often symbolized as a box, a drawer in a cupboard, or a jewelry case.

More vivid dreams seem to coincide with ovulation, which I think relates to the fact that I am more creative in waking life at this time. This dreamer links ovulation with the type and quality of her dreams.

When I ovulate, I seem to have cycles of dreaming that I am pregnant, or I am giving birth, or I have a child. This seems to reflect my concerns at the appropriate time of the month. These dreams are very strong, and waking up is a shock. When you record your dreams, include details of your menstrual cycle. Later, check through your dream journal and see how dream themes reflect hormonal changes at ovulation.

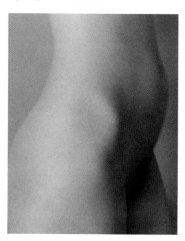

CONNECTION

● Vagina dentate, *"toothed vagina," refers to the idea of the mouth and the vagina being in symbolic sexual relationship. The teeth link to male fear that the penis may be damaged when involved in penetrative sex.*

Penis THE PENIS IS LINKED TO ELIMINATION of waste from the body and to the sexual act. The phallus has been worshiped in patriarchal societies, sometimes openly, at other times secretly. It often represents penetrative power.

Early Gnostic Christian traditions called the penis the "tree of life" and worshiped it.

"Wet dreams," in which ejaculation of semen occurs, happen before a boy has had sexual intercourse. These dreams help the body to become "primed" and are part of sexual development. Similarly, girls may experience orgasm or sexually arousing dreams before having any sexual relationships.

Semen is the seed of new life. If it appears in your dreams, does it symbolize new beginnings for you? It may relate to concerns about fertility and pregnancy. "Spilling seed" symbolizes waste and loss.

"Cock" is a slang term for the penis. If you dream of a cock, or rooster (see page 285), does it have a sexual connection for you?

Some women symbolically take on the role of the male in their dreams, as you can see from this dream extract.

I dreamed I had a penis, and somehow I wasn't surprised.
The dreamer felt quite at ease with this change of sex, and enjoyed the sensation.

CONNECTION

◎ *If you dream of being "pricked" could it refer to "a prick," another word for penis?*

Blood BLOOD IS THE LIFE PRINCIPLE, what keeps us going. Without blood we are lifeless. In dreams, blood may spill and redden the earth as it pours from wounded bodies. If you dream of bleeding, ask yourself whether your life force feels diminished by your current circumstances.

Gladiators had a special place in Roman society, and not just for the blood lust of the battles. The blood of a gladiator was believed to have healing or aphrodisiac powers. Women gladiators wore the costumes of Amazons when they fought.

In the Middle East, brides stepped over blood, from a sacrificed sheep for example, in order to ensure fertility. Many women dream of blood before the onset of a period; often the dreams are violent and involve knives and sharp objects. These may be caused by cramps in the womb that are translated into being wounded in the dream.

> *Just before a period, I always dream about blood flowing from a cut. Either the next day or two days later, I start my period.*

A dream of a blood transfusion may reflect waking reality, for instance, for people who have dialysis. But it may also mean that you need a fresh input of energy, a new lease on life.

Skeleton

OUR SKELETON SUPPORTS US; it is our structure. In dreams, the skeleton often relates to mortality. Death and decay are symbolized by its presence and, in Buddhist meditation rooms, skeletons are sometimes hung up to remind the meditator that life is impermanent.

Ankou, the Breton (French) herald of death, came in the form of a tall, thin man, or as a skeleton carrying a scythe and shading his face with a broad-brimmed hat. In his coach, he kept a pile of stones that he threw out each time he reaped a new soul. The sound of rattling stones symbolized approaching death. Skeletons are also associated with the Mayan god of death and the underworld.

In Britain, an *ossuary* was a place where the bones retrieved from a grave would be placed. This was before permanent "perpetual graves" were introduced in about 1650.

Dreams of bones may symbolize getting to the "bare bones," or reaching the basis of an issue beyond the superficial signs. If someone says, "I've got a bone to pick with you," it means that he or she wants to tell you how you've annoyed them.

CONNECTIONS

- ◉ *"Bred in the bone" means something is part of your intrinsic nature.*
- ◉ *"Bone of contention" is a point of dispute, something to argue about.*
- ◉ *"To bone up" means to improve skills or knowledge.*

YOUR RELATIONSHIPS WITH THE PEOPLE IN YOUR LIFE are crucial. Family, friends, lovers, and colleagues all play a role in bringing breadth and depth to your life. Dreams reveal what is happening below the surface and allow you to go beyond superficial ties to the roots of your connection with others. Dreams can also remind you of those who are important to you and can nudge you to make contact again.

Relationships take us to the limits of our emotional range, from great joy to utter despair, and they can bring us into contact with the finality of death:

I dream of people close to me passing away and leaving me all alone to sort things out that have been left behind.

Though dreams such as these may be upsetting, they act as preparation. These dreams introduce us to the grief we may feel in the future and can act as a spur to tell those we love how much we care for them before it is too late.

After a divorce, one partner may dream that the other has died. This symbolizes the "death" of the marriage or partnership. Whatever the dream content, you can use it to chart your own process of acceptance and recovery. Dreams will give you guidance on ways to ease the pain.

People in
Your Life

People in Your Life

I am walking down a school corridor. There are a couple of cleaners washing the walls. I am puzzled, and comment that they are only going to the level of their heads. "Well," they say to me, "You know you can't go above head level."

Each of us has a set of personal symbols that grow out of our life experiences. The essence of our dreams largely arises from these unique personal experiences. Above is an example from my own dreams.

Many years ago in England, I led a team of teachers helping alleviate and prevent disruption in schools. One particular head (principal) refused to recognize the serious problems in his school and could not or would not make moves to change damaging practices.

I had to write a report for a crucial meeting where these difficulties were to be aired. I circulated my report prior to the meeting and within hours was summoned to see the Deputy Chief Education Officer. I was told to withdraw the report. "But," I replied, absolutely stunned, "every word is true." "That's not the point," he replied. "I don't doubt what you've written is true, but you can't go above the Head."

So, you can see the personal symbolism of "head" for me at that time.

Dreaming is a universal phenomenon, which is inseparable from life because the only dreamless state is death. Each of us will find that the people and places of our dreams tell us about our culture and environment. Soldiers in conflict dream of war, children who are bullied dream of monsters that chase them, mothers dream of their children, and writers dream up their plots.

In the process of dreaming, past experiences are relived, become assimilated and mastered, and we come to an understanding of those who have peopled our lives. We become enriched as we do this, especially if we actively seek to understand why people appear in our dreams. Ask yourself why your dream person is here in your dream. What does he or she represent in your life at this moment?

Dreams are the key to the storehouse of all your memories and experiences, starting from infancy. All the people who have meant something to you may come into your dreams, and you need to make connections to understand why they appear. As you will see in the following entries, the roles people play will help you decipher your dream's message.

BELOW *A dream of a teacher may indicate new learning for you.*

Mother

The child, tiny and alone,
creates the mother.

ANNE STEVENSON: POEM FOR A DAUGHTER

WOMEN REPRESENT THE FEMALE ASPECT of the
dreamer and the maternal side—the mother
archetype. The archetypal mother has a great
deal of power—the power of life and death.
Without her protection and nurturing, the child
is vulnerable and may die. In a very real sense,
the relationship is about life and death, so in
dreams we see a whole range of mother images.
They include the wicked witch or stepmother, the sad, lost soul, and the defiant
protector. Whether your dreams feature an earth mother, your mother, or you as
mother, use them to explore this crucial relationship. This dreamer had to take
responsibility for all the children in the world, as well as her own:

I have to get the children—all the children—to a place of safety before the
world blows up; I know this is going to happen but nobody believes me.

CONNECTIONS

- *Are you in need of mothering? Do you need to be looked after and cared for?*
- *Do you feel you are over-controlling or over-protective?*
- *Are you burdened by your responsibility as a mother?*
- *Do your dreams show the freedom to have fun with your children as well as take care of them?*

Father

RELATIONSHIPS WITH FATHERS are highly significant. Fathers symbolize authority and protection. Whether you grew up with your biological father, a stepfather, or a father figure, you will have been influenced by the nature of your bond. As we grow up we learn that parents are not perfect and, in dreams, this awareness may come as a shock.

The children's book illustrator Kate Greenaway had a disturbing recurring dream in her childhood after her beloved father died. Her father would appear in the dream, but when she looked at him, his face would change into someone else's. She would desperately try to pull off the false face, but was confronted with another and another until she woke up in tears. In her dreams, she was always trying to recover her lost father.

Some dreams can bring us compensation after loss, as this dream does:

I dreamed that my father came back home to live with us and he was smiling and always happy.
This dream makes up for what the dreamer lacks. Other dreams allow us to meet up with others and ourselves as we used to be:

My father had his leg amputated because of gangrene, yet whenever I dream of him, he is just as he was before his operation.

Sister

SISTERS IN DREAMS may refer to siblings or female friends. Sibling rivalry may cause dreams of competition or aggression:

When I got in the car, my sister got in and started pulling my hair, arguing with me. She could do anything to me but I couldn't do anything to her, my parents wouldn't let me—they wouldn't stop her either.

Early childhood desires for attention, protection, and recognition surface in such dreams where we are ignored or left unprotected.

When I was young, I dreamed that my sister was in my class at school and I got really angry.

If you have similar dreams, it may mean that you are still trying to resolve issues from your past or that there is a current relationship that has similar conflicts.

I used to dream that I was in bed with my elder sister at home in Belfast. A huge steamroller, used to surface roads, was coming toward us and I couldn't rouse my sister.

Here, there is a strong feeling of responsibility. However, such dreams may mask a feeling that it wouldn't be a bad idea if sisters could get flattened now and again! In other dreams siblings join together against parents or in support of each other in conflict situations outside their home.

Brother

AS WELL AS SIBLING RIVALRY, dreams about a brother often relate to taking care of him, of being in a parental, responsible role, with the possibility of failing and being blamed if anything goes wrong. This may produce strange dreams:

I dreamed that my brother changed into a little red hen and I was chasing him down the road.

This was a flashback to childhood when John and his brother lived on a farm. Being the elder, John always felt he had to look after his fast-moving, unpredictable brother.

Fights between brothers, and between brothers and sisters, are far from unusual. The ambivalence of the love-hate relationship shows up in dreams of fights, bullying, and arguments. At times, this can be oppressive, as this dream shows:

I had a dream where my brothers shut me in the living room all night and the light switch and door both disappeared, leaving me in total darkness, unable to get out.

Other dreams about brothers are about being protected and indicate the closeness of shared experience:

I was being chased with my brother on a rocky mountain. At the end I fell and, while I was falling, all I was doing was praying so I would go to heaven.

Uncle

UNCLES MAY HAVE SOME OF THE AUTHORITY of the father, but the added distance allows for more flexibility. Bonds of family loyalty still apply and dreams may highlight this aspect of your relationship.

I feel that dreams hold the key to how I feel about my family, but I wish the dreams were more pleasant and not so disturbing.

If you have disturbing dreams about any member of your family, then ask yourself what is wrong with the relationship. What would you like to change? What do you need to address?

Male characters in dreams often represent masculine energy for a woman dreamer, so think about how the dream uncle acts, what his strengths are and what he might have that you need. What qualities does he have that you could use to bring greater balance to your life?

CONNECTION

○ *"Uncle Sam"—Slang term for the United States government.*

Aunt AS THE SISTER OF YOUR FATHER OR MOTHER, or the wife of your

uncle, your aunt has family connections that could influence your life. Also, aunts are often second mother figures, who may be less strict than mothers. The following dream was set in the home of the dreamer's aunt:

As an adolescent, I had different dreams about sex. In one, I was at my aunt's house, trying to have sex with a male or sometimes a female.

I either succeeded in doing it while eating cookies and drinking tea and my aunt did not notice, or I was left unfulfilled because of an interruption.

The dreamer feels inhibited at home, so her dream gives her a different setting to explore her sexuality.

CONNECTION

◎ *"Aunt Sally"—The figure of an old woman's head that used to be a target at fairgrounds and fêtes. Today, it refers to anyone who is a target for undue criticism, especially if they have been unfairly set up by others.*

Grandfather

GRANDFATHERS GIVE A SENSE OF CONTINUITY IN FAMILY LIFE. They are part of the line that connects us to the past and, for some people whose fathers are unable to give much attention to a child, the grandfather becomes a surrogate father figure. Like grandmothers, grandfathers are traditionally viewed as protective, caring, and more indulgent than parents.

Grandfathers act as guardians to family traditions and, as such, may dislike modern developments. If you dream of a disagreement, decide whether it is personal or whether it symbolizes conflict between the different generations.

Ancestor worship plays an important role in Chinese religions. People regularly visit gravesides to pay their respects to those who have died. Families also have shrines in their homes to honor their dead relatives. Grandfathers are especially venerated. Therefore, dreams in which they appear are particularly auspicious.

When my grandfather died, I dreamed he came to say goodnight and goodbye.

CONNECTIONS

◉ *Do you need the wisdom of an elder to guide you on your way?*

◉ *If your grandfather is alive, could your dream be a reminder to visit him?*

Grandmother THE MATRIARCHAL LINE shows itself in

dreams and may reveal the sense of shared responsibility toward frail grandparents, as this dream does:

I dreamed that my grandma (who is 88 years old) was in bed and my mother and myself were washing her and she was dressed, but her clothes were dirty.

Mother and daughter look after the aged grandmother as women have done since time immemorial. Grandmothers are wise elders who, after death, return to us in dreams to guide us or to accompany us through difficult times. They often bring great comfort, as this recurring dream does:

I'm seven months pregnant. As soon as I found out I was having a baby, I have dreamed of my grandmother. She's been dead for three years and I was very close to her. In my dream, she is young and smiles at me, though she doesn't say anything.

Grandparents bring the wisdom of their experience, and symbolically, as in this dream, they reassure the dreamer:

After the death of my grandmother, I used to call her to me: She would sit and stroke my hair and say comforting things to me.

Daughter

THE BIRTH OF A CHILD may reactivate anxieties about our own childhood experiences. A client, who was six years old when her sister (aged four) died from leukemia, had distressing dreams that her daughter would also die of cancer. Though unpleasant, such dreams do help us face our deepest fears about mortality and help us recognize previous grief.

I dream of wandering in the Lake District, my childhood home, with my daughter and sisters.

A daughter in a dream can indicate a desire to have a daughter or may represent yourself as a little girl, perhaps your "inner child." What about the age of the girl? If she is seven years old, for example, think about what was happening to you at that age. Were there any significant events in your life then? As your own children grow, forgotten memories and connections may arise, surfacing first in your dreams. These trigger earlier experiences, which may need reexamination and reevaluation in the light of how you are now.

CONNECTION

◎ *Can you accept the dream daughter who comes to you?*

Son **THE PRODIGAL SON IS A PARABLE** told by Jesus, involving a rebellious son who goes his own way, then returns to his father, who kills "the fatted calf" to welcome him back. The son and his brother, who had never strayed, continued with their sibling rivalry. Do your dreams of sons relate to this form of disagreement?

My dreams about "neglecting" my new baby have given me insight into the need to stop fussing over my family as they become adults. Worrying about children is natural and is often intensified when there are health concerns. This dreamer had a twenty-year-old son who suffered from epilepsy, and one night she had this dream:

I dreamed he was at the grotto in Lourdes, and my own mother, who died four years before he was born, was attending to him. I knew that she wanted him to go with her, but I didn't know where to.

I pleaded with her to leave him with me, since I was the one who should look after him.

The dreamer felt that, if she had agreed, she would have lost her son. He died two years later, but she blessed the time they had together.

Husband

DREAMS IN WHICH YOUR HUSBAND APPEARS usually relate to pleasures and pains in your daily life, as well as pointing out hidden conflicts. As marital bliss may turn sour, so dreams dramatize this change:

When my marriage started to break down, I had a recurring dream of maggots burrowing in potatoes.

The maggots symbolized the invasion of the marriage by another woman, who was eating away at the relationship the dreamer had with her husband. The mundane potato, a food staple, is ordinary, just as the dreamer thought her marriage was, but it turned rotten.

Before I met my husband, I used to dream of having great sex with different men, but once we got together, the dreams stopped because there was no need for them any more.

In the world of dreams, you may enter a different time dimension, whether past or future. Many people who have suffered illness or injury that has left them without a limb, for example, or with limited movement following a stroke, find that in their dreams they are able-bodied once more. Similarly, partners and family also dream of the person when he was fully able.

If you have a close bond with your husband or partner, you may find that you dream of the same subject on the same night:

There have been several occasions when my husband and I have dreamed identical dreams on the same night.

Wife

CLOSE RELATIONSHIPS ARE THE SUBJECT of most women's dreams, and as wives we dream of husbands and children. Sometimes, women dream of being married, about the wedding and the ceremony that is involved, but less frequently they dream of being the "wife." However, where you are the "other woman," dreams may change:

When I was having an affair with a married man, I used to dream of meeting his wife.

These dreams, which revealed anxiety about the clandestine relationship, added to the dreamer's difficulty of maintaining contact with her lover.

Wife is also an archaic term given to any woman, so if the term *wifely duties* appears in a dream, this refers to the traditional female roles.

"Wife-swapping" dreams, in which married couples swap partners for sexual gratification, may reflect a longing for another partner or a desire to spice up your sex life. If the dream involves a couple you know, think about whether you are attracted to either partner. However, remember that in dreams there is no censor, so the wild fantasies that you dream about can exist without you having to put the dream into practice in your waking life.

Friend THERE IS A SAYING THAT FRIENDS are what God gives us to make up for our families. While this may not be true for many people, it does acknowledge the importance of friends. They are there to sustain us in the worst times and to celebrate the best times. However, we may hold back from them. One of my clients dreamed that she was with a group of friends. She was crying, but no one noticed, and the friends continued to speak to her as normal. She thought about the dream and realized that she needed to tell her friends how she felt, rather than hide her sad feelings when awake. She needed to stop putting on a brave face and be honest with those whose friendships she valued.

Your dreams will give you guidance about what to do when you have arguments, as this one did:

Recently I had an upsetting dream about someone I am no longer friends with. In the dream, we talked through all the issues and I woke up feeling relieved.

CONNECTIONS

◉ *"Fair-weather friend"—Is one of your friends there when the world is wonderful, but not when you need more support?*

◉ *"A friend in need is a friend indeed"—Does a friend want your help? Are you able to give it?*

Lover

IN DREAMS, LOVERS MAY BE YOUR WAKING PARTNER, your ideal, or your wish-fulfillment partner, or they may even compensate for a waking situation that is unsatisfactory.

I dreamed I went to Sea World with my ex-boyfriend. We had to hold our breath while in an underwater tank and swim forward to leave the place. Then we were back in a café in Glasgow getting dried off in front of lots of people. My ex said that it was a lousy vacation and I said that they made us hold our breath too long.

The dream reveals how the relationship with her lover went on too long. They had metaphorically held their breath, hoping that some improvement would take place. The pun in "Sea World" relates to the fact that the relationship ended when the ex-boyfriend decided to go traveling and "see the world." You can recognize that there is still some vulnerability in that they are "exposed" in a very public place. When relationships end, we all feel vulnerable. Sharing a dream with your lover can be highly beneficial.

Recently, I was troubled about my relationship with my lover and I had a dream in which he featured, so we talked about it. The discussion brought to light insecurities we both had and it helped us become closer again.

Neighbor

THEY SAY THAT FENCES make good neighbors. In other words, when everyone knows where the boundaries are, the relationship will be good. Good neighbors can help you feel secure in your home and be a source of help when life goes awry.

I dreamed that someone came to my door and told me that I shouldn't have my house. He threatened me and I rushed to my neighbor's house.

This dream came at the time when the dreamer was separating from her husband. He had threatened her, and told her that they would have to sell the house if they divorced. The dreamer's neighbor had been supportive throughout this difficult time, so the dream accurately reflects where she can run in an emergency.

Disputes with neighbors can cause anxiety dreams, and sometimes, aggressive conflict. If you regularly dream that a neighbor is putting you down, for example, or that you are being passive and not asserting your rights, then consider whether you need to find a way to address the problem—perhaps through mediation. You could also try to act differently in the dream, rehearsing a situation in which you stand up for yourself and act assertively.

Colleague

WHEN YOU DREAM OF YOUR WORK SETTING and the people that you work with, your dream may be linked to a rerun of an ordinary day. However, when it takes an unusual twist, be alert for deeper meanings. This dreamer found herself in an unusual situation, which she found amusing:

It was like a mixture of The Kama Sutra, The Joy of Sex, *and the company's Monday morning staff meeting. All my colleagues were dressed oriental style, and ready for real orgies. The end was a flop—even in the dream, I couldn't join in the fun because the faces of the people reminded me that I wouldn't touch them.*

This type of dream, where a colleague is put in a sexual role with the dreamer, can indicate that there are sexual tensions at work, that someone is sexually attracted to you, or vice versa. However, they can also reinforce the boundaries that keep business and pleasure separate.

I work in a factory in the evenings and don't finish until 10 P.M. When I get to bed, depending on what sort of night I've had at work, I dream I'm still at work. My mind must get overactive with working so late. I sometimes sit up in bed and I can see the people I've been working with and I think to myself, "Am I in bed or at work? I just don't know where I am."

Such confusion may be as a result of stress. Certainly, working shifts alters both sleep and dream patterns. If you have this type of dream, record when they happen so that you can see if there is a pattern.

Boss THE PERSON OF AUTHORITY, the boss, may represent leadership, although much depends on what he or she is doing in the dream. In some dreams, it may be figures such as a king, queen, president, or premier that symbolize the head of an organization.

If you dream about your boss at work, it may be linked to problem-solving or relationships, so think about the situation and what it may symbolize. If you dream that you are having raging arguments with your boss or inflicting brutal blows, it probably indicates a high level of stress or conflict at work. If such dreams are recurring, then work out what it is that is making you so distressed and try to address it—otherwise, your waking situation may further deteriorate.

Recording and analyzing my dreams has helped me to get a far greater perspective of the problems that confront me at work and shown me that I can do something on a practical level to alleviate problems.

As the boss, you may have mixed feelings about delegating work. One woman had a series of dreams in which she was giving tasks to junior staff with excellent results, so she successfully set up a new procedure for delegating work.

CONNECTIONS

◎ *"Being bossy"—Have you been ordering other people around and not showing much consideration for them?*

◎ *"Bossed about"—Have you been ordered around and feel aggrieved about it?*

Doctors and Nurses

DOCTORS AND NURSES are traditionally linked to caring and healing. A nurse accompanies the patient through a journey of illness, whether simply to bandage a wound or to offer palliative care in terminal illness. Dreams may symbolize a longing to be cared for or may represent the dreamer as caregiver.

Dreams that nurses have may reflect their practice or previous concerns when they were students. This nurse told me about a dream she had just before she took her final exams:

I was in a graveyard and all the tombstones lifted up and bodies, which were falling to pieces, were chasing me.

This dream reveals that the dreamer has fears that not all medicine is beneficial.

I dreamed that the doctor gave me a prescription but I was convinced it was poison. I wouldn't take it, although I pretended I would.

Maybe it's time to find a new doctor.

CONNECTIONS

◎ *Does your dream indicate that you need a physical check-up?*

◎ *Has your dream doctor given you advice? If so, what does it relate to in your life at present?*

Police **POLICE SYMBOLIZE POWER AND CONTROL.** They are the law enforcers, the rule upholders, and so represent how we are bound by our culture and society. Clearly, the actions of your dream police will tell you what is being emphasized. What is the situation—an arrest, an interrogation, a routine car check? Is the police officer directing traffic, showing you the best way to go? Is their manner pushy, bullying, calm, or caring?

In the following dream, you can see how the authority of the father has declined. His symbolic uniform no longer has the polish and presence it once had:

I dreamed that I saw my father dressed in a policeman's uniform. It was covered in dust and he looked tired, as if he had lost all his energy.

In China, newly appointed magistrates used to sleep in the temple of the City Good to receive instruction on how to be exemplary judicial servants. This dream incubation ritual (see page 25) shows how the power of dreams was respected and used to uphold society.

CONNECTIONS

◎ *Are you worried about a situation that could get you into trouble if the "police" found out about it?*

◎ *Do you need to "police"—keep under surveillance—someone close to you?*

Firefighter

SINCE SEPTEMBER 11, 2001, when the World Trade Center's twin towers were destroyed in New York, firefighters have taken on a mythic role. In their attempts to rescue so many people in horrific circumstances, they became true heroes. If you dream of firefighters, is it this heroic dimension that is involved?

Dreams of fire can indicate a feeling of being "burned up" or "burned out," possibly indicating underlying stress. If you are starting the fire or setting fire to yourself, it can indicate severe distress, so it is important to ask yourself what in particular you want to destroy. If a firefighter comes to put out the fire or comes to rescue you, who do they represent in your life? Who can you turn to who will support you in difficult times?

Firefighters represent those who have faced ultimate danger—"walked through fire"—and survived. On a symbolic level, it can be anyone who has had to face real or possible tragedy and who is still filled with hope.

CONNECTIONS

◎ *Are you facing difficult times ahead through illness or because of "fiery" relationships?*

◎ *Do you need to douse a situation so that it does not become inflamed?*

Shopkeeper

WHETHER IN A SUPERMARKET or a corner store, storekeepers exchange goods for money in their business transactions. In interpreting dreams about them, much depends on the type of store involved.

I dreamed of a store where I could get anything I wanted and where money didn't seem to be a problem.

When we are short of money, this type of wish-fulfillment dream compensates us.

CONNECTIONS

- *Hardware—Are you getting advice on the correct way to build or repair something? Does this link to a waking project?*
- *Clothes—Are you being given, or do you want, a new image?*
- *Produce—What types of fruit and vegetables are offered? Do you need to include these in your diet to bring more balance?*
- *Real estate agents—Are you thinking of buying a house or apartment? Is it time for you to move on?*
- *Liquor—Are you buying for a celebration? Do you have any concerns about the amount of alcohol you drink?*

Teacher

TEACHERS, INSTRUCTORS, LECTURERS, AND MENTORS appear in dreams when we need guidance. They may be real people who have taught us at school or college, or they may be symbolic.

You can use dream incubation techniques to receive guidance from a teacher, although you may have to be patient. You do not need to go to a special place as they did in Ancient Greece; you can do it in your own bedroom. Before you go to sleep make a request for help through a challenging situation. Be specific about what you need to know and write the question down in your dream journal. Record your dream immediately on waking and you will find that your dreams bring you insight from your inner guide or teacher. It is still called *dream incubation*.

If you are a teacher, you probably dream of your students as well as your school or college. At the start of a new term, it is not unusual to have disturbing dreams as you wonder what the term will bring and whether you've lost your ability to teach:

I dream that my class at school has gone completely crazy and that I'm having no success whatsoever in calming them down.

CONNECTIONS

◉ *"To teach someone a lesson"—Are you about to give someone a hard time, to make their life difficult?*

◉ *"Teaching your grandmother to suck eggs"—Are you trying to tell someone what they already know or preaching to the converted?*

Soldier

SOME WOMEN DREAM THAT THEY ARE SOLDIERS going into war zones. One dreamed that she came out of a pine forest and was relieved that the enemy was behind. Then, she felt a wet patch on her chest and knew that she had been shot, although she was not afraid. This dream may relate to a situation in which the dreamer thought that she was "out of the woods," or in the clear, but that at another level she knows she is still vulnerable. Her emotions are under control, but she may still "pine" about something or someone.

I was in my house and the atmosphere was very tense. The streets were deserted. I was alone hiding from an army. They came barging in and our house turned into a battlefield. I ran into my room and my brother appeared. He locked the door to hold them back, but they were too strong. I opened my window and jumped—my brother didn't come—and I ran down the street trying to hide.

The battlefield may symbolize difficult relationships at home. Are you fighting a personal war at present?

Guard

GUARDS ARE USUALLY CONNECTED WITH PRISONS, but there are also bodyguards and security guards in stores. A military guard of honor may also be of significance.

I'm on a dark hillside with jailers and a lot of fierce guard dogs, almost like bears. Some women tell me I can get away if I take a stone that will make me invisible.

The dreamer feels trapped in a situation at home; she feels "in the dark" about her future. In the dream, she did finally escape and on waking felt as if she had been through an ordeal and survived. It gave her an increased feeling of confidence to cope and carry on.

Where there is a guard, think about what is being protected. Is it treasure, money, a secret, or a private party? What does it symbolize in your life? Guards protect entrances and exits, so if these feature in your dreams, it may indicate that you feel your access to something is being hindered. Who is holding you back? Are you preventing yourself from moving?

CONNECTIONS
◎ Do you need to be "on your guard" right now?
◎ Perhaps you have to "guard your tongue"?

CONNECTION

Do you feel that you are being held prisoner by your present circumstances?

Prisoner

TO BE A PRISONER involves confinement, loss of privileges, lack of power, and loss of freedom. The imprisonment may be legal, following conviction by a judge and jury, but may also be illegal, the result of being abducted by a maverick kidnapper or hostage taker. Take these factors into account when assessing the message of a dream, whether the prisoner is you or someone else.

For years I had a dream of my father. I would be waiting for large prison gates to open, then my father would come out and stand in a row with other men and I would machine gun all of them.

You, like this dreamer, might be shocked by your behavior in dreams. She was horrified by the dream because she and her father were so close. The dream recurred until her father died from cancer two years later, after suffering great pain. In her dream, she may have wanted to help release her father from the prison of his pain. This would have been a merciful release, yet such waking thoughts would be too dreadful to contemplate for this dreamer.

Student A STUDENT

REPRESENTS THE LEARNER, the initiate, or a
person setting off on their apprenticeship
of life. Much can be understood from the
type of student, what they are studying,
and their attitude toward their course.
They may represent someone you know
or an aspect of yourself that requires
new understanding.

A young man dreamed that he was
running around getting nowhere, all the
time being pursued by the British soccer
player Ian Rush. He recognized that in his
first year as a college student, he was
"rushing" around so much that he was
achieving nothing and not reaching any of his goals. He needed to slow down and
adjust to his first taste of independence.

After a workshop for college students, a recurring theme I discovered, not
surprisingly, was romantic encounters.

*Someone I don't know enters the dream. When I wake up, I don't
remember the face, but I know that he is really nice-looking and everything
I want in an ideal partner.*

This is a wish-fulfillment dream as the dreamer longed for a relationship and
found some comfort and reassurance from the positive sensation of the dream.

If you dream of yourself as a student, does it indicate a desire for learning and
new qualifications? Would these help you in your career? If so, what can you do to
make the dream a reality?

Historical Figure

DREAMS ABOUT HITLER ARE common. He symbolizes oppression and the destruction of human life. His is the ultimate controlling, manipulative power. Is there a controlling element in your life that feels unbearable? Do you feel dehumanized, fearful, and helpless?

President Abraham Lincoln had a dream a few days before his death. The dream began with the sense of a death-like stillness, and then he heard sobbing coming from another room. His search for the source of this sorrow led him to the East Room. He said,

There I met a sickening surprise. Before me was a catafalque, on which rested a corpse ... whose face was covered. "Who is dead in the White House?" I demanded of one of the soldiers. "The President," was his answer. "He was killed by an assassin!" Then came a loud burst of grief from the crowd, which woke me from my dream.

He was deeply moved by the dream and recounted it to others, but it did not prevent his assassination, which happened when he visited the theater.

I dreamed of Diana, Princess of Wales. She was smiling and looking at all the flowers that had been left for her outside Kensington Palace.

The death of Princess Diana led to a huge outpouring of grief throughout the world and prompted many dreams of loss and renewal. The death of a young woman with two young sons led to strong identifications by women especially, and dreams reflect the impact of such historical, mythic figures on the lives of "ordinary" people.

Politician

WHILE POLITICIANS ARE CONCERNED with the running of a country, and with government and lawmaking, they are also negatively associated with using office for personal gain. Sleaze and spin indicate an unscrupulous use of their talents. If your dream politician is involved in underhanded dealing, does this raise concerns about someone with power to influence what happens in your life?

Your dreams of political figures may reflect an interest in national or international issues and may be triggered by events in the news. If your dreams focus on particular people, consider their qualities, both positive and negative, and see if you share any of these traits. Accepting your light and dark side, your divine and shadow side, is part of becoming a whole person.

After Calpurnia's dream warned of Julius Caesar's murder, his successor, Augustus (died 14 C.E.), paid great attention to dream portents or warnings. He even made a law that if people in certain countries dreamed anything that concerned the commonwealth, they should advertise their dream in the marketplace.

CONNECTIONS

◉ *Are you "politicking"—seeking votes of support from others?*

◉ *Do you need to be "political," shrewd, and ingenious, in a project that you are involved in?*

Royalty

WHEN A MEMBER OF A ROYAL FAMILY appears in your dream, it may represent that person or symbolize someone in authority. As leaders, royalty indicates political or spiritual strength, or the reverse—abuse of power as birthright and the opposite of democracy.

A queen is a woman of power and influence, the ultimate majesty of the feminine. People make appeals to her, as happens in this dream:

I went to see Queen Elizabeth and Prince Edward. I was scared, and she was a bit annoyed because one group of visitors had just left and she wanted to relax. I wanted to ask her to send a rich doctor to help my sister who was very sick.

Powerful queens appear throughout history and legend. Isis, the great goddess of Egypt, was known as Queen of Heaven, from whom all life arose. The queen represents fecundity, the ripeness of growth, and the power of nature to provide.

The king represents power, masculine energy, creation, and procreation. In dreams, he may advise or command, so if words are spoken, what is the message?

CONNECTION

If you dream about a king, ask yourself what kingly qualities you possess or wish to possess.

Stranger STRANGERS SYMBOLIZE THE FOREIGN

or unknown. They can bring threat or new ways of looking at the world. They can bring diversity to your life. In your dreams, you can also be a stranger to yourself or connect other strangers.

In a dream, I was introduced to two people, both with the same name, who were different parts of the same person. I introduced them to each other. I woke up seeing the two as halves of the same person, saying, "Confront yourself with yourself."

Strangers can be anonymous people who the dreamer feels they should take care of:

I dream I am walking with strangers when we have to climb a mountain. We get halfway up, then realize there is no turning back, so we climb farther up. I am helping the other people to get to the top, then I find if I don't hurry I will fall down. I make a desperate effort and make it to the top.

The dreamer is scared of "backsliding"—slipping down and losing her place—yet puts others before herself.

Charles Dickens used to take a nap each afternoon to help him with his writing. He said that in his dreams new characters would stand in front of him and give him ideas for his latest work. Your dreams can inspire you, too.

UNIVERSAL DREAM THEMES connect us with those who have gone before and with generations yet to come. These themes—which include falling, being chased, and losing teeth—are reported in North America just as they are reported in Africa, showing that we share basic dreaming patterns, although our cultures and environments may differ. Universal themes are usually attached to the natural environment, weather, animals, basic human situations, and life processes such as birth and death.

Carl Jung believed that dreams could put us in touch with emotional, spiritual, or intellectual potential, and he showed how universal themes come from what he called "the collective unconscious." As you read this section, you will find that others share your dream themes. For example, crossroads figure in dreams universally. Whether you are in New York City, in the heart of a sleepy English village, or in the jungles of Borneo, you will find a junction of two paths. Crossroads represent a meeting point—an intersection where choices have to be made about a journey. The cross is found on tombstones and flags and relates to the marrying of physical and spiritual, the synthesis of active and passive.

As you explore these dreams, remember that you are part of the web of humanity and that you share your dreams with everyone.

Universal Dream Experiences

Universal Dream Experiences

Nightmares are always helpful because sometimes, when things are getting me down, I refuse to think about these problems consciously. The nightmares force me to assess everything—they don't stop until I do something about it all.

The common experiences we share with other human beings show up in all kinds of situations. In their drawings, children frequently depict universal images that they cannot explain or are unlikely to have seen, yet could have been described by a child living two thousand miles away. These images, whether in drawings or dreams, reinforce the idea of a collective unconscious. For example, during the research for my book *Children Dreaming*, Vikki told me:

My happiest dream was when I was in a garden. It was sunny. I saw a gate and went through it, and there was a very old man, saying, "Go back—you have a lifetime before you come through here."

Wherever she was, the dreamer was reluctant to turn back, just like the hundreds of others from every cultural group who have reported such dreams or had near-death experiences. It appears we are all capable of tuning in to a universal level of connection, since

LEFT *Terrifying nightmares are "wake up" calls. They alert us to worries we may deny when we are awake.*

Universal Dream Experiences

the archetypal symbol of the wise old man is well-known in every culture.

It is a universal truth that trauma profoundly affects dreams. A significant symptom of post-traumatic stress disorder (PTSD) is recurring nightmares that force the dreamer to relive an event. They are intense, terrifying, and cause strong physical responses such as raised heartbeat and sweating. Dreamers describe PTSD dreams as being different from anything experienced while awake. Fear wakes the dreamer suddenly, still gripped by the terror of the nightmare.

Captain W. H. Rivers (1864–1922), a British doctor in the Royal Army Medical Corps during World War I, was also a noted anthropologist. During the war, Rivers became convinced of the power of dream interpretation to help in the recovery of soldiers suffering from what was then termed "shell shock" and is today known as PTSD. At the time, he raged against the fact that "the psychology of dreams was not deemed worthy of inclusion in a course of academic psychology."

Dr. Rivers pointed out that dreams confront us with difficulties that we encounter in waking life but translate into dream terms. At Craiglockhart Mental Hospital in Scotland, he treated shell-shocked victims whose dreams were so distressing, that they would wake up vomiting. The poet Siegfried Sassoon's atrocious nightmares decreased under psychoanalyst Sigmund Freud's "talking cure" used by Rivers. In this treatment the patient decribed the dream and any feelings associated with it, and so was helped to face and overcome the difficulties in his waking life that disturbed and disabled him.

Chase

IN ENGLAND, "THE CHASE" RELATES TO the act of hunting an animal, usually a fox. Many places, for example Cannock Chase, are so called because hunting took place there. If you dream of a chase, consider whether you feel "hunted." Are you the pursuer or the quarry? If you have been feeling a victim in waking life, you may dream of being the subject of other people's unwanted attentions and feel vulnerable. For this dreamer, whenever she has her recurring dream of a chase, she is the hunted one:

In the dream, the chase ends with me sinking in quicksand. I cannot escape no matter what I do or how hard I try.

The quicksand provides a swift ending because it is "quick." However, the dream indicates she needs some power to find a positive way out of her difficulties. She may need to seek the help of others since the recurring dreams reveal that she cannot overcome whatever is pursuing her alone.

CONNECTIONS

- *"Cut to the chase" means to get to the point. If you dream of a chase it may mean you need to take swift action.*
- *The chase is part of a gun which encloses the bore. Could your dream mean you are about to "go off," to shoot into action or target someone?*

Chasing

BEING CHASED, OR BEING OVERTAKEN, evokes our earliest fears of someone or something coming from behind to overpower us. These dreams often involve being chased by an unidentified male, a group, or an animal. Men and women dream about being chased by men, but rarely do women feature as the aggressors. However, in tribal groups where hunting for food is the norm, there are more dreams about being chased by animals.

In the following dream, set in an urban environment, generalized fear stalks the dreamer. Many young people are aware of street crime and fear personal attack, which features in dreams such as this. However, this dreamer recognizes that support is offered by another so she has a rescuer in her dream, though they must "go underground"—become less visible—to get away.

I was in a club with a friend, then I got caught for some reason and was going to be killed. I escaped, then they chased after me. I kept being caught and escaping, until a boy came and saved me, and we ran away together through an underground tunnel.

Sometimes, chasing dreams may indicate oncoming illness, as this one did:

When I'm off-color or ill, I have my childhood dream where giant letters of the alphabet chase me to a low brick wall. I never get to climb over. Often, this dream is accompanied by a feeling of sandpaper rubbing on my skin.

The dry, scratchy feeling of sandpaper reflects changes in the surface of the skin due to a rise in temperature, or fever.

CONNECTION

⊙ *Could your dream about being chased refer to being "chaste"?*

Conflict & Attack

CONFLICT IN DREAMS IS HIGHLY REVEALING. Is the conflict between yourself and others, between family and friends, or are you at war with yourself? Conflict can be positive, when it allows difficulties to be aired and, through discussion, leads to resolution. It can also be negative—conflict can fuel more discontent, for example, when we refuse to negotiate or compromise because of fixed attitudes and beliefs.

I dreamed that a friend asked me out. I didn't want to go, but I did in the end, and I got drunk. We were surrounded by buildings, with no one else around, when the friend turned violent and started smashing beer bottles. He was going to attack me, then I woke up.

Harry Bosma, a noted dream researcher, has written extensively about aggression in dreams. In his personal experience of chronic fatigue syndrome (CFS) he described how vivid dreams and terrible nightmares plagued his sleep. Although medication helped his sleep pattern, the aggressive dreams continued to disturb him. His advice to similar sufferers is to face your fears and consider how your dreams represent your disease. This could help you to accept your illness and so begin the process of recovery.

CONNECTION

◉ *Are you about to "attack" a new project?*

◉ *Does your dream conflict represent a disagreement you do not want to address when awake?*

Being Held Hostage

IF YOU ARE HELD HOSTAGE IN A DREAM, it may indicate that you feel someone else has a hold on you—some power that prevents you from doing what you want, or need, to do. In nearly every case, hostage-takers have demands: They want a ransom, political recognition, or an exchange of some kind. Can you relate this to your life at present?

Sometimes, the relationship with the hostage-taker in the dream changes. For example, a rapport may develop, which causes the victim to feel a bond of connection.

I was completely rooted to the spot. I knew I could escape, but somehow I didn't want to leave.

This dream may symbolize a love–hate relationship in which the dreamer is involved.

As well as being physically held prisoner, you can also be held hostage by your fears, as this dream clearly illustrates.

My sister was waving a large spider in my face. I was terrified of it. Even though I was crying, she would not stop.

Something frightening was literally under the dreamer's nose, or "in her face," and holding her hostage in an emotional sense.

CONNECTION

◉ *Do you feel that someone is manipulating your emotions? Could they be making you feel guilty in order to get something from you?*

Love

Dreams have helped to move me on when talking hasn't helped. All dreams are acts of love in that they are a uniting of energies ... I am always full of gratitude to them. DWAYNE

LOVE, THAT VITAL PART OF LIFE, finds its way into all aspects of our dream world, whether in relationships, acts of creativity, or pure bliss at the stunning landscapes through which we travel. Dreams help us appreciate our world, once we give ourselves time to breathe in their power.

Love brings agony and ecstasy. Your dreams may expose your unconscious desires, your secret passions, and your longing for different dimensions in your life. Listen to the messages they bring about love and see how you can transform your life. If you dream that someone you love is being hurt, think about the source of the pain. Are you or another member of your circle inflicting damage? To see someone you love in pain sometimes feels worse than experiencing the pain yourself, especially if it is your child who is hurt.

CONNECTION

If flowers can grow through the strongest cement, love can find you at any point in your life. You cannot keep the spirit of love contained.

Betrayal

WHEN WE ARE LET DOWN, when our trust has been broken, or when we have betrayed others, dreams of disappointment and anger come to visit.

The act of adultery causes dreams of anger and loss. If you are in a relationship that seems stable, but you dream of being two-timed, see your partner with another lover, or sense infidelity, then you could explore your feelings of insecurity. Is your dream warning you about things that you do not acknowledge when you are awake? Rather than indicating that a partner is physically straying, your dream may be a metaphor of your anxiety that he or she is less attentive or is losing affection for you.

If you dream that you are having an adulterous affair, ask yourself if this is what you'd really like to do. Does it symbolize a desire for more creativity? Can you find ways to express and satisfy all kinds of passion in your life?

When I am depressed, I dream that someone I trust has turned on me. Betrayal by another may represent displacement. You project onto another person what you feel subconsciously. It may be too hard to accept that we betray ourselves, so we move the feeling, or displace it, onto someone else.

Feeling Guilty

GUILT IS A POWERFUL EMOTION that crops up in dreams involving close family members or friends. When her sons were small and she was going through an unhappy time, Lisa had this dream:

I'm in Canada by a fast-moving river where logs are rushing along. My small sons walk across the logs. I watch, knowing the danger, but do nothing to stop them. They fall into the water, but still I do nothing. Then I feel guilty. I jump up, run across the logs, and frantically search for them. They are gone and I cry.

The "log jam" that threatens Lisa and her sons represents the dangers that she faced at a time when she was depressed and felt powerless to look after her sons.

In this dream, my father has grown very old and is really ill. He later dies. I feel guilty, as if it is my fault, and I get really upset.

Many of us feel guilty when our parents die since part of us thinks we ought to be able to save them. This dream reflects that common reaction after bereavement.

Dreams in which you are accused of a crime—such as robbery or murder—may be linked to unconscious desires to steal or to kill someone who has made you angry. In waking life, we suppress these strong emotions, and in dreams, we still feel guilty or awkward even when we have not committed any crime at all.

Vulnerability

BEING ABANDONED IN A DREAM may reflect feelings of loss or separation or fear of being left behind on an emotional or physical level in waking life. These dreams often come at times such as divorce or death of a loved one. Abandonment dreams may help you realize what it is you fear. Do you fear being abandoned by a lover or by a child leaving home or going away to college? Recalling these dreams can help you acknowledge emotions that you avoid during waking life, such as vulnerability.

When I was six, my father died suddenly. We left Germany, where we were living, and I had recurring dreams of complete solitude, where everyone was dead except me.

More positively, such dreams may indicate that you are ready to abandon your old habits and attitudes, and anxious to take a new direction in your life.

Glass may feature in dreams of vulnerability; it is transparent and associated with windowpanes or even "pains." "Walking on glass" in a dream may foreshadow pain by being pierced in waking life. Broken glass indicates that all is "in pieces." Such dreams may reflect your emotional state.

CONNECTIONS

◎ *Are you "cut up" about something?*
◎ *Do you feel threatened or no longer whole?*

Fear

Those things which have occupied a man's thoughts and affections
while awake recur in his imagination while asleep.

THOMAS AQUINAS

DREAMS OFTEN REFLECT FEAR ABOUT WAKING ISSUES. During the day, we may
unconsciously deny our fears, but when we sleep, the defenses are down, and we
come face to face with them. Dreaming of rape, or of being violated, may relate to an
area of your life in which you feel violently forced to do something against your will
or better judgment. If you have suffered a sexual assault or had a narrow escape in
waking life, your dreams may reenact the trauma. This is typical of PTSD and you may
need professional help to recover from your ordeal. Amira had this dream after a spate
of arson attacks was reported in her area:

I dreamed that I was sitting on the couch and that, all around me, small
flames broke out. They were on the furniture, on me, and on the carpet. The
door was across the room, and I was really scared.

Courage

IT TAKES COURAGE TO UNDERTAKE DREAM WORK,
to explore your dreams, and to be willing to see aspects of yourself that have lain hidden in the dark for years. The pay-off for this courage is the discovery of a mine of rich potential, a new understanding, and the knowledge that you can face your dream monsters and survive intact. The feeling of courage in dreams has a special role in empowering the dreamer.

Perhaps the most important questions that you can ask yourself are: "Why am I having this dream now?" and "How does this dream serve my health and wholeness?"

Courage in dreams includes turning to face someone who threatens you, standing up for someone you care for, or outwitting those who have the potential to harm you. In some cases, in order to escape, you may become lucid in your dream (that is, you know that you are dreaming) and can take courage in both hands to do whatever you want to direct the outcome of the dream.

I've had dreams where I've been in personal danger. At a certain point, I was able to devise a way to get myself out because I knew it was a dream.

Universal Dream Experiences

CONNECTIONS

- How do your dreams reveal your courage?
- Are they telling you about something that you don't recognize in waking life?
- Is your dream about the courage of your convictions?

Triumph

WHEN YOU SUCCEED AT A TASK, or in a competition in which you thought you would fail, it brings a sense of great elation. If you have such a dream, is it because you undervalue your abilities? Is it a wish-fulfillment dream to compensate for recent failure? Staying alive at all can represent a great triumph:

There is a struggle of will with some awful "being." Sticks are pushed through my body to my eyes. I try to control my eyes and therefore my thoughts. I have an almighty struggle to free myself and manage to move a limb, breaking the spell.

The dream was filled with fear, but winning against this potentially overwhelming force left the dreamer much more confident about succeeding in her waking life.

Victory in a dreamed conflict sometimes involves great sacrifice, as in the wars of waking life. If you have been in such a situation, your dreams will remind you of the horrors as well as the triumphs. When you wake, recognize the victories and your role in winning a just peace. If you have not experienced a conflict situation, ask yourself what your dream victory relates to in your waking world.

Machines
WHEN MECHANICAL OBJECTS OF ANY KIND appear in

dreams, their function is highly significant. They can relate directly to the condition of machinery you use at home or at work or may symbolize mechanical, routine aspects of life. First, think about the physical machinery and whether you are worried that it has a fault or that it might break down. If this is not the case, then consider whether it is a symbol of your emotional life

Vacuum cleaner—Do you want to clean up your relationships? Do you have to suck up some "dirt" that is bothering you?

Electric mixer—Are you feeling mixed up about something? Do you want to combine elements of your life that are separate at the moment?

Juicer—Do you need added "juice" or energy?

Washing machine—What needs cleaning at present? Do you want to freshen up, and make a clean start?

Clothes dryer—Do you feel dried up, either physically or emotionally?

Crane—Do you need a lift, to get to a higher vantage point?

Digger—Does your path, or road, in life need an overhaul, or does it need to be repaired?

Steamroller—Do you feel that you are being flattened? Is something weighty bearing down on you?

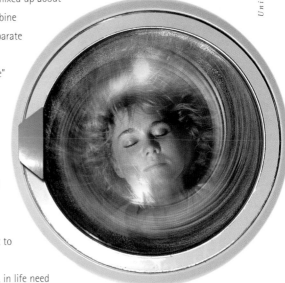

Technical Expertise

TO BE EXPERT AT SOMETHING affirms your self-esteem and confidence. The nature of the technical expertise gives you clues to its significance. For example, if in your dream you are making clocks, this has some link to time and your management of it. If you dream of writing a computer program, it may relate to waking use of a computer.

Technical expertise may also relate to physical skills. For example, if you dream of an acrobat or trapeze artist—a performer in a balancing act—what does this have to do with your current situation? Are you trying to keep your footing on a "high wire," perhaps at work? Is the acrobat performing confidently or anxiously? Does this reflect your feelings about a task that you have undertaken? Acrobats train to improve their balancing skills in order to be successful and so avoid danger. Is there some training that you need to prepare you for a future venture?

Acrobats stand on their hands, and so invert the normal human position. Could this be linked to a reversal in your life? Is some aspect "upside-down"? Consider any emotional reversals that you might be feeling.

Death

DEATH IS THE END of one stage of existence and the beginning of another. It may represent the end of an affair. Frequently, dreams of death at, or after, divorce mark the end of marriage, yet also the beginning of a new phase of life. According to Tibetan spiritual tradition, the recognition of death is central to the enhancement of life.

Many symbols of death appear in dreams. A harpist is regarded as bringing news of death. Similarly, an hourglass symbolizes time running out. Paintings that include the figure of Death often show him holding an hourglass and a scythe, signifying the reaping of the harvest at the end of the season.

Some cultures make death masks to retain an image of the deceased. The Aztec culture had a triple-death mask, which represented the cycle of life. It depicted old age and death overshadowing life.

In 1827, the murder of Maria Marten by her lover at Polstead in Suffolk, England, was reputed to have been discovered by her mother, who dreamed three times of the "red barn" where her daughter's body was eventually discovered.

CONNECTION

● *Banshee—A Celtic spirit particularly linked to Irish families. The banshee is said to wail as a warning that death is approaching and also when there is a death in the family. In dreams, she may appear as a woman with long hair, flying through the night sky.*

Rebirth

REBIRTH IS ALL ABOUT new beginnings and fresh chances. Sometimes, in order to continue with life, we have to adapt to survive.

In stories and myths, we find the tale of the hero who has to face a grueling journey in order to find some truth or save the world. In the process, he or she undergoes a transformation, a symbolic rebirth. Luke Skywalker, the hero of *Star Wars*, and Clark Kent, who became Superman, are two examples. They faced death but survived against the odds. In dreams, you may witness rebirth, see someone coming back from the dead, or be reborn yourself.

In Hinduism, the cycle of birth, death, and rebirth—*samsara*—is governed by *karma*, the moral law of the Universe. Reincarnation may occur thousands of times as the soul progresses, until it is free of all attachments to worldly pleasure.

CONNECTIONS

◉ *Do you feel that you need a new beginning?*

◉ *"Born-again Christians" are those who lost their Christian faith but come back to it with renewed evangelical commitment.*

◉ *Ushabti, figures carved from stone, were overseers of the dead. They symbolically carried out the work of their master in the afterlife, where he would be reborn.*

Falling

FALLING DREAMS CAPTURE A PRIMAL EMOTION. As babies, we have to learn to walk, but falling over is part of that learning process—and it can hurt. As we learn to stand upright and move freely, this represents the beginning of our independence. When we have falling dreams, we recapture the feeling of being out of control or the feeling that the ground has gone from under us.

When you have falling dreams, think about what support in your life feels shaky. You may be "falling for" someone—a new love in your life—or the opposite, "falling out" with someone. Falling can also be about feeling compelled to jump:

I am in a big room, like a warehouse. The room is very high. There are big archways and light glares through them. There is no glass, and I am terrified of falling through the archways, even though I am well away from them. As well as the fear of falling, I seem to feel I might jump.

Physical sensations that wake you are sometimes set off by the following type of vivid dream:

We were traveling through a tunnel in a car. We seemed to be going faster; then suddenly, the road ended and we fell. I could feel my stomach turn and that woke me up.

CONNECTIONS

◉ *Do you feel on shaky ground about a decision you need to make? Seek more information to increase your confidence.*

◉ *Have you recently experienced any trauma which makes you feel as if your world has "fallen apart"?*

Flying

Since he weighs nothing,
Even the stoutest dreamer
Can fly without wings.

W. H. AUDEN: THANKSGIVING FOR A HABITAT

FLYING DREAMS USUALLY CONCERN ESCAPING, RISING ABOVE DIFFICULTIES, or having
feelings of empowerment.

All of the walls were covered with insects. I tried to get downstairs to get
away from them. I tripped and started flying. I flew all around my house.

Many early childhood dreams of floating downstairs transform into adult dreams
of taking off and soaring through the sky. Flying can take a variety of forms: arms
outstretched like a superhero; cycling through the air; flapping arms like a bird, or
being carried by thermal drafts. In some cases, it involves changing shape.

I had the ability to change into a butterfly, and be able to fly to safety
whenever I felt threatened. The dream ended with a feeling of acute terror
at not being able to undergo the required metamorphosis, as an evil presence,
in the form of an old lady, approached me.

Though flying dreams give a sensation of power
and exhilaration, they may also symbolize the need for
an overview or a higher point of reference.

My dreams of flying unaided bring me total
joy—euphoria. I feel that I am in total
control of my own life.

Vehicle WHATEVER FORM THE VEHICLE TAKES, it usually symbolizes

the dreamer's personal state and life journey. Think about the direction in which the vehicle is going, whether it is on the right track or stuck in a dead end. Either way, does it represent your life at the moment?

When you have dreams about accidents, ask yourself what feels out of control in your life. Often, accidents are caused by a lack of concentration, being careless or reckless, or not giving yourself enough time to weigh the risks. Typically, such dreams involve losing control of a car, falling, being in the wrong place at the wrong time, being involved in a disaster such as a flood or earthquake, or being hurt by machinery that is not being driven properly.

If you dream of an accident in a vehicle, check on the cause of the accident when you wake. If your car's brakes failed in your dream, make sure they are roadworthy—sometimes, dreams warn us of things that we've noticed at a subliminal level in waking life. If poor brakes didn't trigger the accident dream, work out what they signify in your emotional life. Maybe you need to slow down or take break before you "break down."

Performance Driving

WHEN YOU ARE DRIVING successfully in your dream, or when you are competing in very fast races and feel thrilled with your performance, enjoy the pleasure of your success. You may have such an affirming dream after you have "driven through" a particularly difficult negotiation.

Whenever you have enhanced performance in dreams, it indicates that you are feeling empowered or that you have the potential to improve. Before interviews or examinations, many people dream that they have performed better than they anticipated. The dream leaves a residue of confidence that influences their waking actions.

Driving cars is often linked to sexual performance, so if you are driving excellently does it relate to your sexual prowess at present? Also, consider the condition of the car you are driving in your dream. If the car is a "high-performance" model, it will have a different connotation from a jalopy.

CONNECTIONS

◉ *Do you feel that your confidence is at a high point?*

◉ *Have you been pushing yourself in training, and now feel at peak-performance level?*

Missing Your Travel Connection

THIS CAN BE CAUSED BY LOSING YOUR WAY, or by being trapped and unable to progress. Whatever the cause, such dreams are usually related to feeling frustrated and held back in some way. When you are on a journey, the place where the connection is to be made is significant:

Airport—This is connected to arrivals and departures and may symbolize birth and death. Also, airports are transition points. If you miss your connection, does it represent an interruption in plans to bring about changes?

Railroad stations—Has someone gone off the rails? Are your plans being derailed, so you cannot make the connections you desire?

A connection links places and people together; however, when you miss a connection, it indicates some sort of failure. This may be because of an error on your part, misinformation from some other source, or because an outside force, such as bad weather, has disrupted the connection. If the missed connection is your fault, ask yourself if you give yourself enough time to do things in waking life. Do you leave things until the last minute or fail to make adequate preparations?

CONNECTIONS

◎ *Do you feel disconnected or alienated?*

◎ *Are you missing someone to whom you were connected in the past?*

Journeys

THE JOURNEY IS A POWERFUL IMAGE. Think of Adam and Eve—expelled from Paradise and doomed to travel forever outside the place to which they longed to return. In a sense, all life is a journey—from age to age, from known to unknown, and from birth to death.

A journey indicates movement in your life, which may be physical, emotional, or spiritual. It may be collective—in a group or on public transport, such as a train or bus. It may be alone—on foot or by car. The type of journey, method of transportation, and type of terrain all provide clues to aid interpretation. Companions may appear in the form of birds, animals, or guides. The atmosphere—safe or threatening—will tell you of your inner feelings.

At some point on a long journey, memories of home flood in. Travel writer Pico Iyer spent his childhood in England. His book *The Global Soul* describes how, when he reached Kyoto, he fell asleep. In this deep sleep, he dreamed of England with its

"green, green hills." His poetic words spoke the truth of his feelings of homesickness at the end of his travels. Even though he shares his time between Japan and California, his dreams always take him back to his childhood home.

Universal Dream Experiences

Discovering New Places

I dreamed that I was at a conference center with a group of people, waiting for the speaker (Jeannie) to arrive. Somehow, I knew that I had to "entertain" the other people until Jeannie came, and I took them into a room that I had never seen before. There were portraits on the walls, but there were also some empty spaces. We began to make portraits to complete the interior of the room.

I HAD THIS DREAM JUST BEFORE I WOKE so it stayed fresh in my mind. For me, it symbolizes the discoveries that I'm making as I write this book, and the new people that I meet while carrying out my research. I would describe it as a very affirming dream, and it set me up for an inspiring day of writing.

When you discover new places, ask yourself if you are ready to expand into new projects or into new dimensions in relationships. Consider the climate in the place—the lighting, and all the elements that make up the scene—and relate these to your present desires or needs. If it is a particular place, perhaps a landscape that is different from your usual setting, ask yourself what it has that you need. If you dream of a desert (see page 174), is it because you need plenty of open space, or perhaps some time alone? Or maybe you are feeling dehydrated and you need some water?

Finding New Rooms in Your House

THIS RELATES TO UNCOVERING NEW ASPECTS OF YOURSELF, because houses typically symbolize the dreamer.

I have the recurring dream that I am in a huge house—sometimes one known to me from my past, but not always. I am looking, or searching, for all the rooms in the house. I am always surprised, pleasantly I have to say, at the infinite number of rooms—there are too many for me to look into—and by their contents. They are often bedrooms, and the light is an orange color.

The dreamer has a great deal of unexplored potential, which she recognizes that she has to uncover. What she finds is pleasant, and the contents bode well. The orange color is also significant. Orange is linked with energy. It is a combination of yellow and red—the color of the life-giving sun and also the color of passion—and is an apt color for a bedroom.

CONNECTIONS

If you discover a new room, think about the function of that room:

- *Bedroom—Rest, sexual relationships, and sleep.*
- *Bathroom—Washing, bathing, hygiene, and elimination.*
- *Dining room—Feeding yourself, interaction with others, the sharing ritual of breaking bread together, and communication.*

Damage to Buildings

ON OCTOBER 21, 1966, nine-year-old Eryl Mai Jones told her mother about a terrible dream that she had had during the night. In the dream, she had gone to school, but it was no longer there because "something black had come over it." She was very distressed by the dream and tried to persuade her mother to let her stay at home that day. But Eryl Mai went to school, and was one of 144 students and teachers who died at Aberfan, South Wales, when tons of coal waste slid down from a slagheap and engulfed the school. Other dreams of damage to property may not be as predictive or dramatic as Eryl Mai's, but they are always worthy of attention.

If your property is damaged in a dream, first consider if you are worried about the physical condition of your home, and then look at the symbolic significance.

- Damaged walls allow outside elements to get through and undermine the stability of the roof. If they are damaged, it may signify that you feel undermined and unable to help yourself, and you may well be in need of external support.
- Broken doors cannot keep people out and so may indicate vulnerability or the inability to maintain boundaries.
- Broken windows leave you open to intruders and may affect your view of things.

Accidental damage is different from malicious damage, so consider the cause and who is responsible for the harm.

Home Improvements

DREAMS IN WHICH YOU MAKE CHANGES TO PROPERTY often relate to physical changes that you are making, or would like to make, to your home. Sometimes, wish-fulfillment dreams are triggered by television home make-over programs.

At first, I thought the house was a mess, but when I got inside, it was like a palace—everything was beautiful. My friend said, "Well, what did you expect? We've only just moved in."

This dream reflected the dreamer's disagreements with her husband about a house she wanted to buy, but he didn't. The conflict in the dream represents the two views about the house which is ultimately resolved once the dreamer had the opportunity to make changes. Her dream affirmed her vision that the house could be turned into a beautiful home, which is what happened.

Your home may symbolize you, the dreamer. Are there any improvements that you need to make to yourself?

CONNECTIONS

◉ *Could you do with a new "coat of paint" to brighten yourself up and project a fresher image?*

◉ *If you dream of building an extension, does this symbolize the need to expand your horizons?*

◉ *Putting on a new roof may relate to raising your sights and reaching higher levels than you currently achieve.*

◉ *Clearing or laying a new path may relate to new ways of making your way in life.*

Universal Dream Experiences

Burglary

BURGLARY INVOLVES TRESPASSING into a house or other building with the intent to commit robbery, rape, or some other crime. It involves an invasion of personal space and threatens the inhabitants.

Always, I am asleep in my own bedroom, and alone. In my dream, I awake, it is very dark, and there is a burglar in the house downstairs. I can hear the intruder rummaging through our belongings. Sometimes, there are two of them because I am aware that they are communicating, although I can hear no speech. I am so frightened that I cannot scream or even move from the bed. My legs are like lead, and I cannot move to warn my family ...

Dreams featuring loss of possessions or valuables often follow a waking robbery. However, they may also be caused by a recent, major upheaval, such as moving to a new house, a change at work, illness, or a family member leaving home. Symbolically, something you value has been taken away, and this feels like a violation.

CONNECTIONS

- Do you feel that your home is at risk in some way?
- Are you taking care of the "valuables" in your life, including yourself?

Toilets

TOILETS SYMBOLIZE ISSUES CONCERNING WASTE, both physical and emotional. However, on a practical level, toilet dreams may be triggered by a full bladder, which acts as a stimulus to wake up and visit the bathroom.

Dreams featuring problems with toilets—toilets that are too dirty to use, toilets that are flooding, toilet stalls without doors or with walls of glass—can indicate that the dreamer wants to eliminate waste material but is frustrated in some way. This "blockage" may relate to the dreamer's own psychological inability to "let go," to release negative, toxic feelings. Where this happens the retention of "waste" negative feelings damages the well-being of the dreamer and such dreams may be a warning call to clean up emotionally.

I dream that I must find a toilet to clean myself or remove stained underwear. I used to know where the bathroom was in this building, but everything has changed ...

This dream may represent a hidden part of the dreamer, which she thinks is in some way "dirty." This may be something she is ashamed of, and what removed the "stains" in the past won't work now. The dreamer has to find new ways to be cleansed.

CONNECTIONS

- *If you are observed using the toilet, who is the viewer? Can you make any connection to feeling overexposed to this person?*
- *Do you need to declutter—to get rid of material that is no longer useful to you?*
- *Pleasurable dreams of using the toilet may represent healthy self-expression and the symbolic release of outdated or completed aspects of your life.*

Meeting the Famous

FAMOUS PEOPLE APPEAR in our dreams just as they do in the media. When Diana, Princess of Wales, died, hundreds described how they had dreamed of her. Whenever there is a major event involving a celebrity or public figure, you can expect an upsurge in this type of dream. Usually, they are wish-fulfillment dreams, in which the dreamers meet their heroes. In others, the hero appears as a friend and gives helpful advice.

I dreamed that I was wandering around a derelict house with Kate Moss. I asked her what she'd wanted to be before she was a model. She said that she'd wanted to be a doctor.

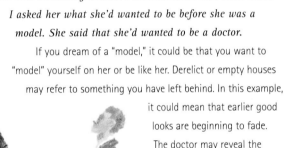

If you dream of a "model," it could be that you want to "model" yourself on her or be like her. Derelict or empty houses may refer to something you have left behind. In this example, it could mean that earlier good looks are beginning to fade. The doctor may reveal the dreamer's own early desires, which were unfulfilled.

CONNECTIONS

◎ *Do you long for fame and fortune?*

◎ *Would you like more recognition for your "star" qualities?*

Loss of Sight

IF YOU LOSE YOUR SIGHT in a dream, it may relate to waking problems with your vision, or a fear that a visit to the optometrist will bring bad news. If you are worried after such a dream, then arrange to have an eye examination.

Losing sight may indicate that you have lost your sense of direction or that you are blind to your potential.

I was playing lacrosse, but I went blind, and I couldn't carry on.

You may want an excuse to give up an activity, so being blind gives you a way out.

Another aspect of the inability to see may be formed by the idea that there are invisible, spiritual presences. Christians are taught that, although they cannot see God, he can see them, and that Jesus is always present.

The Irish word for poet—*file*—originated from the Indo-European root meaning "to see." This is also linked to the idea of being a "seer." Dreams may allow you to

glimpse the future, in the way in which poets can connect ideas that take on a different dimension.

Evil eye—the widespread belief found in Europe, the Middle East, and Africa that certain people could inflict harm simply with a glance—was also known as "overlooking." So, is being overlooked a way of receiving pain or damage? Has this happened to you recently?

CONNECTION

◎ *Have you lost sight of the path forward?*

◎ *Are you blind to opportunities that are available to you?*

◎ *Have you been "blinded" by an unexpected event that has turned your life upside-down?*

Loss of Hearing

A DREAM WHERE ALL sound has stopped may indicate problems with your ears or your hearing. If there is no physical trigger for such dreams, then consider the symbolic significance. Have you heard something that has upset you? Are there words that you would rather not hear right now? Selective deafness, or choosing not to hear, is a form of self-defense. It protects us temporarily from that which feels potentially overwhelming.

Ears represent our openness, our receptivity, and the willingness to listen to our inner selves, as well as to others.

In my dream, everyone seemed to be talking to one another, but for me it was totally silent. No one noticed, and I was terrified.

CONNECTION
◎ *Is your dreamed hearing loss related to avoiding unpleasant criticism?*

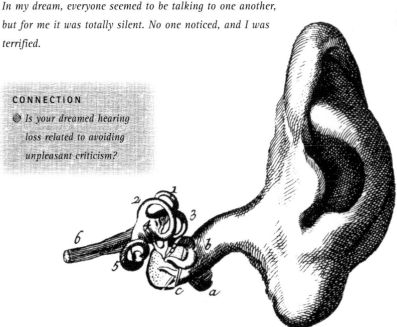

Loss of Voice COMMUNICATION IS THE FOCUS

whenever the voice is involved in a dream. Some of the most distressing dreams are when you cannot call out for help—when you open your mouth to scream, but no sound comes out.

I was in a coffin, supposedly dead, but I could hear everything that was going on around me. I could hear my mother saying that it was time to put the coffin lid on. But I couldn't move or speak. Fortunately, this dream ended quickly.

Take a look at who else is in the dream. Who cannot hear you? Do you have difficulties communicating with this person in your waking life? In the examples above and below, one dreamer's mother and another dreamer's colleagues reflect different areas of concern.

In my dream, I was arguing with my fellow teachers. I was shouting so much, trying to be heard, that I lost my voice.

CONNECTION

Do you need to give your voice a rest? Should you listen more and say less?

Teeth Falling Out
LOSING TEETH IN A DREAM

may reflect waking problems, but may also symbolize loss, the breaking of attachments, moving out, or moving away. This may also be linked with the image that you present to the world at large.

This short dream seems to occur within other dreams. I realize that my teeth are crumbling, just like chalk pieces. I put my hand up to my chin, and my teeth fall out into my hand, in brownish-white crumbs.

In some dreams, the teeth become loose but stay in the dreamer's mouth and begin to choke her. If this happens to you, does it mean that you are choking something back, forcing yourself to keep your feelings and thoughts to yourself at the expense of damaging yourself?

Dreams of losing teeth happen when there are major changes in your life, for instance, when you move away from home, take a new direction, or separate from your partner.

CONNECTIONS

◎ *If your teeth are crumbling in a dream, does it represent something that is breaking down and being crushed so that it no longer has any form or strength? Is your spirit being crushed?*

◎ *If you have root-canal work, does this link to the root cause of a problem in your life?*

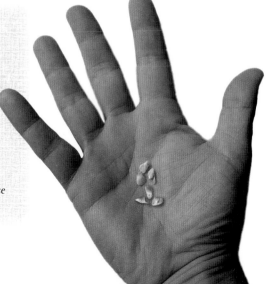

Loss of Belongings

WE INVEST IN WHAT BELONGS TO US. So, whether it is a car, a wallet, a purse, or clothing, it has personal relevance for us. The nature of the loss is important. Has it been stolen? Lost after a flood or other natural disaster? Lost in transit while you were on a journey? Taken away from you as punishment? Explore the circumstances and see how they fit with your waking life.

Any container, such as a purse, is the "holder" of private documents that identify us, such as credit cards or a driver's license. This may be linked to secrecy. In losing the purse, our personal details go into the public domain, enabling others to take advantage of us. Also, losing such things may symbolize loss of identity.

CONNECTIONS

- *Have you changed your appearance or undergone surgery that has affected your sense of identity?*
- *Has a member of your family been "lost" through a disagreement?*
- *Do you no longer feel as if you belong somewhere?*

Recovering Lost Property

FINDING WHAT YOU HAVE LOST brings feelings of relief and joy. The property recovered will indicate the focus you need to follow. Consider the following:

Purse—Linked to identity, since it contains so many personal possessions. Recovering a lost purse may indicate a renewed sense of self and security.

Wallet—Money, driver's license, and credit cards may be contained here. Have you been concerned about finances but feel in a stronger position now?

Camera—Taking photographs lets us hold onto experiences, but they are not authentic and may indicate an attempt to hold onto the status quo, or to seek a false sense of security.

Clothes—Recovering lost clothes may indicate a renewal of security, since clothing provides protection.

Shoes—Finding lost shoes can mean that you are recovering your lost footing.

Keys—Loss of keys means that you cannot access your home or car. Recovering them means that you may enter once more.

Cell phones—The return of phones signifies reconnection and renewed communication.

Healing

WHEN ZENA WAS DIAGNOSED WITH CANCER, she was given two surgical options. She was left with the decision either to have "everything taken away" or to have minor surgery and wait to see how she fared.

Before Zena made her decision, she dreamed that she was in an airplane, taxiing for take-off. As she looked out of the window, she saw a woman running alongside, shouting, "You can't take off—it's gone to the belly of the plane. Get everything out!" She took this to mean that she had to choose the radical operation. Otherwise, her recovery could not "take off." When the operation was carried out, the surgeon discovered that the cancer had spread much farther than they had realized, and told Zena that her decision had probably saved her life.

Clarissa Pinkola Estes, Ph.D., described a healing dream in which a woman who was having open-heart surgery realized that there was no roof and that the overhead operating light was the sun itself. The sun touched the woman's heart, and the surgeon said that no further surgery was necessary. On waking, the dreamer felt healed and reassured that her operation, when she had it in waking life, would be as successful as the one she experienced in her dream.

John had a recurring image whenever he was unwell. In the middle of an ordinary dream, he said that a Chinese man might pop up from nowhere and hand him a glass of white liquid, which he would drink. The morning after this image had appeared in his dream, he always felt better.

Being Paralyzed

NIGHTMARES CAN BE SO

DISTRESSING that you may force yourself awake with such speed that the brain has not fully switched into waking mode. This gives rise to the sensation of being paralyzed— you cannot shout for help, but you can open your eyes and see. Although this is frightening and distressing—since you are physically locked into the fear of the dream—it is not unusual. However, if you wake up this way frequently, you could spend more time trying to identify the underlying cause of your nightmares and so reduce their impact.

If you are paralyzed in a dream, it may indicate that you are stuck in some aspect of your life. Being unable to move makes you vulnerable and powerless.

People who have been paralyzed following an accident frequently dream that they are able-bodied once more. The dreams compensate the dreamer by taking them back to previous capabilities. Robert Haskell, a dream researcher, described a woman whose arm was paralyzed. In her dream, an animal was attacking her pet dog and she was beating it off with her arm, which was no longer defective. When she woke, her arm was completely restored in reality.

Illness

PRODROMIC DREAMS are those that occur before illness. They may serve as a warning, or a wake-up call, for the dreamer. If you are having treatment for an illness, these dreams may reflect your concerns. In dream groups for cancer patients, participants reported an upsurge in anxiety dreams just before routine check-ups, or chemotherapy. Such dreams help us to recognize anxiety and give it an outlet.

For I had lost the right path ...
DANTE

Dante described as "a dark mood" what we call depression—an illness that blights many lives. People suffering from depression have dreams with a higher masochistic content and more subdued, grayer colors than in others' dreams. These colors reflect the gloom of their waking lives.

Shamans, or *kahunas*, of the South Seas, routinely use dreams when working with people who are ill or disturbed.

Communication with the Dead

THE APPEARANCE OF A DEAD PERSON IN A DREAM can cause terror or joy, depending on the dreamer's perspective. Does the dead person come to threaten or advise you, to comfort you or remind you of the distress of the death, as it does for the second dreamer below?

After my father died, I had a series of dreams about him. First, I dreamed that he wasn't actually dead. Then, I dreamed that he wouldn't accept that he was dead. Next, I dreamed that he was getting better in the other world. Finally, I had a lovely dream where I met him. He looked years younger than while he was dying of cancer. He put his arms around me, told me that he was fine now, and that he loved me, and not to worry about him anymore.
I felt good when I woke, and have felt good about him ever since.

This dream is in stark contrast to the first.

After my friend committed suicide,
I dreamed that he was in a revolving
door. He didn't come out and the door kept
revolving, although his face appeared with a ghastly
haunted look on it—sort of tortured, mocking, with
a half smile. With each revolution, his face would
decay more and more.

Your dreams will replay the action, especially after an emotional "revolution," such as a friend's suicide, that has turned your safe world upside-down.

Communication COMMUNICATION INVOLVES SIGHT,

HEARING, AND SPEECH. Difficulties in communication indicate frustration.

I dream that I am at home and that someone is trying to break in. I pick up the telephone to dial for help, but no matter how many times I dial the number, it just won't connect.

The mailman, bringer of news, is our modern equivalent of Mercury, the messenger god. Where mail is lost or the mailman cannot get through because of bad weather, for example, it may indicate feelings of being isolated, not getting the message or being left out. This also relates to communication via e-mail, where your Internet provider goes down or there is a fault with your computer. If this happens, ask yourself about the effectiveness of your communication.

I met an old boyfriend. We agreed to exchange phone numbers.

I started to write his number down, but, after a few digits, he said that he'd forgotten the rest. In the dream I kept thinking, "He doesn't want to give me the rest."

The original communication problems in the dreamer's previous relationship are still evident in the dream.

CONNECTION
Do you feel blocked, inhibited, or held back from getting your message across?

Forgetting

DREAMS OF FORGETTING WHERE WE LIVE, or where we left the car or the baby that we are responsible for, are common. On a simple level, they reinforce our sense of responsibility and perhaps the waking stress to which we are subjected. For instance, if you dream that you have forgotten to complete a report at work, it may indicate anxiety about work. Perhaps you feel that the task is beyond you or that others will see you as incompetent.

On another level, such dreams may symbolize an unconscious desire to leave something behind. We may forget where we live because, on an unconscious level, we don't want to go home. Or we may leave a baby behind because we are tired of the responsibility of looking after someone else. The baby may represent anyone who depends on us, not just a small child.

I'm far from home, and suddenly realize that I've left the baby in the house alone. I hurry back, fearful at what I'll find, but the baby is fine, playing or crawling about quite happily. Then I realize that I had arranged for someone to look after him. I'm so relieved.

This dream expresses anxiety yet reinforces the dreamer's sense that she is a responsible, caring person.

DREAMS ABOUT TAKING A TEST show that a situation is causing you anxiety. The stressful impact of tests at school stays with us and may recur at other "testing" times. For example, one dreamer told me about her dream of showing up for a Latin test, only to find that she has forgotten to study an important topic. If you have this kind of dream, think about how it relates to testing situations in your life at present.

I'm in a large audition hall trying out for a big part. I'm scared but excited. In the acting section, I fluff all my lines. I feel embarrassed and humiliated. All the others, including the judges, start laughing at me.

This dream expresses the fear of looking foolish or becoming a laughing stock. When you make the transition from one state of consciousness, or awareness, to another, you can expect dreams in which you have to undergo a ritual test or examination of some kind.

Judgment

THE COURTROOM IS A PLACE OF JUDGMENT. This may be linked to judging yourself, feeling self-conscious, or being judged by others. If it is not related to a waking situation, for example, with court attendance, could it be that you are feeling exposed and that you are being made to defend yourself?

When we are judged, whether in a competition, an examination, or a court of law, we are either accepted or rejected—we pass or fail. Is there a situation in which you are being tested at the moment? Moving from one stage of life to another often involves having to pass a test of acceptance and adaptation.

Justice is depicted as a blind woman, holding a sword and scales. The Virgin Mary is also known as the Mother of Justice. If you dream of a female figure holding weighing scales, it could represent your own search for justice or be related to a decision you must make.

CONNECTION

◎ *If you dream of a lawyer, are you concerned about a legal situation, or does it reflect an interrogation of some kind?*

House on Fire

RECURRING DREAMS that began in childhood often indicate that the source of the dream also began during this period. This dreamer has felt insecure for most of her life, although she now has her childhood dream infrequently.

I am in a house on fire; it is always my mother's house. I stand at the top of the stairs, with the fire behind me. At the bottom of the stairs, I am confronted by snarling dogs. I don't know which way to go. The dream always ends the same way: I die and wake up feeling hot and exhausted.

As a young girl, the dreamer felt divided loyalties when her parents split up and didn't know which way to turn. The dream dramatically portrays her sense of being caught in the middle. Fire in dreams may represent anger that we suppress when awake.

Fire may also be linked to post-traumatic stress disorder (PTSD). Diarist Samuel Pepys recorded an entry for September 2, 1666, in which he described the terror of the Great Fire of London and how he had tried to save his own valuables. Later, he began to have "dreams of fire and falling down of houses." Six months later, he was still having problems sleeping because of "terrors of fire."

Drowning

IF YOU LIVE BY THE SEA, or close to an expanse of water, it is quite natural to dream of water, since it is an important feature of your environment. You may dream of drowning because of warnings of possible danger, as this woman did:

I used to dream that my brothers and I were all in the sea, that they were drowning, and that I was desperately trying to keep their heads up.

This could also reflect the dreamer's feelings of responsibility toward her brothers. Dreams of being submerged and unable to breathe may indicate that you feel smothered or out of your depth.

If you dream of someone you love drowning, it may be because you recognize that they are involved in some activity that may "swamp" them, causing them to lose their balance and, in the worst-case scenario, be "washed away" or "washed up."

Drowning may also be linked to floods, so consider whether you are feeling inundated and overloaded.

CONNECTION

◎ *Do you feel submerged by what is going on in your life? How can you reach the surface to get yourself some air?*

Being Lost LOSING YOUR WAY and finding yourself in a

strange place, unable to find your way home, is a common anxiety dream. The father
of the following dreamer died when she was six, and she has had many other
separations since—events that have left her feeling very insecure.

I always seem to be lost and alone, even if I start off with a crowd of
people. I always end up wondering where I am, and I'm never able to find
the best way to get home.

Sometimes, dreaming that you are locked out of your home indicates a feeling of
rejection and exclusion.

My friend, my home, and all points of reference have disappeared. I'm
wandering around trying to find someone I know, so that I will be safe. I'm
panicking but trying to appear calm, so nobody will know how distressed I am.

Symbolically, the house or home may represent the self, so being locked out may
indicate feelings of loss of self or alienation and insecurity.

The experience of being lost can have also have a positive outcome. An Irish
legend tells of the hero Cormac who became lost in a mist and, when it finally cleared,
found himself next to a well. Inside the well, he
saw five salmon, which survived by eating
the hazelnuts that dropped from nine
hazel trees surrounding the well.
Five rivers flowed from this source
into the five provinces of Ireland—
representing the five senses from
which all knowledge comes.
Cormac realized that being lost
was a blessing because he had
found the Well of Knowledge.

Being Trapped

I dream that I am in a room, and the walls are closing in on me. I'm not frightened because the walls are made of sponge.

THE NURSE WHO HAD THIS DREAM said that it came when she was feeling stressed. The sponge symbolized the fact that she felt she could not "soak up" any more, literally or emotionally. Although the walls seemed to "cushion" the impact, nonetheless she knew that she would be squeezed to death if the dream continued.

When you have dreams of being trapped in a confined space, ask yourself if you feel constrained in waking life. What do you need to do to get outside your "box"? Sometimes we feel trapped by our circumstances, and dreams highlight this fact.

In dreams where people have trapped you, think about why this has happened and what they want from you. Does it reflect a waking situation—for example, feeling trapped in a loveless marriage or a dead-end job?

I had a recurring dream that my friends and I were stuck in the back of a truck. We were being kidnapped. Every so often, a couple of people would get out, but I was always the last to leave.

Being held against your will indicates fear about the potential power of other people to control your life.

Escaping Danger

I dreamed that I was in a car, driving very fast. The setting was in somewhere like a jungle. Suddenly, an elephant started charging toward me. I was terrified but kept hooting the horn, and, at the last moment, the elephant swerved away.

THE DIFFERENT ELEMENTS OF ANY DREAM in which you are escaping danger are significant. If we consider them in this dream, we have:

Car—If you are driving very fast, are you out of control?

Jungle—This may reflect feelings about the dreamer's environment, as in, "It's a jungle out there."

Elephant—This animal is wild but can be domesticated. The elephant is big, which signifies power, has a long memory, and is associated with strong libido.

This dreamer has to "deflect" a threat, which she does successfully:

I dream that I can't get out of the house. Then, when I do, I am chased by a giant man. He can cover twice as much ground as I can. I always wake up before he catches me.

The threat is from a larger-than-life person, with twice as much power. The only way to escape is to "wake up." If this is how you escape in your dreams, what do you need to "wake up" to? What are you missing, or avoiding, when you are awake? Things won't improve until you face up to them.

Surviving

FOLLOWING TRAUMA, dreams frequently repeat the disturbing event. Though the person has survived, their dreams remind them that there is an emotional scar that needs further healing. The American writer Russell Banks still dreams of his violent, alcoholic father, who abandoned the family when Russell was twelve. Although his father died in 1979, Russell still dreams of him two or three times a week, especially if he is feeling betrayed, upset, or abandoned. That early experience of violence has left a marker in his dreams. However disturbing such dreams are, ultimately they reinforce the fact that the dreamer has survived.

Antoine was seventeen when he told me about the following dream, which greatly disturbed him.

All I can remember is that my dad died. I think he was shot. I was so distraught that I held a shotgun under my jaw and pulled the trigger. I felt my life going away from me. I was right on the brink of death, or possibly just past it, when I started to recover. I was in immense pain, and realized that I was in very bad shape, with a horrible disfigurement to my head.

Unspoken fears about death, suicide, and loss in general, are dramatically portrayed in nightmares such as Antoine's. They access feelings covered up in our waking life and allow us to face what troubles us most.

Whatever the source of fear, survival is of paramount importance.

Man-Made Disasters

IN A RADIO INTERVIEW, novelist Nina Bawden explained how she recalled the horrific Potter's Bar railway crash in England in 2002. For a week, she was in intensive care, and did not know that she had been in an accident in which seven people were killed, and seventy injured. The first hint that she was involved was when she dreamed that her husband was dead. When she finally woke, to find her family keeping vigil around her hospital bed, she asked if her dreams were true. They were.

Often, our dreams will give us information that our conscious mind cannot allow. Survivors of disasters find that dreams give details, and allow the dreamer to come to terms with the event.

British author Graham Greene wrote about a dream he had when he was five years old. It happened on the night of the *Titanic* disaster.

I dreamt of a shipwreck. One image has stayed with me for more than sixty years: a man in oilskins doubled over beside a companionway under the bow of a great wave.

Greene said that he also experienced dreams about shipwrecks on nights when other vessels sank.

War

THERE ARE MANY DIFFERENT TYPES OF WAR, from world war, which is officially proclaimed and fought according to international rules, to holy war, such as a *jihad*, in which people defend or attack in the name of their faith. If you dream of war, it may reflect events that are happening in the world or may reveal an inner conflict that is disturbing you.

Disturbances in your neighborhood may trigger dreams of conflict, as they did for this Muslim dreamer:

There was a sense of imminent "war" between my family and devils in human form. There were feelings of inevitable defeat, but the dream ended on a high note when, with the help of a group of angels, we won the war.

When the dreamer's family moved, the racially-motivated conflict was left behind.

In war, the recognition that friend and foe are not so different can give rise to this type of dream:

I dreamed I was in a Balkan country, in a huge castle. I was running around trying to find old clothes so I could stay warm. There was a war going on, and I was given an enormous bazooka gun that fired grenades. I kept firing them into the middle ground, close to "my people"—not at the enemy.

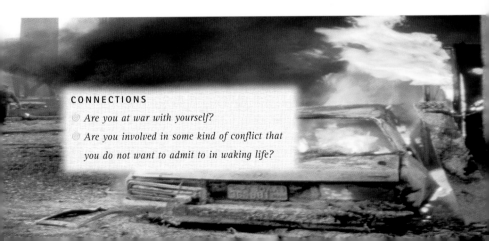

CONNECTIONS

◉ *Are you at war with yourself?*

◉ *Are you involved in some kind of conflict that you do not want to admit to in waking life?*

Natural Disasters WHEN EVENTS SUCH

AS EARTHQUAKES, FLOODS, AND HURRICANES take place, those involved report
nightmares that reenact their fears. In the disaster at Aberfan, South Wales, when
a slagheap engulfed a village school, many children were killed. Survivors suffered
recurrent nightmares. Jeff Edwards, one of the pupils, recalled, "I was buried very close
to a little girl and had nightmares for a long time afterward." Many of those involved
still have disturbing dreams years after the event:

*This is a recurring dream about being engulfed by a tidal wave. Sometimes
I am by a beach and other times I am walking down a street from my
childhood. I know that the wave is coming, and I have to prepare for it.
Sometimes I am successful, and the water washes over me. I know I am
underneath it, but mostly I feel calm. Sometimes I die, and then I wake up.*

After a traumatic event, recurring nightmares are eventually transformed into less
direct replications of the actual event. After September 11, 2001, people began to
dream of tidal waves, instead of towers on fire. The tidal wave is a similarly life-
threatening event that comes out of the blue.

Magical Creatures

I used to dream that I was in my garden, searching for something.
Lots of fairies were helping me.

MAGICAL CREATURES TURN UP IN DREAMS THROUGHOUT LIFE. They highlight fears and connect you to stories and myths that have a strong impact on you. When she turned seven, Sally dreamed that she arrived home from school and knocked on the door:

A dragon came to the door and told me, perfectly politely, that my parents had moved and didn't live there anymore. I felt annoyed with the dragon.

Such dreams reflect childhood fears of being deserted.

Giants may represent spiritual as well as physical powers. "A giant among men" in your dream may be a guide who comes to give you superior insight.

It was once believed that the unicorn's horn could detect or neutralize poisons and cure many diseases. The tusks of narwhals were often passed off as unicorn horns.

Many dreamers report feelings of a great weight on their chest and a sense of great evil. Sometimes, the dreamer sees a figure that is sexually rapacious. These figures are known as *incubi* and *succubi* and are demons in the form of imps. They were often included in paintings in medieval times and symbolized the uncontrolled world of dreams and desire.

Wearing Special Clothing

IF YOU DREAM OF BEING DRESSED IN CLOTHES THAT YOU DO NOT NORMALLY WEAR, consider what they represent. Often, different clothes symbolize the removal of everyday restraints, the opportunity to display a hidden part of you.

To be dressed as a shaman may indicate a mystical, healing dimension. A clown's costume may show the need to bring more fun and humor into your life.

Being dressed as a Native American shows links to a natural existence, where animals and the land are cherished and respected.

If you are dressed in disguise, as for a carnival, it may provide a license to do mischief—where the usual rules are overturned and anything is possible.

Dressing in clothes from a historical period may reveal an interest in that era or connect you to some ancestor who lived at that time.

Masks allow you to act differently— they can mask your feelings.

If you are wearing a uniform of any kind—such as policeman, nurse, or soldier—it may symbolize a desire for authority or knowledge.

Wearing animal disguises, such as leopard skins or antlers, can represent a need for the strengths and characteristics of those animals.

Being Naked

BEING NAKED IN YOUR DREAMS is not unusual. The key feature is to recognize what you feel about your situation. If you feel at ease and comfortable, it reflects your sense of confidence about yourself in relation to others. Where you feel embarrassed or on show, it may indicate a sense of being at a disadvantage.

A common, upsetting dream is where you find yourself walking down the street wearing inappropriate clothing that leaves you exposed.

I dreamed that I went to school wearing only a tiny shirt. I tried to cover myself up, but never could.

Being naked may allow you to discover completely new dimensions, as it did for this female dreamer:

I am not always female in my dreams, or even human, although I am always "me" in different bodies—male, child, different female body, animal, etc. I can be a man after swapping to a woman and vice versa.

The dreamer finds that she embodies all of these aspects—just as we all do. To find balance and feel complete, we have to integrate the different facets of our selves.

Erotic Encounters

EROTIC DREAMS MAY BEGIN IN EARLY ADOLESCENCE, as they did for this dreamer:

From the age of eleven, I used to have masochistic, sexual dreams of being a slave in Ancient Egypt.

By being the "slave" the dreamer is relieved of responsibilty for the sexual events and so avoids feelings of personal guilt that may arise.

Giving yourself sexual pleasure in dreams may relate to an actual act or may indicate an area of your waking life in which you are concentrating on your own desire. Does it relate to feeling selfish about a waking personal pursuit that excludes other people? How do you feel in the dream—happy, frustrated, orgasmic? It may be a wish-fulfillment dream or may indicate sexual frustration, since dreams can be both symbolic and literal. Sexual fantasies can safely be explored in the dream state.

The partners who feature in my erotic dreams are more likely to be men I don't know, or don't know very well, than to be my boyfriend. In one dream, I went for an interview to be a teacher at a college. After being interviewed by the principal, I had to find a young man who would show me around.

I found him in the library. I thought he was nice-looking, and he smiled at me. As he showed me around, he started putting his arm around me. We ended up forgetting the guided tour and spent the afternoon in his room having sex.

CONNECTIONS

- *Do your erotic dreams make up for a lack of sexual expression in your waking life?*
- *Do they enable you to express your sexuality more freely?*

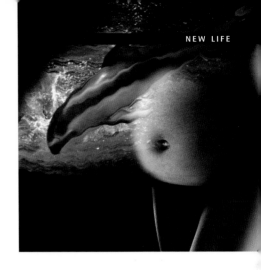

Pregnancy

DURING PREGNANCY, AS THE FETUS DEVELOPS, women's dreams are rich with images of change. For many women, the first indication that they are pregnant comes in a powerful dream. Robert Van de Castle, American dream researcher and author, described how his wife, Susanna, dreamed that she was looking for a baby thermometer in a department store. Suddenly, she saw a circular indoor swimming pool, in which a dolphin and a woman were swimming, and Susanna climbed into the water to join them. Symbols of conception—the "fish" and the circular, water-filled pool—were obvious to Van de Castle. The pregnancy test taken after this dream confirmed that there was a baby on the way. During pregnancy, dreams can be a very useful way of releasing fear:

I dreamed that I was having a baby, and complaining to my family and friends because it would hurt so much—and that I didn't want it. I felt terrified, but when I had the baby, it came suddenly, and didn't hurt at all.

An American obstetrician found that his rate of premature deliveries dropped from 6.5 percent to 2.8 percent, after he began paying attention to anxiety dreams of pregnant women. If you are pregnant and have anxious dreams, talk to your doctor, partner, or midwife. They should be able to reassure you and help you to address your natural concerns.

My mother always dreams of fish when someone is going to have a baby. Many women dream of fish when they become pregnant. This may fit in with the idea of the embryo in the amniotic fluid swimming in its watery world like a fish.

Birth

DREAMING OF BIRTH may be the result of seeing someone who is pregnant, being pregnant yourself, or may relate to the whole process of fertility.

I dreamed that I gave birth to a skinny, black-haired baby, who was fragile, and extraordinarily beautiful. He was so lovely that I felt it to be one of the happiest dreams I have ever experienced. When I did give birth, my baby was exactly like my dream baby.

On a symbolic level, birth is about the emergence of a new self—a bringing forth of new awareness and fresh talents.

CONNECTIONS

- *Was the labor itself easy or hard? Do you need to labor at a project to bring it to a successful conclusion?*
- *Birth certificate—These dreams concern identity, and being given rights in a society.*
- *Birth control—Are you concerned about your fertility, or about becoming pregnant accidentally?*
- *"Not born yesterday"—Worldly wise, neither stupid nor easily taken in.*
- *"Born with a silver spoon in his or her mouth"—When a baby is born to wealthy parents.*

Babies

I had a recurring dream during pregnancy that I had had a baby, but forgot about it for several days. When I went back to it, it had died of starvation and neglect.

A NEW BIRTH MAY BE FOLLOWED BY DREAMS OF BABIES, in which anxieties are released. However, the dreams are frequently linked to new development in the dreamer's life—the release of dormant potential or the discovery of new talents and capabilities.

I'm suddenly aware that I have lost my baby. He has been taken by an unknown "them." I can't believe that I've handed him over and let him go. The remorse and fear are terrible.

Dreams about neglecting a baby, or failing to protect him or her in some way, may be related to fears about your children, or may reflect the fact that you are not paying enough attention to yourself. It can indicate denial of potential. The opposite is indicated in dreams of finding a baby, where you are connecting to previously hidden personal abilities or potentials. New babies symbolize fresh starts, new opportunities, or learning new skills.

If you dream of people leaving babies with you— for you to look after—without asking you or without leaving adequate food and clothing, it may indicate that you are being given other peoples' responsibilities.

Sometimes dream babies surprise and disturb because they act out of character and not as ordinary babies do:

I dream of babies who are able to talk and behave like adults—not a very pleasant sensation.

Being Invisible INVISIBILITY IN DREAMS

can offer protection against pursuers, for example when you have a magic cloak or possess the power to disappear from view. On the other hand, when you are invisible in a dream, it can indicate that you feel ignored—that you and your life are insignificant to others who claim to care for you.

I sometimes dream of being in a room where nobody remembers me. It's as if I am invisible, and I'm completely ignored.

If you dream of being invisible, it may indicate that you are hiding from others or yourself. By hiding your views, hopes, and wishes it is impossible for others to truly

"see" the real, authentic you. If you have this type of dream, it may be time to look at how you present yourself to other people and to make changes to take up your place in the world.

CONNECTIONS

- *Do you feel overlooked and left out?*
- *Do you keep your thoughts and feelings hidden so no one can see the real you?*

Shapeshifter

DREAMS IN WHICH PEOPLE WE KNOW CHANGE INTO SOMETHING—or someone—else can be very disturbing. They almost always involve facial changes, for example, where someone may suddenly look menacing. In other dreams, it is the "monster" that changes.

I dreamed a long, involved dream in which I was captured by a "monster" that was capable of metamorphosing into different and odd forms. Then, when I thought I was free, it appeared in front of me in different guises. It was an amorphous dark blob—very evil, but with a personality.

Sometimes, these shapeshifters represent unpredictable people with whom we are intimate—the bond and the threat are symbolically represented. There is no escape for the dreamer, no matter how hard she tries. Where this happens, it is useful to think about who, in your life, has different facets that disturb you—one minute kind and at another time hurtful. For example, someone might be loving yet change under the influence of alcohol. Try to make a connection to your waking life

As in the fairytale *Beauty and the Beast*, a beast may be transformed by love. In this case, the shapeshifting is a form of moral test: Can the heroine uncover the beauty behind the beast's monstrous appearance?

CONNECTIONS

- *What lies below the outer skin of your dream beast?*
- *Is your dream beast related to a "beast of burden"?*

WE ALL LIVE IN THE NATURAL WORLD, with the sky above us and the ground beneath our feet. Whether the sky is gray or blue, and whether the ground is desert or pavement, we live in an environment that fills us with images and sensations. We are influenced by, and dependent on, the elements, and our dreams reflect this relationship.

In your dreams of the natural world, look for connections between

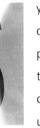

yourself and the earth. Although, consciously or unconsciously, we store knowledge of physical, spiritual, or emotional significance, the deep wisdom that comes to us from our connection with the natural world often goes unrecognized. In this chapter you will see how vital the symbolic links are.

In New Zealand, there is a Maori creation story that captures the power of nature and reflects our human need to understand and explain our world. According to the story, Sky Father and Earth Mother embraced each other in the deep darkness. In between them were their children, the gods of the sea, wind, forest, and food—and one other god called *the fierce one*. In order to reach the light, these children had to separate their parents. Although this separation was necessary for the sake of humanity, it made everyone sad, and tears in the form of raindrops fell from the sky.

Natural Phenomena

Natural Phenomena

I want to keep my dreams, even bad ones, because without them I might have nothing all night long.

JOSEPH HELLER: SOMETHING HAPPENED

The Taoist philosophy emphasizes the importance of our respectful relationship with nature, particularly mountains, trees, waterfalls, and lakes. You can see this in classic Chinese paintings, where landscapes have a timeless beauty, and people, if included, are seen as tiny figures against the majesty of the mountains.

Over millennia, natural objects have taken on symbolic meaning: In dreams, it is important to consider the symbolic, as well as the surface, meaning. For instance, if you dream of a pineapple, it may be because you ate pineapple before you fell asleep, but there are other aspects to consider too. During the seventeenth and eighteenth centuries, sailors returning to England from the South Seas would impale a fresh pineapple on their gatepost, as a sign that they had come back. Stone-carved pineapples are still used to decorate entrances. So, earthquake can change lives. Rain may not come and crops may fail. In order to exert some control, humans have built up rituals to influence the natural world. In African traditions, the "trickster" symbolizes this realization that life is subject to unexpected changes, fateful events, and the influence of chance. Eshu, the trickster god of Nigeria, ensures that everyone is aware that life is unpredictable. In your dreams, you may meet a trickster figure symbolized in the chaos of natural events, as well as in people. Native Americans make masks that can open up to reveal a different face. Like the trickster, they show that there is another facet to be aware of.

We honor the natural world in the festivals and seasons that we celebrate. We discover symbols in our dreams of, for example, eggs at Easter, signaling the start of spring, or evergreens in darkest winter that remind us that life continues even though all growth seems to have stopped. Every time you dream of the natural world, reflect on how you relate to the natural world.

ABOVE *Dreams of natural disasters remind us of the awesome power of nature, on which we depend.*

pineapple has a deeper meaning too, symbolizing a traveler's return. In colonial America, pineapples were also known as a symbol of hospitality.

The world is not a predictable place—anything can, and does, happen. At any moment, an unexpected storm or

Amber

AMBER, A FOSSILIZED RESIN from primitive pine trees, is the symbol of the sun, illumination, and immortality. Vikings revered amber's magical qualities. The Latin name for amber is *electrum* and electricity was named after it. If you rub a piece of amber, it carries a static charge, and will make the hairs on your skin stand up. Amber was considered by alchemists to be a symbol of the sun. It was linked to healing and used to be rubbed on sore eyes and sprained limbs.

Amber can hold life itself. The movie *Jurassic Park* is based on the idea that dinosaurs can be cloned from the DNA trapped in amber. In the movie, an insect caught in the resin held the blood of the dinosaur in its proboscis and so provided the DNA from which extinct life could be resurrected. In China, amber is called the "soul of the tiger," reflecting the orange and black-brown of its colors.

In Baltic countries, amber beads were known as "the tears of the goddess Freya" and were used as a cure for arthritis. In Ancient Greece, amber was believed to be formed from the tears of the sun nymphs called Heliads, possibly because amber seems to capture the color of the sun in a condensed form. Amber is also referred to as "lynx stone," based on an early belief that it was formed from the urine of a lynx, as described by Barbara G. Walker in her book *The Woman's Dictionary of Symbols as Sacred Objects*.

CONNECTIONS

- *Does your dream of amber concern the need to bring a charge of energy into your life?*
- *Do you feel that part of your essence is fossilized, like the small creatures trapped inside pieces of amber?*

Natural Phenomena

Crystal

AS WITH OTHER PRECIOUS STONES, crystal is a symbol of the spirit and was described as such in the Bible: Jesus Christ is referred to as a "living stone." Crystal also represents the higher self.

Today, crystalline elements are used in electronic devices. Early examples include their use in submarine-detector sonar systems and in watches and clocks. In the past, crystals were used to detect future events; they were called "stones of power" because it was believed that looking into them revealed the future. This art of seeing the future, by scrying, or looking into a crystal ball, predates the Greek and Roman eras. Staring into a crystal ball for long enough was also said to empty the mind and create visions.

In Japan, crystals, known as *tama*, are seen as symbols of eternity. In other traditions, shamans use them in their healing work because of the crystals' association with purity and clarity.

CONNECTIONS

◎ *When crystals appear in your dream, does this mean that things are "crystal clear"?*

◎ *Crystal chandeliers often symbolize wealth.*

◎ *A crystal ball may indicate that you have concerns about the future and want to know what will happen.*

Gemstones THROUGHOUT HISTORY, JEWELS HAVE BEEN THE

CURRENCY OF POWER. Jewelry has been worn from earliest times—Egyptian mummies have been found with a treasury of beautiful necklaces, bracelets, and earrings. In myths, gemstones or jewels have been guarded by dragons, serpents, and monsters. Jewels symbolize hidden treasures of knowledge, love, and riches.

Raw gemstones are cut and polished to enhance their beauty, before being set in rings and necklaces for people to wear. In Spain, cut gems are known as *piedras de rayo*, meaning "stones of the light." Diamonds and other gemstones are used in crystal healing. Your dream of gemstones may be linked to its own symbolic qualities:

Diamond—Hardest natural material known, symbolizing light, life, the sun, and constancy.

Emerald—Green, transparent, and highly valued, emeralds symbolize immortality, hope, and faithfulness.

Jet—Black and shiny, jet symbolizes grief, mourning, and safe travel.

Lapis lazuli—The deep blue gemstone flecked with gold and white symbolizes divine power, success, and ability.

Opal—Opals come in many colors and are considered unlucky. They symbolize widowhood and tears.

Amethyst—Pale lavender to deep violet, amethysts are said to prevent drunkenness; they are known as "bishops' stones" because they were worn by cardinals and bishops.

Ruby—Deep red rubies, as other red stones, are associated with blood. They symbolize royalty, dignity, passion, and invulnerability.

Sapphire—The deep blue of this stone was linked to heaven; sapphires were seen as protective stones as well as a cure for anger and stupidity.

Topaz—This comes in a variety of shades and symbolizes friendship, warmth, and faithfulness.

Metals

METALS SYMBOLIZE COSMIC ENERGY in solid form and are also linked to the libido. On this basis, Jung asserted that base metals symbolize desire and "lusts of the flesh." Extracting the essence from these base metals and transmuting them into higher metals is the equivalent of freeing creative energy from the mundane, basic concerns of everyday life. The metal you dream of may indicate what is of most importance to you at the moment.

Gold—The metal of the sun symbolizes kingship, which is why the Three Magi brought it to Bethlehem on the birth of Jesus, the new king. It represents illumination and spirituality. It was once believed to have healing properties and was rubbed on the eye to cure a stye.

Silver—The metal of the moon and the feminine aspect of humanity.

Iron—The metal of Mars, the god of war.

Mercury—The metal of the god Mercury. Also known as "quicksilver."

Copper—The metal of the goddess Venus, whose major shrine was in Cyprus, the Isle of Copper. It is used for warding off rheumatism. In Britain, *copper* is an old-fashioned slang term for "police officer"; this is shortened further to *cop* in the United States.

Lead—This metal is heavy, dull gray in color, and linked to "leaden feelings." It was associated with Saturn, a planet with a reputation for negative influence. Malleable lead was used by the Romans to line coffins and keep them watertight. They also inscribed curses on lead sheets and placed them in temples.

Air ACCORDING TO ANCIENT BELIEF, AIR IS ONE OF THE FOUR BASIC ELEMENTS. It symbolizes creativity, thought, and intelligence. We cannot live without air, so when it features in your dreams, consider its quality. Is it foggy, misty, crisp, clear, or polluted? The answer will give you an idea of the atmosphere that surrounds you in waking life. Can you breathe easily in the dream? People who suffer from asthma sometimes feel constricted and can find themselves gasping for breath in their dreams. In some dreams it is another creature that has trouble breathing.

I dreamed that a fish was on the lawn. Somehow, it had jumped out of the water. I knew it couldn't live if I didn't get it back into the river; it was struggling for breath.

Working on your dream can bring insight and hope. In this dream, when the "sunlight" comes, this clearer air marks the turning point for the dreamer.

One dream I had, of being on the edge of a dark forest that I was afraid to enter, was an early indication of an acute anxiety disorder. When my spiritual adviser prayed with me about the frightening dream, before the illness had taken hold, I "saw" sunlight come into the woods to illuminate the path. This gave me hope as I embarked upon a very difficult time.

CONNECTIONS

◉ *"Air" may also refer to the way in which a person behaves. Are you putting on "airs and graces," or behaving in a superior way that demeans other people?*

◉ *Do you need to "clear the air," or say what you mean so that another person understands your position?*

Earth EARTH GIVES US OUR FOUNDATION. It is one of the four elements of ancient belief. It grounds us and is the source of all that sustains us. "Mother Earth" symbolizes nurturing care; the womb from which life is formed.

When the earth opens up, as it does in this dream, consider what you are afraid of falling into, or what might suddenly "open up" for all to see.

I dream that I am in a garden racing after my brother.
I am always about to win, when the ground opens up in front of me. I fall
into a hole, onto a pile of leaves. There are tunnels leading away from it.

The element of competition between this dreamer and his brother leads to trouble. The dreamer could consider whether his anxiety forces him to strive for less in his waking life. The dream showed his feeling that when he competed with his brother something went wrong—he was "dropped in it"; the ground could not support him.

Everything is part of the universe and so is connected, by energy, to everything else, from the surface of the earth on which we live to the atmosphere we inhabit. This interconnectedness may be symbolized by the earth in dreams.

CONNECTION

◎ *What is the quality of the earth in your dream? Is it richly fertile*
  or a wasteland? Does this reflect your emotional state?

Fire

FIRE SYMBOLIZES THE RATIONAL MIND, the divine spark that led to humans being raised above the rest of the animal world. It is one of the ancient four basic elements that sustains life. It also represents heat, energy, and ire, meaning "anger." Trial by fire, used against witches in medieval Europe, was a torture driven by anger and ignorance.

Fire is associated with purification. *Beltane* is the Irish name for May Day, and means "bright fire." At the festival of Beltane, bonfires were lit to mark the arrival of spring. The Celts would then pass their animals between the fires to purify them.

In the Aztec culture, Heuhueteotl, the god of fire, had human offerings made to appease him.

The fireplace is the heart of the home and the center of warmth. The heart is sometimes referred to as the fire that fuels our bodies. If you dream of a fire, could it refer to your heartfelt emotions? The sacred fire is the central symbol for Zoroastrians, whose religion first arose in Iran in the sixth century C.E. The Olympic flame carried to open the Olympic Games still symbolizes the spirit of fair competition and harmony between competitors.

CONNECTIONS

- *Is anything welling up in you that needs your attention?*
- *Are you dreaming of boiling water? If so, it may indicate that you need to "let off some steam."*

Water   WATER IS THE SOURCE OF LIFE AND ONE OF THE FOUR BASIC

ELEMENTS. In dreams, it symbolizes our emotional life. Water can conceal in murky depths, or reveal in crystal clarity. As one dreamer said:

Now that I have been working on my dreams, I have found that dirty water indicates a problem, and that dirtier water indicates a bigger problem.

Water in bathrooms gives us the opportunity for private cleansing and elimination. If you dream of washing yourself, or your clothes, it may indicate that it is time to "clean up," to "start fresh," or to "clean up your act," and perhaps get started on that project you have been postponing.

Where water is in a contained space, such as a swimming pool, it signifies controlled emotion and restraint.

Wells and water springs were held in particular reverence in many traditions, as the source of fresh water was life-giving. The water emerged from the ground as if by magic, and so it was invested with special powers of healing or revelation.

Deserts

WE THINK OF DESERTS AS BARREN PLACES, which are almost devoid of vegetation or wildlife. However, many plants grow in deserts, sending down deep roots to collect moisture from far beneath the surface and storing it in their leaves. The plants open out only in early morning or early evening, when the worst of the heat is over. Certain animal species have also adapted to survival in this apparently hostile environment.

The sand in a desert seems to be endless, and this sense of infinity is associated with spiritual qualities because of the belief that the universe is infinite and we are part of that. Sometimes the sand is threatening, as it is in dreams in which the dreamer sinks down into it. This indicates a lack of solidity; if your world is shifting around you, you lose your bearings.

If you dream of being in a desert, this may reflect feelings of isolation or of being in a "cultural desert"—a place that holds no interest for you. If you find yourself on a desert island, does this concern a desire to get away and have some quiet time?

CONNECTIONS

◎ To "desert" someone is to abandon them. Could your dream desert relate to a feeling that you have been left behind?

◎ Is your life like a desert—poor on the surface, but rich beneath the ground?

Chasm

A SEEMINGLY BOTTOMLESS CHASM can bring about fear in dreams, as it would in waking life. In the depth of the abyss, you are farthest away from the light. This may indicate a lack of spirituality or a desire for illumination. Often, it is only by sinking all the way to the bottom and experiencing the pit of despair that we can return to joy.

Stories often trigger dreams:

The first nightmare I can recall came after my father read Alice In Wonderland *to me at bedtime. I dreamed that I was trapped in a dire, deep, black, underground cavern. Its walls were closing around me, and I was screaming for release. Beyond it, there was a small passageway, where my mother and grandmother were staring impersonally, all "dressed up."*

Primitive fears of being hurt surface in this dream about an abyss:

I was climbing a very steep staircase that had a precipice on each side. I had just reached the last few steps, when someone ran toward me and threw me into the abyss. When I woke up, I wasn't frightened, just disappointed that I hadn't reached the top.

Valley VALLEYS ARE POPULAR PLACES FOR SETTLEMENTS.

Valleys offer protection, are less exposed than mountain tops, and provide fertile land on which to both grow crops and raise animals.

Typically, a river supplies water to a valley. In your dream valleys, notice how the water is flowing. Is it clear and fast moving? Does this reflect how you feel your energy is moving?

Christian, the hero of John Bunyan's allegory *The Pilgrim's Progress*, has to pass through the valley of the shadow of death in order to reach the celestial city, heaven. The biblical prophet Jeremiah described the valley as a "wilderness, a land of deserts and of pits, a land of drought and the shadow of death." It symbolizes the trials that people have to undergo in their life journey or spiritual quest.

Though I walk through the valley of the shadow of death, I will fear no evil for Thou art with me; Thy rod and Thy staff they comfort me.

PSALM 23

Forests and Woods

Natural Phenomena

TREES MAKE UP THE CHARACTER OF FORESTS AND WOODS and, in their abundance, give us shelter, food, and wood for building. Forests are dark and mysterious. They contain the unknown and so symbolize the unconscious. Many myths and fairy stories support this archetype—characters get lost in a wood, or forest, only to discover great treasures or wisdom.

Pan, the ancient Greek god and guardian of the woods and forests, is represented in figures such as the Green Man, Puck, and Robin Hood.

In Africa, many traditions reflect the close relationship between the land and the people who depend on it. In Cameroon, dancers perform a Juju dance, where they dress as forest spirits and tell the story of the destruction of forests and the natural environment. The destruction of the rainforest typifies lack of respect for earth and bodes ill for the future of our planet. If you dream of this kind of destruction, it may reflect waking environmental worries or a personal feeling of being "cut down."

CONNECTIONS

◉ *If you "can't see the forest for the trees," you could be missing the big picture because you are focusing on details, rather than looking at the whole thing.*

◉ *"Knocking on wood" is a superstition to ward off evil, or bad luck.*

Cliff THE HIGH VANTAGE POINT A CLIFF OFFERS gives us the opportunity to get a wider, bird's-eye view, even though it may be frightening to be so exposed.

I have a recurring dream of climbing a high cliff, where I have nothing to hang onto. It is dark, and I can't see very well. Sometimes, my mother is there, but she never helps me. I always wake up before I get to the top.

Climbing to the top of a cliff may represent ambition and a desire to reach a "top" position in work or in some other area in which you might be in competition with other people.

In dreams where I am falling off cliffs, I try to wake myself up, so that I can stop myself from falling.

The ability to wake yourself from a frightening dream comes naturally to some people, or can be developed as this dreamer found. Usually she could wake herself if she had a disturbing dream.

As with other falling dreams, coming down from a great height can be terrifying. Consider whether you have gone beyond your "comfort zone." Such dreams may indicate anxieties about your ability to cope with success.

CONNECTION

◉ *Cliffhanger—Are you apprehensive about making a decision? Is there a situation that is making you tense? Are you waiting for information, such as a medical test result?*

Cave

AS CAVES WERE THE EARLIEST DWELLING PLACES for many peoples, they came to symbolize the universe. According to Ancient Greek and African myths, caves are places where human beings and gods meet; primitive cave paintings depict all types of beasts and divine beings, such as flying men and creatures who swim through the air. It is also said that all mortal gods and saviors are born in caves, or their equivalent.

Initiation rituals have frequently taken place in caves. This is because caves are secret places, and the entrances can be guarded to prevent intruders from entering and stopping the initiation from taking place.

Like a womb, a cave can protect and conceal. The fact that it is hidden and closed associates it with the feminine principle. It is a place where mysterious events take place, out of the glare of daylight. However, it is not without dangers:

> *I dreamed I was in an ice cave. This thing came up behind me, but when I turned around, it wasn't there.*

In one of the famous Japanese Shinto myths, the sun goddess, Amaterasu leaves her cave to bring light and order into the world. The Celts believed that you entered the *otherworld* (heaven) through a cave.

CONNECTIONS

- *Do you feel that you are about to "cave in," or give way to someone else, in a dispute?*
- *Is someone you know acting as a "caveman," behaving in an unsophisticated and aggressive way?*

Stone A HOLED STONE—a stone or pebble with a natural hole in it—was believed to protect the carrier from a range of misfortunes. For example, a *hagstone*, another term for a holed stone, was traditionally hung over a bed to prevent *hagriding*—being tormented by witches. Hagstones were also used to prevent nightmares by having them close to the bed, and were collected for their healing properties. So, if one appears in your dream, ask yourself what you want to be protected from.

In one of Jung's final dreams, he saw a large, round stone on which was inscribed: "As a sign unto you of Wholeness and Oneness." This is the central image of alchemy, the philosopher's stone, something that was central to his life's work. This symbol represents the full attainment of Jung's goal, which was to explore how our dreams, emotions, and spirituality are symbolized in the personal subconscious and in the collective unconscious.

Millstones are used for grinding wheat. A heavy weight can be a burden like "a millstone around your neck." So if you dream of a millstone, it may indicate that you are feeling "ground down."

Both Anglo-Saxons and Vikings used runes. These were stones or wooden tablets cut into discs, which were carved or inscribed with lines and used to cast spells or to foresee the future.

Mud MUD—THE MIXTURE OF EARTH AND WATER—is usually associated with ground that both hinders progress and dirties our bodies. In many dreams, feelings of frustration are magnified, as the dreamer tries to escape from someone or something, but cannot move forward because the mud sucks them down. It can, as in this dream, threaten to annihilate the dreamer:

I used to have terrifying nightmares where I would try to escape by running through mud, which got thicker and thicker, until it overwhelmed me, and the screams in my throat were unable to surface.

The tendency of mud to dirty and stain has become part of language, in the saying "to muddy your good name." If this happens in a dream it may indicate that you are concerned that your reputation is being ruined.

CONNECTIONS

- *Are you a "stick in the mud"— someone who won't try new things?*
- *"Clear as mud" means that something is not clear at all. Are you unclear about a situation in which you are involved?*

Marsh

BOGGY, POORLY DRAINED MARSHLANDS often signify a place of change, where land and water combine to make a different territory from merely land or sea. In this place, people can sink or become "bogged down." Do you feel stuck at present? Are you caught up in a situation from which you cannot free yourself?

If you dream of a marsh, consider what you see. Many unique flowers grow on marshlands: marsh orchids, marsh marigolds, and marshwort. Marshmallow, which grows in salt marshes, has soft, pink flowers. Its roots were once used to make the spongy-textured confection that is traditionally toasted on fires. What can you associate with this? Are you being "as soft as marshmallow?"

In the past two decades, much of the land belonging to marsh Arabs of northern Iraq has been drained and lost to them. Does your dream have any links to this? Do you feel "drained," or as if you are symbolically losing your home or traditions, which have been dear to you all your life?

Mountain

As morning dew is taken up by the Sun,
so my evil deeds are taken up by the sight of the Himalayas.

TRADITIONAL HINDU PROVERB

MOUNTAIN PEAKS ARE WHERE HEAVEN AND EARTH MEET, the mountain providing passage from one plane to another. The highest point on earth is regarded as the summit of paradise by those who live in the Himalayas. It is a sacred place reaching up to the creator. This is why so many mountains are regarded as sacred places of pilgrimage. They symbolize aspiration, renunciation of worldly desires, and the search for higher potential and spirituality.

I am climbing the side of a mountain with my husband and mother.
I tell them to be careful because it is slippery, then I lose my footing, and
fall into space. I am horrified. I fall to the bottom, where my body splatters
in several directions.

If you dream of being hurt in this way, of falling from a great height, ask yourself what is forcing you up to dangerous heights in waking life. If your body is broken into separate pieces, it may mean that you are not holding onto a sense of wholeness—perhaps your head and heart aren't working in harmony?

Seas and Rivers
NEPTUNE WAS THE ROMAN GOD OF SEAS AND RIVERS. He rode on the sea in a chariot pulled by seahorses, carrying his three-pronged spear, or trident. It was said that when Neptune was in a bad mood, he caused storms, floods, tidal waves, and earthquakes.

I had a series of dreams where I was menaced by the sea. I was very depressed at the time, and the dreams became a focal point. I feel that they saved my life.

The regular movement of the sea, in response to its endless nature and the tides, offers a sense of continuity and hope. For this dreamer, the sea gave her a wider perspective that broadened her focus from herself to her part in the whole of nature:

In the following instance, the dreamer branches out on her own and is rewarded by finding a beautiful place that allows her to look out over the sea:

I go into a house, looking for an apartment. I'm told that there are only a few left to rent, but I break away from the guide and discover lots of interesting rooms. At last, I find one with a fantastic view across the sea and seafront.

The dream indicates that she needs to follow her personal path in order to discover what is important to her. When she does this her view (her outlook) is improved.

$\mathcal{I}ce$ AS WATER
SYMBOLIZES THE UNCONSCIOUS,
ice represents frozen emotions.
It is rigid and prevents
movement—only when it thaws
can water flow once more.

Falling through ice
indicates a breakthrough in emotions, though in a startling and uncomfortable way.

The tip of an iceberg reveals only a small part of a larger mass. For every cubic foot of the iceberg above water, there are at least eight cubic feet below. In dreams, an iceberg may symbolize the visible part of a much larger problem, and can act as a warning to the dreamer, to think more deeply about something that seems to be insignificant. Also, icebergs are so beautiful that their danger can be overlooked.

When we are in relationships or in situations that are superficially enjoyable, we may get seduced by the pleasure and be unaware of hidden dangers, and dreams may reflect this. A large mass or expanse of ice may indicate that the dreamer's emotions are frozen. Hidden below the surface, these emotions can pose a threat, just as frozen water does.

In Australia, an *iceberg* is a colloquial term for someone who regularly surfs or swims, whereas in the United States, it is used to describe someone who is cool and aloof. An "ice queen" freezes others out by her unfeeling attitude.

CONNECTIONS

◎ *Have you submerged your emotions so deeply that people are aware of only a small part of them? Are you hiding your feelings?*

◎ *Are you feeling "icy" toward someone?*

Island TIME OUT, away from all the stresses and strains of life, is what many people crave. Being on an island, far away from everyone and everything, is a dream solution. The type of island will help you to interpret the dream:

- A tropical island, with ripe fruit and running water, indicates relaxation and fulfillment.
- A storm-tossed island with no shelter reveals a sense of threat, with nothing to protect you.
- An island covered in trees or bushes, indicates difficulties pursuing a path or being unable to get through something.
- A remote island may reveal a need to get away from it all, or that you are feeling cut off.

Ireland is also known as "the Island of Saints." Is it possible that your dream is linked to spirituality?

For this dreamer, the overwhelming desire is for solitude.

I am walking with a horse on a beach on an island. My friends are waiting for me at the beach hut, but I just want to carry on walking with the beautiful big horse.

Although you are on your dream island, you may not be alone and may still yearn for a connection with nature and a period of reflective solitude.

South Pole THE MOST SOUTHERLY POINT on the earth's axis

represents inhospitable territory, yet challenges the human imagination. It attracts those who want to test their strength and their ability to endure hardship. It symbolizes survival against the odds, as does the climbing of Mount Everest. If you are not involved in expeditions to such places, then consider what it is that is challenging you at present. Are you facing a potentially dangerous undertaking? Are you providing enough support and backing for a venture?

A Norwegian, who was part of the 1911 Antarctic expedition led by the British explorer Scott, was wholeheartedly committed to reaching the South Pole before Amundsen, his fellow countryman. However, during the expedition, he dreamed that he was in a Chicago street when he opened a telegram, signed by Amundsen, which said he had reached the Pole. The dream offered a solution to internal conflict. It revealed that deep down he wanted Norway to have the full honor.

Many explorers who have endured hardship, such as those who embarked on expeditions to the South Pole, had vivid dreams about food. As Otto Nordenskjold wrote in his book *Antarctica*, "Meat and drink were usually the centers around which our dreams revolved. One of us made a habit of going to banquets and was highly pleased to relate that 'last night I got through three courses.'"

Waterfall

WITH THEIR FORCE AND ENERGY, waterfalls are frequently linked to cleansing. As they cascade down mountainsides, they carry the cool freshness of icy water. They symbolize untainted water, unused by anyone else, which is one reason why they are linked with purification rituals, such as baptism. In the Shinto religion, mainly practiced in Japan, waterfalls are held to be sacred, and purification ceremonies under waterfalls symbolize regeneration.

To be drenched in water, by rain or under a waterfall, may indicate that unconscious material is rising to the surface. This can happen when you are working with a therapist, or when some previously concealed facts are revealed to you.

In the Hindu religion, water has an important role to play. The purification of the body is just as important as purification of the mind, so a Hindu should bathe in running water every day.

CONNECTIONS

- *Do you want a fresh start?*
- *Are you about to undergo an initiation, for example, in a spiritual dimension of your life?*
- *What would you like to wash over you, and pass you by, so you no longer have to think about it?*

Lake

In my dream, I was in a watery world, then literally shot upward into a light-filled world. It was like a breakthrough.

THE ENCLOSED WATER OF A LAKE may represent restricted, contained emotion that holds the dreamer back. The quality of water is important: Is it clear or murky? Is the water too deep for safety? Is the surface of the lake calm or wind-tossed? As it is entirely surrounded by land and not directly connected to the sea, the lake may signify the lack of an outlet, either emotional or spiritual.

Mythology links include "the lady of the lake," who appeared in the Arthurian legend, symbolizing any female, supernatural being. The Loch Ness monster is said to dwell in deep waters and is supposedly always present, yet never found. In your dream, could a lake represent mysterious forces at work deep in your psyche?

CONNECTIONS

◎ *If you dream of swimming in a lake, consider how easy or difficult it is to make progress. Does this relate to a waking situation in which you are trying to move forward?*

◎ *Does your dream lake represent security, as it is self-contained and the boundary is clear?*

Volcano

THE VOLCANO MAY BE DORMANT, burned out, or active, explosively erupting over the surrounding area. If you dream of dormant or burned-out volcanoes, this indicates that past troubles have died down, and the fires have been quenched. If you dream of an active volcano that still smokes or erupts, this symbolizes emotional activity at a deep level that may burst out. If this happens, the lava, or emotional flak, may reach anyone who happens to be in its path. Are you feeling angry and about to explode? If so, take care that innocent people are not injured in the process.

I had a nightmare in which a wise old man, complete with black cloak and long white hair, led me into a place of blackness. There, he stood with his back to me, hands raised in the air. The blackness was filled with glowing mouths and volcanoes. The invisible ground beneath me was uneven, but I had to follow where he led.

This dream included both the danger of volcanoes and treacherous ground, but also the promise of insight from the archetypal "wise man." The dreamer knows that if he holds onto his courage in the darkness, he will come through it a wiser person.

Sky and Clouds PEOPLE HAVE ALWAYS VIEWED

THE SKY as a mystical realm, the home of the gods and the path to heaven.

The Hindu god, Vishnu, who is responsible for controlling human fate, is often portrayed as riding across the sky on an eagle. Garuda, the Hindu golden-winged sun bird, often carries a discus, which symbolizes the sun. Indra, the most celebrated god of the *Rig-Veda*, the holy book of the Hindus, is the Hindu sky god. The weather is his responsibility.

Clouds are connected to celestial or heavenly matters. Angels are shown sitting on clouds, and in Michaelangelo's painting in the Sistine Chapel the hand of God reaches from clouds. In the *Torah*—the five Books of Moses—there are many references to God symbolized as a cloud.

Then a cloud covered the tent of the congregation,
and the glory of the Lord filled the tabernacle.

EXODUS 40:34

In the time of the Vikings, clouds were known as the steeds of the Valkyries.

I once had a dream where I was way up in the sky. The whole of
Australia was edged in bright lights, illuminating the continent. It made
me realize how big the world is.

Clouds release rain and so are linked with compassion for the earth. In many traditions, rituals are carried out to bring about rain and insure that crops grow.

CONNECTIONS

⊚ *Are you living "under a cloud," fearful of misfortune?*

⊚ *Is your head "in the clouds," which means you are unable to concentrate*
and cannot think clearly?

Stars and Constellations

THE CONSTELLATIONS ARE A RESULT OF HUMAN CLASSIFICATION. Long ago, as people stared at the stars and the patterns they created, they made pictures out of what they saw and named these star groups. This made the dark skies friendlier, as they gave reference points for navigators. In 150 C.E. the Greek astronomer Ptolemy published a list of 48 constellations, based on much earlier records. In star maps, you will find constellations named after many animals and mythical creatures.

The Celts venerated the stars. They called them "the Court of Donn" (Donn being the Lord of the Dead) and viewed them as ancestor deities. Stories tell how the different constellations and stars came into being. For example, it is said that one of the Celtic god Donn's children, Gwydion the Magician, made a woman from flowers to be the wife of his son. When the flower woman murdered her husband, Gwydion created the Milky Way as a road to heaven to help him find his murdered offspring.

The five-pointed Star of David was first used as a symbol of Jewish identity in the fourteenth century. A five-pointed star, drawn without taking a pen off paper, is also known in the Middle East as "Solomon's Seal," or "the endless knot." This is a powerful protective symbol, representing a perfect universe and the four traditional elements of air, earth, fire, water, plus spirit. First found in Ancient Greece, this star is now seen as the mark of a magician.

CONNECTIONS

- *Do your dream stars relate to heavenly aspirations?*
- *Are you about to star in something or to perform in an event?*
- *Are you "star-crossed"—not favored by the stars, or unfortunate?*
- *Do you have "stars in your eyes" about someone?*

Planets

EACH OF THE PLANETS IN OUR SOLAR SYSTEM has different connotations. The connections listed below will help you to decipher your dream.

Venus—In astrology, this planet is associated with the moon and with love. Venus is the morning or evening star, and represents the unification of opposites.

Saturn—Originally ruler of the Golden Age and Seventh Heaven, Saturn is now shown as an old man carrying a scythe, a tool of destruction that may bring about rebirth.

Neptune—This planet represents the source of all things—the primordial ocean from which life was formed.

Jupiter—Associated with expansion, creativity, and energetic organization, Jupiter is depicted as a venerable figure who sometimes rides in a chariot.

Mars—An armed man, sometimes known as the god of war, Mars represents masculine energy, passion, and fearlessness.

Mercury—In ancient mythology, Mercury was the messenger of the gods and is associated today with communication. The bodies of gladiators slaughtered in the arena were dragged away by slaves dressed as Mercury. This was a sign of respect for the gladiators who were now free to go to their heaven. Mercury is also the name of the liquid metal known as "quicksilver."

Uranus—Symbolizing boundless space, the planet Uranus stands for that which is not fully formed, and can indicate latent potential.

Pluto—Unknown to the ancients, this planet may symbolize hidden forces.

Moon THE MOON REPRESENTS THE FEMALE

intuitive side, the mother, emotions, the reflective principle, and psychic connections. It is linked to silver and the gemstone selenite. The goddess of the moon was called Selene in Ancient Greek culture.

The four quarters of the moon (New Moon, Waxing Moon, Full Moon and Waning Moon) influence the tides and the menstrual cycles of women.

The moon played an important part in the Celtic calendar, with lunar fire festivals marking the four quarters of the year:

Samhain (November 1) marked the beginning of the Celtic year, when the herds were brought in for the winter. It signalled the harshest time of the year and the time when the Celts felt closest to their gods in the "otherworld." Today, we celebrate this time as Halloween and All Saints' Day, when we remember the dead.

Imbolc (February 1) indicated early spring and new beginnings, symbolized by lambs. Today, Christians mark this time at Easter.

Beltane (May 1) marked the beginning of the summer, when the herds were let out to graze. From the Celtic festival comes the maypole, a symbol of fertility. This is a time of rebirth.

Lughnasa (August 1) marked the end of harvest.

CONNECTION

◎ *Moon tree—A symbol from the moon cults of Ancient Assyria that is a female deity. The moon cults revered the female principle.*

Sun

Welcome, Sun of the seasons, as you travel high in the skies;
your steps are strong on the sign of the heights,
you are the glorious mother of the stars.

TRADITIONAL CELTIC SONG

THE SUN REPRESENTS SUPREME COSMIC POWER. As it is the brightest, most important object in the sky to us on earth, it is equated with divine power. It has been worshiped throughout the world, from the Incas to the Australian Aboriginals, as Helios, the god of light in Ancient Greece, and in Rome as Apollo, the sun god. It represents masculine energy and is connected to the metal gold.

The sun was seen in ancient cultures to have two aspects, named as the "Black Sun" and its twin, the "Solar Sun." The Black Sun journeyed through the dark, once the daytime or "Solar Sun" had set. People used to believe that the Black Sun traveled to the darkest depths, to rise again as the golden sun of daylight. This is an example of the idea of duality, the yin-yang of life. The Black Sun came to signify the gods of the underworld.

CONNECTIONS

◎ *Could your dream "sun" represent your "son"?*

◎ *Where your dream sun is concealed, does it indicate that you are hiding your sunny side, your brightness and warmth?*

◎ *If you are burned by the sun in a dream it may be a warning to take more care when sunbathing.*

Rainbow

THE RAINBOW IS A SYMBOL OF HOPE AND RESPITE after a period of upheaval. It is the bridge between heaven and earth, between secular and divine. In Native American legends, the rainbow is the ladder to other worlds. Similarly, in Scandinavian traditions, it is the *Bilforst*, "the tremulous way over to Asgard," or heaven. On the journey from earth to heaven, mythologies tell us that those who have led a good life have an easy passage, while those who have not are consumed by fire.

In Australia, the rainbow is associated with the Divine Snake, one of the most powerful creative forces in the universe. For the Aborigines, the Rainbow Serpent is as vital to their understanding of creation as Adam and Eve are to the Christian culture, or the "Big Bang" to a scientific one.

The Aborigines of Arnhem Land, Australia, believe that the Rainbow Serpent Mother made the world and gave birth to all the people in all their varying shades. In Western society, the rainbow has been adopted as a symbol of gay pride. Just as the rainbow contains a range of color, so humans come in many colors and so the rainbow symbolizes the interconnection of all colors and all humankind.

CONNECTIONS

◎ *Is there a pot of gold waiting at the end of the rainbow—a reward after a difficult time?*

◎ *If you dream of a rainbow, it may represent new hope after difficult times.*

Rain

The rain falling from the sky impregnates the earth,
so that she gives birth to plants
and grain for man and beast.

AESCHYLUS

RAIN IS A LIFE FORCE—a source of fertility, like the sun. Rain is essential for the growth of all plant life, on which we ultimately depend, and is seen as a divine blessing after a period of drought. All sky gods fertilize the earth with rain.

The double-headed serpent was a symbol used by the Tlaloc Aztecs to represent rain. The fringes on Native American garments and moccasins symbolize falling rain.

Water is a symbol of the unconscious. Water as rain, falling down on us from above, signifies higher thought or intention. Although, to some extent, we can control bodies of water, we cannot control the elements. Rain comes when it will. Falling rain is sometimes seen as a metaphor for the shedding of tears.

CONNECTIONS

◉ *Does falling rain in your dream relate to farming or fertility?*

◉ *Does anything that has "come out of the blue" need your attention now?*

CONNECTIONS

◎ Do you feel "thunderous,"
or really angry about
something?

◎ Does your dream relate to
pace—do you need to speed
up and "strike like
lightning"?

◎ Does your dream of thunder
and lightning symbolize a
stormy period in your life?

Thunder and Lightning

THUNDER AND LIGHTNING WARN OF IMPENDING STORMS and can highlight "stormy"
times in waking life. The fork of lightning illuminates the sky, while the clap of
thunder forces us to pay attention.

In Nordic cultures, thunder was known as "the voice of the gods" and "divine
anger." In mythology, thunderbolts were the weapons that the gods hurled to earth.
Shamans believe that being struck by lightning indicates that initiation has occurred.
This is why some shamans paint a zigzag of lightning on their foreheads when taking
part in rituals.

Lightning symbolizes flashes of inspiration, spiritual revelation, and the sudden
realization of a truth. Like the rays of the sun, lightning represents powers of both
destruction and fertilization.

In British folklore, there is a belief that if you hang eagle feathers from a tree in
your garden, it will prevent lightning strikes.

Snow

LIKE ICE, SNOW ALSO RELATES TO FROZEN EMOTIONS; however, there is some movement, as snow falls, drifts, and is softer. Melting snow may symbolize the unfreezing of rigid attitudes, or a release of feelings.

Falling snow covers the landscape with a white blanket and muffles sound. In dreams, this represents a desire for a fresh start—"virgin snow" gives us the opportunity to make a new mark where none has been made before, and to make the first impression on a new landscape. Are you embarking on an innovative venture? Do you want to make your mark?

We also play in snow, making snowballs and snowmen. If you dream of this, it may indicate a need to make the most of natural opportunities when they arise, for, like snow, they can melt away and disappear before you've made the most of them.

CONNECTIONS

◎ *"Snowed under"—Are you stressed out by having too much to do in too little time?*

◎ *"Snow job"—A Canadian and U.S. term to describe deceiving or overwhelming someone with elaborate or insincere remarks. Is anyone doing this to you?*

Storm

A STORM MAY MERELY THREATEN, before passing over, or it may be destructive. In your dream, you need to consider whether the storm was just a threat, or if you were caught up in the maelstrom. Symbolically, a storm represents the discharge of pent-up emotions, or emotions that get out of control and cause havoc. When we "storm out," it signals such a state of heightened emotion.

Sometimes, other people in your dream may see a storm coming, while you remain unaware:

My dream started with me setting off for town on the bus. But I took the bus in the opposite direction. I was aware of this, but continued with the journey. On the bus, I met up with two friends who were not usually together. They were talking about the storm outside, but every time I looked out of the window it seemed sunny and warm. They eventually got off the bus, while I continued with the journey.

CONNECTIONS

◎ *"Storm in a teacup"—A lot of fuss over something that is quickly forgotten.*

◎ *"To storm a building"— To rush in, usually in a hijack situation or where hostages have been taken, to set them free.*

Seasons

Four seasons fill the measure of the year;
There are four seasons in the mind of man.

JOHN KEATS: THE HUMAN SEASONS

CHANGES FROM SEASON TO SEASON are part of the cycle of existence, and in dreams symbolize change in human life.

Spring—Youth, new beginnings, fresh starts, and potential yet to be fulfilled. It brings gentle warmth to drive away the cold of winter.

Summer—The height of fecundity, when everything is in full bloom. To keep summer eternally in your soul means to keep hope alive. It is the time of the height of productivity or performance in life.

Fall—Harvest time, when life and nature bear their fruit. This is a time to reap the benefits of all past efforts.

Winter—A time when darkness falls, when we retreat to the warmth of our homes. This is a time of reflection and completion, as the wheel of existence makes ready for the darkness in order to germinate new life.

The Celtic festivals of Samhain, Imbolc, Beltane, and Lughnasa mark the seasons of the Celts' year. They celebrated with fires, food, and rituals to bring protection and fertility.

The Celtic god Dagda, the "good god," had a special harp, and his music helped to bring about the changing of the seasons. He could play three special melodies on his harp, to make people sleep, laugh, or grieve.

Flood

FLOODS HAVE THE POWER TO WASH AWAY structures, ground, and people. As they wash away the soil—as in the Nile Delta, which regularly floods—they also bring new nutrients, so helping to regenerate the land. They represent the end of one cycle and the beginning of another. However, on an emotional level, dream floods represent being overwhelmed by the unconscious.

Myths about great floods abound. In the biblical story of the flood, Noah was instructed to build his Ark so that life could be preserved. Afterward, God sent a rainbow as a sign that there would never be a world-destroying flood again.

I dreamed that a water pipe burst, and that dirty water was gushing up into the air. Water flooded everywhere, and we were surrounded.

CONNECTION

◎ *Are you overwhelmed by events or emotions at present?*

Drought

WHEN WE ARE WITHOUT WATER, extinction threatens, because we cannot survive without it. As water symbolizes the emotions, to suffer a drought indicates that feelings have dried up and that we are lacking in emotional fluidity. This may be caused by a withdrawal of other people's affections or could be caused by a major loss, such as a bereavement.

As our skin becomes drier—as we age, or after too much time spent sunbathing—dried-up riverbeds or cracked landscapes may appear in our dreams. This dramatically portrays the drying effects of the sun on the skin and aging.

Climate change has led to increased incidence of drought, as well as floods; many people find that their dreams reflect concern about these detrimental changes. In such dreams, we mourn the devastation caused, or find ourselves trying to bring about positive changes. Do your drought dreams spur you on to become actively involved in environmental issues?

CONNECTION

Drought *is an old-fashioned term for thirst, so if you dream of this, does it indicate dehydration? Are you drinking enough water to maintain good health?*

Hurricane and Tornado

LIKE EARTHQUAKES, HURRICANES AND TORNADOES bring calamitous change. On a symbolic level, as the hurricane sweeps away everything in its path, it signifies the sweeping away of the old and, once calm is restored, the opportunity to build anew.

The energy of a hurricane is applied to people who bustle about with such speed and noise that they, too, clear everything in their path. Could this relate to you or your colleagues? Do you feel that rushing around means that things of importance could be brushed aside or destroyed?

CONNECTIONS

◎ *Do you feel that you have been swept along against your will, by someone else's pressure?*

◎ *Are winds of change about to alter your life?*

Earthquake

BEFORE JESUS DIED ON THE CROSS, he said, "Father, into Thy hands I commend my spirit." (Luke 23:46) Immediately, there was an earthquake and part of the Temple in Jerusalem was destroyed. To this day, earthquakes are interpreted as signs of God's anger and power.

If an earthquake appears in your dream, this may represent a complete upheaval in your life brought about by major changes at home or at work. Frequently, after a traumatic event such as a railway disaster or an airplane crash, you will have dreams in which you are overwhelmed by natural disaster, over which you have no control. An earthquake is an eruption of energy that occurs suddenly because of underground activity, usually along a fault. Are there some metaphorical "faults" that you think might suddenly break through to the surface?

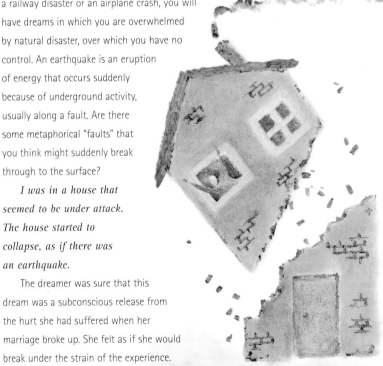

I was in a house that seemed to be under attack. The house started to collapse, as if there was an earthquake.

The dreamer was sure that this dream was a subconscious release from the hurt she had suffered when her marriage broke up. She felt as if she would break under the strain of the experience.

Avalanche

THE ORIGIN OF THE WORD AVALANCHE is the French phrase *à val*, meaning "something that goes downward". Usually, it refers to a mass of snow, ice, and earth that suddenly slips down a mountainside, covering everything in its path. It can indicate feelings of being overwhelmed, being taken by surprise, and being suffocated under the weight of something.

If you dream of an avalanche when you are in snow-capped mountains, it may indicate anxiety about being caught in an avalanche, or may be in response to avalanche warnings. However, if this is not the case, you may be concerned that you are not able to cope with the volume of work you have to complete. People talk about "an avalanche of paperwork." If this is causing you concern, look at practical strategies to reduce your workload.

On a positive note, we can also have "an avalanche of applause" or "an avalanche of bouquets." If you dream of these, it indicates that you are being rewarded for your talents, or for efforts you have made in the past. Success has come and your hard work has been recognized.

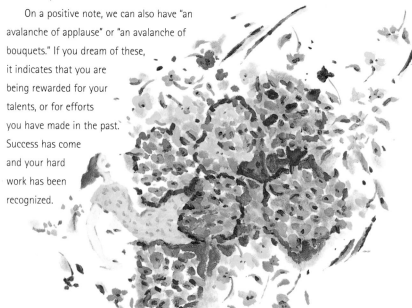

Tidal Wave THE APPEARANCE OF A HUGE WAVE that could

sweep away the dreamer represents a sense of threat, possibly from a sudden disturbance to the psyche. The dreamer may feel overwhelmed by strong feelings that threaten to "sweep her off her feet." These unknown, or unexpected, inner forces may wash away previous security.

I dream about a big wave suddenly appearing from nowhere. I can't get away, and it rushes over me.

A *tsunami* is a destructive sea wave produced by submarine volcanic eruption or earthquake. If this is in your dream, what concealed or submerged activity do you feel is threatening you?

I am coming along a ledge, a rocky outcropping, which is partly artificial. It seems safe enough, but a huge wave is approaching, and it will sweep over everything. It is high above me, green and powerful. I brace myself to receive its force, and hope that if I cling tightly to the rock, I will not be swept away,

and that there may be an air pocket beneath the overhanging rock face.

A tidal wave can clear away the debris of old beliefs, and self-defeating habits. New shores may lie ahead, to which the tidal wave can carry you.

Fossil

**FOSSILS ARE RELICS FROM
PREVIOUS AGES.** They are
pieces of history and
geography, showing us what
used to exist. To dream of
a fossil indicates an interest
in what has gone before. The
fossilized creature or plant
that features will give you
clues to the meaning of
your dream.

"A fossil" is also
a derogatory term for
someone whose ideas are
out of date and who is stuck
in the past. Does your dream
fossil symbolize a person
you know, or do you feel
behind the times yourself?

CONNECTION

◉ *Fossil fuel—Naturally occurring carbon fuel such as coal or oil. To dream of
this may indicate a need for more natural personal "fuel," such as fruit and
vegetables to increase your energy level.*

Shell

SHELLS OF SEA CREATURES AND TORTOISES offer protection (see pages 275–276). They allow the animal to retreat when danger threatens, or when it needs to rest.

The scallop shell is the accepted symbol of Saint James. Pilgrims to his shrine at Compostela in Southern Spain wear a scallop shell on completion of their pilgrimage. On Saint James's Feast Day—August 5—children traditionally built grottos, or artificial recesses, decorated with oyster shells. This still happens today, though to a lesser extent than previously.

Legend tells us that Aphrodite, the Greek goddess of love, arose from the sea standing on a scallop shell. The scallop shell, like the cowrie shell, symbolizes the vagina and so is linked to sexuality.

One of the most ancient symbols is the spiral, which appears singly, in pairs, and in all sizes, and goes clockwise or counterclockwise. It may represent natural forces in spiralling smoke, tornadoes, and shells. In many sacred sites throughout Europe, spiral shells are buried or found on decorated surfaces.

CONNECTIONS

- *Do you need to come out of your shell?*
- *If you dream of a shell, does it represent a need for a retreat?*

Web

THE SPIDER'S WEB SYMBOLIZES TIME AND FATE. A web captures all that enters into its finely structured trap. So, if you dream of a web, you may feel caught up in something from which it feels impossible to escape.

In Greek mythology, a young girl named Arachne excelled at weaving and was changed into a spider after challenging the goddess Athena to a weaving competition. *Arachnophobia* describes a morbid fear of spiders—if you dream of them, it reflects this phobia. As spiders are largely found in cellars and basements and dark places, they may symbolize the underworld or the unconscious mind. Many people have told me about nightmares in which they are covered by spiders and wake up trying to brush them off the bed. However, not all dreams of spiders are negative.

There was an enormous spider. People were poking it, but I wanted them to leave it alone. It span a huge web and wrapped it around me, as if thanking me for my protection. I forgot my fear.

The dreamer felt as if she'd been wrapped in gossamer and that the strength of the thread brought her a sense of respite after having to manage so many problems on her own. She also recognized the thread that connected her to the web of creation.

Color

IN DREAMS, COLOR PLAYS AN IMPORTANT ROLE in highlighting and emphasizing things of particular significance. In some dreams, there may be only black and white or sepia tones, apart from one person or a significant piece of clothing that appears in red, for example.

Here are the main attributes of colors that feature in your dreams (for a more in-depth guide, you will find my book *Creative Visualization with Color* helpful):

Green—Lusty, fertile, fecund. This is a healing color, linked with fertility and nature's riches. The floors of temples in the Nile Delta were painted green to ensure the successful sowing and reaping of crops.

Red—Passion, danger, heat, and power.

Blue—Eternity, loyalty, purity, and infinity. As both the sea and the heavenly sky, it symbolizes celestial matters too.

Yellow—The warmth of the sun, the power of light, spring and its flowers. This color is negatively linked to cowardice and treachery.

White—Associated with purity, innocence, and virtue, white is also linked to deathly pallor and shrouds. In many religious traditions, including Sikhism, white is the color of mourning. Red and white flowers together, without any additional color, are said to be unlucky, because they represent blood and bandages. In the Catholic liturgy, white is associated with the feasts of Christ, Mary, and saints who were not martyred.

Indigo—Associated with the psychic, intuitive side.

Black—Represents night, mourning, depression, and potential not yet realized.

Northern Lights

THE AURORA BOREALIS, also called the northern lights, is a shifting curtain of lights caused by atmospheric phenomena found in the northern hemisphere. Sometimes known as the "veil between worlds," the northern lights exist between earth and the celestial spheres as a glorious shimmering array of color. (The southern lights appear in the southern hemisphere and are known as the *aurora australis*.)

In the time before it was known that they were caused by electrical charges, these lights were said to portend battles and pestilence. Now, travelers visit remote places in order to experience their wonder. If they appear in your dream, it may indicate that a completely unexpected event is about to happen—something that will startle and amaze you. As with all aspects of light, the northern lights are linked to illumination and insight, so think about any new wisdom that has come your way lately, or what knowledge you would like to gain.

Eclipse

WHEN HEAVENLY BODIES BEHAVE IN AN UNUSUAL WAY, this may reflect a change in the natural order of things and indicate that chaotic times prevail. The Ancient Greeks and Romans considered eclipses to be bad omens. Nicias, an Athenian general, was so terrified by an eclipse of the moon that he would not fight against the Syracusans. The result was that his whole army was cut to shreds and he was put to death by the enemy.

In many *cosmologies*—ways of understanding the nature of the universe—the sky monsters were blamed for eating the sun or moon and so causing a solar or lunar eclipse. On a symbolic level, these may represent our own internal "monsters" that undermine our ability to shine.

Ancient peoples of Mexico believed that eclipses were caused by quarrels between the sun and moon. The heavenly bodies beat each other black and blue, so no light could shine.

CONNECTIONS

- *Are you feeling overshadowed, or do you feel that your light has been dimmed?*
- *After an eclipse, new light emerges. Have you gone through a dark time and are coming out the other side?*

IN ANCIENT GREECE, THE DREAM BOOK OF ARTEMIDORUS recorded a particular meaning for each bloom used in wreaths and garlands. The language of florigraphy, the meaning of flowers, was taken very seriously. Flowers were included in every ceremony, and people understood their symbolic significance. When flowers appeared in dreams, their meaning was always important. Likewise, in dreams today, trees, flowers, and plants carry many symbolic meanings.

Deciduous trees lose their leaves each fall and remind us of the never-ending cycle of birth, death, and rebirth. Evergreen trees represent our deepest roots and highest aspirations. Fruit trees are symbolic of the bounty of nature that comes to us when the time is ripe.

Flowers bring color into our lives and are associated with beauty and grace. Cultivated flowers symbolize how we can influence and control natural growth, while wild flowers and weeds show how nature's abundance comes in all shapes and varieties. The flowering of any plant represents the peak of performance.

Climbing plants, in their ability to spread upward and outward may indicate a widening of our horizons, while prickly plants sometimes represent sticking points in our lives.

Trees, Flowers, and Plants

Trees, Flowers, and Plants

Many plants were used in the illustrated manuscripts of the Middle Ages, in the carpet designs of Iran and Turkey, and in the fabrics of France and China.

In the Celtic manuscript known as *The Book of Kells*, the patterns made by twisted vines inspired Celtic knotwork, in which images of birds, plants, and animals are woven together in highly decorative patterns.

When we dream of plants and vines, we are responding to them as an essential feature of our world, both in terms of our physical need for them as food and their connection to archetypal symbols (see page 17).

Alchemists and healers have used plants to bring about change. Alchemilla (also called lady's mantle), found originally in Europe, was used by alchemists. They collected dew from its leaves for their preparations and used it for healing wounds. Alchemilla was dedicated to the Virgin Mary.

Your dreams may include weeds as well as flowers. Some say a weed is a wildflower growing in the wrong place. Certainly a weed is an undesirable plant in a garden, particularly when it is invasive, reducing the survival rates of delicate, cultivated specimens. If you dream of weeds, consider whether you are being pushed out, overtaken, or overshadowed. "Weed" is also a term for cannabis, which may be linked to drug taking or fear of loss of control. To "weed something out" is to remove something undesirable. Is that what you need to do in some part of your life or with your friends? Perhaps you feel that you are the one who is unwelcome?

The Tree of Life is recognized world-wide as a potent symbol and represents the cross to Christians. The Muslim Lote tree represents the boundary between human understanding and divine mystery. In Christianity, the tree is the symbol of both life and knowledge. In China, the Tree of Life was Kienmou, which grew on the slopes of the earthly paradise of Kuen-Lou. The Buddha gained enlightenment beneath the Bodhi tree. Thus, again and again we see symbolic links between trees and spirituality. As you explore the significance of individual trees in your dreams, bear in mind their spiritual significance across different traditions.

Flowers and other plants remind us of the natural world of beauty and growth. If plants are potted, it may indicate constriction or lack of care. If they are blooming vigorously, they may symbolize energy and healthy growth or the threat of rampant excess.

Rosemary, now 13, had this dream when she was 8:

The most frightening dream I have ever had was when I had chickenpox. It started in my sleep, but I woke up and it carried on like a hallucination. It was like trees and enormous plants grasping at me, trying to hold me, trying to kill me. I screamed. I was really upset and scared.

Whatever form plants take in your dreams, learning more about their natures will help you interpret your dreams successfully.

ABOVE *Prickly plants in dreams may signify thorny problems.*

Ash

ASH REPRESENTS SOLIDITY, a stability that holds things together. In Norse mythology, Ygdrasill, the mighty ash, is the World Tree that unites heaven, earth, and the underworld. It is known as the Tree of Prudence.

Rowan, also called mountain ash, wittern, and quickbeam, is credited with protective magical powers. In Lancashire in England, rowan twigs were put over the bed to repel nightmares. In some areas, rowan twigs were put in a newborn baby's crib to ward off malevolent witches and fairies. In old folk tales, rowan berries were said to ease childbirth.

Rowans were often planted near Celtic standing stone circles to protect the stones from any misfortune. Today, people still plant rowan trees near their houses to guard their homes and families. To cut down a rowan is to invite disaster.

CONNECTIONS

- *Does your dream ash tree connect to "ashes," something that has been destroyed by fire or cremation?*
- *Are you in need of the protective qualities of ash?*

Beech and Birch FOR THE ANCIENT CELTS,

the beech was the most venerated tree because it held all the knowledge of the world.
They associated the beech with Ogma, the powerful warrior figure of Tuatha De
Danaan, who became the early Celtic god Ogma Sunface. It is said that he invented
the Ogham alphabet used by the Celts. In some traditions, beech is the symbol of the
written word. In German and Swedish, there is a linguistic link between the word for
beech and the word for *book*, just as there is in Anglo-Saxon. In many European
cultures, beech is the tree of ancient wisdom and is associated with the gods of
learning and human intellect.

The beech is also associated with many other
gods, including the Greek god Hermes the Messenger;
Thoth, the Ancient Egyptians' god of mathematics
and wisdom; and the Norse god Odin, who was given
the gift of the runes (an early Germanic alphabet).
Like the Ogham alphabet, runes were used for
divination. The wood and leaves of the beech were
carried as a talisman to increase creative powers.

Native Americans used birch bark to make
canoes, and birch was a sacred tree for many tribes.
In England, to be "birched" was to be lashed with
birch twigs. If you dream of birch, is it related to
punishment in any way?

CONNECTIONS

- *Do you want to develop your potential with more "book" learning?*
- *Is your "beech" dream really about a "beach"?*

Hawthorn

HAWTHORN IS REGARDED AS A MAGICAL TREE in British folklore. Legend has it that witches' broomsticks were decorated with may, the small white flowers of the hawthorn. The time of Beltane, the ancient festival of the death of winter, was determined by the blossoming of the hawthorn, since may blossom is the symbol of the coming of summer. Maypoles, symbols of fertility, were traditionally made from hawthorn or oak.

To cut a hawthorn down is regarded as unlucky. Sometimes, hawthorn is linked to death because of its powerful smell. This may be because one variety, *Crataegus monogyna*, contains a chemical in its flowers that is identical to a chemical found in rotting meat and corpses.

The tradition of *bawning*, a dialect term for "adorning," in Appleton, Cheshire, England, used to involve the whole village. Today, it is mainly the children who decorate the hawthorn with red ribbons and flower garlands. After decorating it, they then dance around it, singing a special song. It is believed the Appleton hawthorn was planted in 1125 C.E. and was taken from a cutting of a sacred tree at Glastonbury.

The hawthorn is linked to fertility and rebirth. The British poet Geoffrey Grigson says that its musky aroma is suggestive of sensuality and sex. When a hawthorn appears in dreams, it may indicate a new sense of personal regeneration or that you are about to be more creative physically or mentally.

Trees, Flowers, and Plants

Weeping Willow

THE WONDERFULLY GRACEFUL WEEPING WILLOW TREE is just one variety of the willow family. The willow can regenerate by seeds or, if a branch breaks off and is swept down a river, it can root itself in muddy banks. The propensity of willow to survive against the odds and bloom once more makes it a happy omen in dreams.

Willow has many uses apart from its use in building. This abundance of uses is another positive sign for the dreamer. Willow strips are made into ropes and used as osiers for basket weaving, and willow wood is burned to make charcoal.

The willow tree is also associated with water and weeping, sadness and lost love. *To wear the willow* means "to go into mourning," and people whose sweethearts had died wore garlands made from willow leaves. The Hebrews in captivity hung their harps on a willow tree to show they were in mourning for their homeland.

The Celtic god Esus is traditionally depicted cutting a willow. In Chinese mythology, the weeping willow is the tree of the goddess Kwan-yin, who sprinkles the waters of life with a willow branch. The willow, an important symbol of wisdom, was seen to connect to the heavens through its branches and to the lower world through its roots.

CONNECTION

Does your dream of willow symbolize the loss of someone or something you loved?

Oak THE OAK WAS A SYMBOL OF STRENGTH AND LONG LIFE and long ago was seen as a sacred tree throughout Europe. It was also sacred to the Norse people and to the Celts. Oak leaves symbolize the strength of faith. In Ancient Rome the patriot or victor was crowned with garlands of oak.

The word *druid* means "knowledge of the oak," and the Druids practiced their religion in oak groves and woods. Their oak woods provided sanctuary from the Romans, who threatened to overrun them. Mistletoe, a parasitical plant that uses the oak as its host tree, was also a holy plant for the Druids. Mistletoe was valued for its healing properties and was used as a cure for infertility, perhaps because in deepest winter when its host tree seems dead, this parasite thrives. At Christmas, it is customary to bring mistletoe indoors and hang it up so that people can kiss underneath its creamy white, highly poisonous berries.

If you dream of oaks or acorns, it may indicate that you are about to start on a new phase of life. The saying "from little acorns great oak trees grow" represents the idea that successful ventures come from small beginnings.

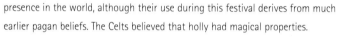

Evergreens

EVERGREENS SIGNIFY the unbroken, unconquered life force, which is why they are used in Christmas celebrations and at funerals. At the birth of Jesus, the Magi brought frankincense and myrrh, which are the sweet-smelling resins of evergreen trees. Frankincense and myrrh have healing properties and were also used in embalming dead bodies. At Christmas, the holly and ivy that are used to decorate the home are now said to symbolize Christ's eternal presence in the world, although their use during this festival derives from much earlier pagan beliefs. The Celts believed that holly had magical properties.

Evergreens reflect the belief in life after death and symbolize immortality. Bay, a member of the evergreen laurel family, is linked to resurrection, since it can revive after dying back to its roots. Bay is traditionally used in funeral wreaths. In English folklore, a bay tree in the garden was believed to protect the house from lightning and to keep away evil spirits. In Ancient Rome, emperors wore bay wreaths as a charm against thunderstorms.

Though poisonous, the evergreen yew tree symbolizes earth and immortality and is almost always found in British churchyards. The yew lives to a great age and can reroot its branches to produce offshoots. It is considered unlucky to damage a yew.

CONNECTIONS

- *Does your dream "yew" represent "you"?*
- *Does your dream of an evergreen tree represent your belief in the eternal cycle of life?*

Fir

THE WORD FIR is used to describe a whole variety of cone-bearing conifers found throughout the world.

Silver firs produce turpentine in blisters on their trunks in summer. The balsam fir of North America produces a turpentine known as Canada balsam, which is used to mount specimens for the microscope because its optical properties are like those of glass. If fir trees appear in your dream, it may be this clarity that is important.

The Ancient Greeks used turpentine to add to new wine to make it keep, and so the fir was added to the many symbols of Bacchus, the god of wine.

As with other trees, the felling of the noble fir was seen as an act of disrespect, since the soul of the tree was destroyed. However, firs are traditionally brought indoors and decorated at Christmas, which falls near the winter solstice. The evergreen tree is the symbol of rebirth and immortality and so at this darkest point of the year it reminds us that life carries on and lighter days will come. It is also known as the Yuletide Tree, deriving from the Anglo-Saxon word *geol*, meaning "wheel." The wheel represents the turning of the sun, and the death of the old year and the beginning of the new.

CONNECTION

◎ *Does your dream of the fir symbolize the end of one part of your life, as you move toward a new beginning?*

Cedar of Lebanon THE EVERGREEN CEDAR

is the sacred tree of Lebanon and symbolizes strength, durability, and immortality. The Lebanon was once covered with forests of cedar, but the wood was in such demand that many of them were cut down. Then war devastated the country, which was once known as the "jewel of the Mediterranean."

The first Temple in Jerusalem was built with the wood from cedars of Lebanon. The timber from these trees is so strong and long-lasting that it represented prosperity and long life for the biblical poets and prophets. King Solomon ordered that cedarwood should be used to build the Ark of the Covenant, a chest containing the Ten Commandments. The cedar of Lebanon is also associated with the Virgin Mary.

In Ancient Egypt, cedar wood was prized as the best wood for building boats and coffins because it resists water and, thus, rot. Cedar is mentioned in one of the earliest books in history, *The Epic of Gilgamesh*, which records the dreams of the heroes as they search for immortality.

CONNECTION

◎ *Does your dream of a cedar of Lebanon reassure you that you can endure any difficulty facing you?*

Giant Redwood

GIANT REDWOODS ARE AMONG THE TALLEST CONIFEROUS TREES ON EARTH. Also called sequoias, there are some specimens that are over 2000 years old. Instead of dropping their cones every year, redwoods hold on to them for two decades. They dominate the landscape in certain parts of California, where Redwood National Park is located.

If you dream of giant redwoods, it may relate to a deep connection with nature and other people long since dead, for these trees have lived longer than any person. Redwoods carry the history of the earth and represent continuity.

Redwoods are held to be sacred by some Native American tribes, who venerate their heavenly connections. The crowns of the trees are so high that they are thought to be imbued with mystical qualities beyond the reach of humankind. The color of the trees is also significant, since red is the color of blood, the heart, and passion.

CONNECTION

◎ *Does your dream of a redwood link to feelings of longevity?*
   Such a dream can be reassuring if you have been ill or are
   awaiting the results of medical tests.

Fruit Trees

FRUIT TREES PROVIDE US WITH FOOD AND GRACE THE LANDSCAPE. Whichever fruit tree you dream of, the condition it is in, its stage of development (is it a young sapling or a mature tree?), and how much fruit it bears will all add to the tree's meaning for you.

In Christianity, apples are symbolically connected to Eve and the temptation of Adam; they are thus linked to knowledge, sexuality, and the fall from grace that forced Adam and Eve out of the Garden of Eden.

At the festival of Rosh Hashanah, Jews eat apples dipped in honey to wish each other a sweet New Year. A Halloween tradition in the United States and in Britain is to "bob" for apples floating in water.

If you dream of apples, are the apples ripe and whole (a positive omen) or fallen and worm-eaten (indicating that there is something in your life that you are neglecting)? Is your dream linked to the Big Apple (New York), or the "apple of your eye," a favored person in your life?

Pear trees may signify a "pair" of some kind. Can you relate your dream to any person you need to pair up with?

Fruit ripening and seeds developing may symbolize conception. *To bear fruit* can mean "to bring a task to completion," as well as "to have children."

CONNECTION

Are your hopes about to come to fruition?

Trees, Flowers, and Plants

Palm Tree IN ANCIENT

EGYPT, the date palm tree was used to make planks that were used in the construction of important buildings, such as temples. The erect growth and stateliness of these trees symbolize righteousness, fame, and triumph. The palm is also a phallic symbol because of its shape, but may represent the female too in its clusters of dates, which can resemble breasts.

The palm continues to bear fruit until old age and so represents longevity and fruitfulness. In the Arabian traditions, it is the Tree of Life; to Christians it symbolizes Christ's triumphal entry into Jerusalem, remembered on Palm Sunday. Palm branches signify glory and victory over death and were an emblem for any Roman Christian who had traveled to the Holy Land.

The palm, never shedding its foliage, is continually adorned with the same green.

This power of the tree men think agreeable and fit for representing victory.
PLUTARCH

In the Hebrew tradition, palms represent a moral man, and the palm is the emblem of Judea after the Exodus.

CONNECTIONS

Could your dream palm tree represent success in an enterprise that you have undertaken?

Do the dates of the palm symbolize important dates for you? Is there an important date coming up?

Olive Tree LEGEND HAS IT THAT THE GREEK GODDESS

ATHENA was given her temple, the Parthenon, after she gave an olive tree to the people of Athens. The Greek god Heracles, known to the Romans as Hercules, cut his favorite wooden club from an olive tree. Since ancient times, the growing of olives to make olive oil has been an essential part of the Greek economy.

Immortality, fruitfulness, and peace are qualities associated with the olive. It indicates plenty because olive oil was such a valuable commodity. With the dove,

the olive branch symbolizes peace. The olive leaf represents renewal of life, while a dove carrying an olive twig symbolizes the souls of the dead who are at peace.

In Ancient Greece, a crown of olive leaves was given to victors after competitions and battles. The victor of the Olympic games in those days was crowned with olive branches. In Christian iconography, some scenes of the Annunciation to the Virgin Mary depict the archangel Gabriel bearing an olive branch.

CONNECTIONS

- *Have you recognized a recent success that you can "crown" or celebrate in some way?*
- *Do you need to offer a peace token to someone?*
- *Have you been "pouring oil on troubled waters," trying to restore calm?*

Eucalyptus Tree THIS AUSTRALIAN TREE HAS

THE BLUE GUM and the ironbark as part of its family. Both are cultivated for the medicinal oils that are produced in the leaves. The leaves are dotted with holes or pores from which the straw-colored oil emerges. The strongly scented oil, which smells like camphor, is used as an antiseptic as well as for treating a cold.

Emblematic of Australia, where its leaves provide the staple diet of the koala bear, the eucalyptus is one of the largest trees in the world and has a very striking appearance. The young saplings sometimes grow as much as fifteen feet (four meters) in one year. Eucalyptus is used for making furniture and ships, and beekeepers value it for the quantity of nectar it provides to bees.

The eucalyptus is also known as the "gum tree " because of the sticky gum that oozes out of its trunk. If you dream of a eucalyptus, the tree might represent a sticky situation you are facing.

CONNECTIONS

- *Do you feel blocked in some way and need to "clear your head" in order to move forward?*
- *Are you experiencing fast development at the moment?*

Trees, Flowers, and Plants

Forget-Me-Not

Hope's gentle gem,
the sweet forget-me-not.

COLERIDGE

THE DELICATE BLUE FORGET-ME-NOT IS A SYMBOL OF LOVERS who are separated. In a story dating from the Middle Ages, a knight was walking with a lady of the court. She saw some blue flowers growing on the bank of the river, so the gallant knight went to gather a bouquet for her. He was reaching for the last one when he lost his footing and fell into the river. As he was being dragged away by the forceful current he shouted, "Forget me not! Forget me not!" This is how the flower got its name.

If you dream of forget-me-nots, think about how the dream relates to your present relationships. You may feel that a lover is being less than interested or is forgetful about your feelings.

CONNECTIONS

◉ *Do you feel that a relationship is coming to an end?*
◉ *Do you need to make more of an effort to insure*
  that people remember you?

Foxglove

THE NAME FOXGLOVE IS A CORRUPTION OF FOLK'S GLOVE, a reference to little folk such as fairies, goblins, or other magical creatures. The elegant foxglove is known as the flower of insincerity. Within the bright exterior of the foxglove is a substance called *digitalis*, a natural heart stimulant that can kill if an excessive amount is taken. This is why the foxglove is sometimes called *dead men's fingers*. Digitalis (from the Latin word *digitae*, "fingers") is used as medicine for heart conditions and other illnesses.

Foxgloves are also called *finger flowers*, because the flowers are like the fingers of a glove. When you dream of foxgloves, think of the significance of a glove, which can protect or conceal a hand. Perhaps your dream indicates that there is something you are trying to keep hidden. You should also consider the "fox" aspect (see page 260) of the flower—are you being stealthy and wily in pursuit of your desires?

CONNECTIONS

- *Are you concealing anything beneath a bright exterior?*
- *Do you need some form of stimulation for your heart?*
- *Are you "foxed," or puzzled, about anything at present?*

Daffodil

DAFFODIL IS THE COMMON ENGLISH NAME FOR THE
GENUS NARCISSUS, which belongs to the amaryllis family. The daffodil is sometimes
called the *Lent lily* because it flowers during the Christian season of Lent. Its cheerful
yellow flower heads bring brightness to spring, when it is one of the first flowers to
appear, showing that winter is over. In this setting it symbolizes hope and renewal.

In Greek legend the asphodel, a lily-like flower similar to the daffodil, is the most
famous of the plants connected with the underworld. Persephone, daughter of the
goddess Demeter, was wandering in the springtime meadows of Sicily gathering
flowers when Hades, god of the underworld, snatched her. His touch turned her white
flowers yellow, and legend has it that daffodils bloomed on the fields ever after.
Homer describes the flowers covering the great meadow as "the haunt of the dead."
Since Persephone refused all of Hades' advances, the daffodil is also a symbol of
unrequited love.

In Iran the daffodil is called "the golden," and in Turkey it is known as "the golden
bowl." The daffodil is also the national flower of Wales.

CONNECTIONS

*Do you need an input
of uncomplicated
cheerfulness to brighten
up your life?*

*Does your dream of
a daffodil symbolize
a new spring, a bright
beginning for
a new project?*

Iris

PERSIAN IRISES ARE FAMED FOR THEIR PERFUME and have such a range of colors that together they can resemble a rainbow. Thus the flower was named after Iris, the goddess of the rainbow, who brought only good news. In Greek mythology, the gods let down a bridge, or rainbow, between heaven and earth so the goddess Iris could act as a go-between to ease discord when there was friction between men and gods.

In Virgil's *Aeneid*, Iris is sent to gather the souls of women and so is associated with the concerns of women and with completion. The iris is often depicted as a fleur-de-lis, symbol of France, and shares the symbolism of the lily, indicating purity, peace, and resurrection.

The gladiolus is related to the iris. The word *gladiolus* means "little sword" in Latin and the flower is so called because its leaves resemble the shape of a sword. As the "sword iris" it symbolizes the sorrow of the Virgin Mary, to whom it was prophesied that her heart would be pierced by a sword of sorrow.

The common yellow iris is called the flag iris. If you dream of a yellow iris, it may mean you want to call attention to or to "flag" something you are concerned about.

CONNECTIONS

- *Does your dream iris refer to the iris in your eye?*
- *Are you like the goddess Iris—the peacemaker?*

Lily THIS MAJESTIC FLOWER IS ASSOCIATED WITH PURITY, peace, and resurrection. It is the sacred flower of all the virgin goddesses in mythology. In nearly every Catholic country, the white lily is dedicated to the Virgin Mary. Dante described it as "the lily of faith."

The lily also represents the fertility of the earth goddess and is dedicated to Hera, Queen of Heaven. In the West, the lily carries the same symbolism as the lotus in the East (see page 241). In the Hebrew tradition, the lily is the emblem of the tribe of Judah and symbolizes trust in God.

Christ told the Jews that Solomon, their monarch, dressed in all his sumptuous finery, could not equal the majesty of the lily and told them to "consider the lilies of the field"—beautiful though unadorned. The lily is also known as the "Easter Lily," after the goddess Eostre, whose name gave us Easter. The beautiful white arum lily is associated with funerals and is considered unlucky if brought into a house.

Lily of the valley, also known as *fairy bells*, was associated with witches, who used it for healing. Lily of the valley contains a substance called *convallatoxin*, a digitalis-like chemical, and more than twenty other substances used in the treatment of cardiac patients.

CONNECTIONS

◉ *If you dream of lilies in a church, could this be linked to a wedding or funeral?*

◉ *Could your dream be linked to cardiac treatment you are receiving?*

Poppy

THE POPPY IS A SYMBOL OF DEATH AND REGENERATION. Remembrance Sunday, also known as *Poppy Day* in Britain because people wear paper or plastic poppies as an act of remembrance, originally commemorated those who died in World War I on the fields of France and Belgium, and now commemorates all those who have died in wars. In the United States, Veterans' Day has traditionally served the same purpose, when people also wear poppies for remembrance. Poppies bloomed in the fields that soldiers dug for their trenches, which were later caked with their blood. Red poppies are used in wreaths for war dead as a reminder of their sacrifice.

Sleep and unconsciousness are also associated with the poppy, as is Morpheus, the Greek god of sleep. Opium, from which morphine and heroin are made, is extracted from the unripe capsules of the opium poppy and furthers this connection of the poppy with rest. Poppy seeds contain no opium and are a good food source. Since the poppy produces an abundance of seeds, the flower is also associated with fertility. Poppy seeds can remain dormant for hundreds of years, then germinate when conditions are suitable.

The poppy is also a symbol of the Great Mother and is sacred to all lunar and nocturnal gods and goddesses.

CONNECTIONS

Is your dream of poppies related to addiction?

Are you in need of a period of rest and relaxation? Are you getting restful sleep?

Rose

Some flowers are only lovely to the eye,
but others are lovely to the heart.

GOETHE

THE FLOWER OF THE SUN, the rose is universally used to symbolize love and passion.
The rose also symbolizes the heart and unity. As the flower of many goddesses, it
represents femininity, fertility, and beauty. The red rose may symbolize desire and
consummation as well as passion. It is also the national flower of England. The white
rose symbolizes innocence, virginity, and the blossoming of spirituality. The golden
rose symbolizes perfection. In the United States, yellow roses are given for friendship,
white roses are associated with weddings, and red roses with funerals.

A rose garden is a symbol of paradise, so if you dream of being in a rose
garden, it may indicate that you are feeling blissful contentment about your
waking situation. In Roman times, roses were grown in funerary gardens as
a sign of resurrection after death. At the Roman Rosalia festival in spring,
rose petals were scattered on the Three Graces, the sister goddesses who
were associated with beauty and charm.

Roses also have thorns. In dreams, a rose with thorns may symbolize
a thorny problem you have to tackle to gain the reward represented by the
rose. A dream of thorny roses may link to a difficulty in a romantic relationship.

CONNECTIONS

◉ *Does a fragrant rose in your dream conceal a thorn, or danger, that may
hurt you?*

◉ *If you are given roses in a dream, consider the significance of their color
and number. Twelve red roses are a sign that the giver is in love with you.*

Snowdrop

A FIRST FLOWER OF SPRING, this dainty white flower symbolizes hope, new life, and fresh opportunities after a period of darkness. In Victorian England, the snowdrop was regarded as the flower of friendship in adversity because it pushes through the snow each spring to bring a sign that new life is flourishing and winter is retreating.

The botanical name for the snowdrop is *Galanthus*, meaning "milk flower," because of its color. In Christianity, the snowdrop is an emblem of the Virgin Mary. It also represents Candlemas, a Christian celebration that takes place on the second of February to mark the day when Mary took the child Jesus to the Temple and made an offering. You may dream of a snowdrop after a fall of snow. So, the falling, or "drop," of the snow becomes "snowdrop," which may have particular significance if you are a farmer or a skier. Your dream could be an indication that you are concerned about the impact that a heavy snowfall could have on your plans.

CONNECTIONS

- *Does your dream of snowdrops represent a glimmer of hope after a difficult time?*
- *Are you returning to good health after being unwell?*

Trees, Flowers, and Plants

Tulip

THE TULIP IS A SYMBOL OF FERTILITY. It is believed to have originated in Iran, where it signified perfect love or a declaration of love. It is the emblem of the Turkish House of Osman and the national flower of Holland, where over 5000 varieties are grown for export all over the world.

The wonderful colors of tulips so desired by Europeans brought on "tulip mania" in Holland in the seventeenth century. People vied with each other to possess rare tulip bulbs, and the price for a single bulb was so high that buying one made some people bankrupt. It seems that anyone with money went to extreme lengths to get a bulb of the gaudy-petaled flower. One sailor, mistaking a tulip bulb for an onion, ate it and was later imprisoned for six months!

In Chinese symbolism, the tulip is the "perfect man" who is associated with harmony and refinement.

CONNECTIONS

- *Is your dream tulip a sign that you need more color in your life?*
- *Are there links with Holland associated with the tulips in your dream?*

Orchid

MAGNIFICENCE, OPULENCE, AND LUXURY are the characteristics associated with orchids, so if you dream of this flower, consider the riches that surround you. *Orchid* comes from the Latin word *orchis*, which means "testicle," because its double bulbs resemble testicles. In England, the orchid was termed *dog's stones* for the same reason. This link with male sexual organs insured the use of orchids as a symbol of potency and as a charm to aid performance and fertility. Parts of the plants were used in the preparation of love potions. Pliny the Elder, who wrote the encyclopedic *Historia Naturalis* (Natural History), said that if a man held the bulbs in his hand it would arouse sexual desire.

If a man gave a woman an orchid, it represented his intention to seduce her or showed that he certainly hoped for sexual favors. Today, this erotic association has not been lost, and orchids are still given on significant dates such as high school proms.

Orchids need great care if they are to flower, which they are able to do for months on end in the right conditions.

CONNECTIONS

- *Do your dream orchids symbolize a sexual relationship?*
- *Do you feel that, like an orchid, you need care to reach your full potential?*

Lotus

THE LOTUS IS SEEN AS A POWERFUL SYMBOL throughout the world, but particularly in the East, where it represents all aspects of creation. The lotus is seen as the product of the union of the sun and the waters, and it represents spirit and matter, fire and water. It is a symbol of divine birth coming unsullied from the muddy depths.

Early Hindu texts say that before creation all the world was a golden lotus, known as the *Matripdama* or *Mother Lotus*—hers was the womb of nature. The Indian lotus links to the goddess Lakshmi or Patma, and the red lotus is the emblem of India.

The lotus flower, which is a water lily, is characteristic of Buddhist imagery. With its roots in the mud, it symbolizes the belief that enlightenment—the flower in blossom—can be achieved in the midst of human suffering, represented by the muddy water. The lotus represents the unfolding of spirituality as the flower grows toward the sun.

The Buddhist "thousand-petaled lotus" symbolizes the final revelation and enlightenment.

CONNECTIONS

- *Are you using all aspects of your creative power to the fullest?*
- *Does your dream lotus inspire renewed interest in spirituality?*

Wildflowers

ANEMONES ARE KNOWN AS WIND FLOWERS and are
named after the Greek god of wind, Anemos.
The red anemone is said to have sprung
from the spot where a drop of blood fell
from the god Adonis, who represents
death and rebirth. Buttercups, with their
bright yellow heads, represent simple
pleasures, sunny days, and the shining
riches of the golden sun.

The pansy, also called *cupid's delight*
and *love-in-idleness* or *heartsease*,
represents undying love.

The daisy symbolizes innocence and
childlike simplicity.

Bluebells flower in abundance throughout
woodlands. Like all flowers with "bells," they
represent the bringing of news for the dreamer, since
bells traditionally were rung throughout Europe to announce
news prior to the introduction of mass communication systems.

CONNECTIONS

- *Do your wildflowers indicate the need for a simpler life, one in which
  nature's simple charms have greater significance for you?*
- *Do you feel you are about to flower, to fulfill your potential or to complete
  an undertaking?*

Trees, Flowers, and Plants

Herbs

ST JOHN'S WORT, A HIGHLY EFFECTIVE ANTIDEPRESSANT, has the beneficial side effect of lucid dreaming when used in systemic treatment for depression.

For centuries, herbs have been used medicinally and as flavorings. Betony, a plant of the mint family, was once used to give relief from fearful visions and nightmares. Mugwort is used to ease tension and depression. Aloe vera has many uses. As "bitter aloe," it was painted on fingernails to stop nail-biting. Aloe vera leaves placed on sunburn stop the stinging.

Sage has medicinal properties to keep teeth clean and relieve sore gums. It also denotes wisdom or sagacity.

Chamomile has a calming effect and is known as "patience in adversity."

In the seventeenth century, "parsley bed" was a euphemism for the female genitals and *parsley* for pubic hair.

Rue is the herb of remembrance and symbolizes grief and repentance, hence the expression "to rue the day."

CONNECTIONS

- *Do your dream herbs link to herbs you are using in waking life?*
- *Do you think that your dream of chamomile tea may indicate a need to calm down?*

Climbing Plants HONEYSUCKLE SYMBOLIZES

EROTIC LOVE because of its enticing smell and the way it twines around other plants.

Ivy is a clinging, hardy climber that is found in all parts of the world. It is evergreen and so symbolizes immortality and everlasting life. In early civilizations the ivy leaf was associated with Dionysus, the Greek god of wine. It was believed to cause, as well as cure, drunkenness. Its clinging habit sometimes represents needy dependency.

Clematis, also known as *traveler's joy*, is like a vine because it climbs over everything in its path. It is sometimes called *lady's bower* or *virgin's bower*, because it makes thick canopies to shade and conceal arbors in gardens.

Vines represent fertility and reproduction. In Christian art, the vine with wheat represents the body and blood of Christ, the Eucharist. In Greece, the vine is the symbol of the god Bacchus, famed for his wine drinking and revelry.

Virginia creeper climbs to great heights. Its leaves turn red in fall and so it is planted for its stunning color at this time of year.

CONNECTIONS

- *Do your dream climbers represent your hopes concerning advancement at work?*
- *Are you a "social climber," with aspirations to increase your social standing?*

Prickly Plants

THE CACTUS THRIVES in the most inhospitable conditions and its prickly spikes protect it all year round and act as a warning to people and animals to keep away from it.

Thorns are found on many plants, including roses, broom, and hawthorn. They offer protection to the plant but injure animals and people who get too close. Jesus Christ was forced to wear a crown of thorns when he was mocked by the Romans as the "King of the Jews."

Thorns symbolize injury and hindrance and often appear in myths and fairy tales. Nettles can sting very painfully. Shakespeare includes them in the garland that Ophelia wears at her death following her rejection by Hamlet. Although they can sting, nettles can also be made into tea and soup.

CONNECTIONS

- *Have you got a thorny problem to solve?*
- *Is someone being a thorn in your side, constantly causing you pain and annoyance?*
- *Are you on the defensive about a situation, erecting a protective barrier around yourself?*
- *Are you feeling "nettled" or irritated at the moment?*

ANIMALS, BIRDS, INSECTS, AND SEA CREATURES as well as strange creatures from legend and mythology, come to us in dreams. They represent not only their unique characteristics but also the symbolic qualities that have been ascribed to them over thousands of years. They also represent the animal nature within us. Animals have been venerated from Ancient Egypt to Celtic Britain, from Aboriginal peoples in Australia to the Inuit tribes in Canada. Animals play a central role in our lives. Domesticated animals, such as cows and sheep, may provide us with food, or they may provide materials, such as leather or wool, which protect us. Animals such as dogs and cats are treasured as pets. Wild animals are both beautiful and mysterious, and in some places we need to be protected from them. The symbolism of fish is an important part of the Christian religion, and they feature widely in legends and ancient stories.

Birds are viewed in many mythologies as having a connection between earth and heaven because they are at home in the different elements of air, earth, and water. Birds may also be seen as messengers because they can fly high, out of view, to the heavens.

All Creatures
Great and Small

All Creatures Great and Small

D reams that include living creatures may take on mythic proportions, as does this one told by Vicki:

I am in a library trying to reach out for a particular book. There is a snake about ten times as big as me wrapped around a post, preventing me from getting the book. The scene in the library changes to my house where I find lots of little snakes tangled in my hair.

Like the legendary Gorgon's, Vicki's hair becomes a writhing mass of snakes. She is still "tangled up" by something related to her studies, since books and a library feature in the dream. She has escaped the enormous snake, but there are still minor issues, "little snakes," that are bothering her.

It is not surprising that a host of creatures are found in dreams. Animals symbolize our instinctive, primal qualities, which is why they fascinate us. We may take on their power when we wear their skins. Norse warriors used to go into battle wearing bear skins and the term *berserk*, originally a reference to the ferocious fighting style of the Norsemen, comes from this. *Bern* meant "bear" and *serkr* meant "coat."

In the Middle Ages, a type of illuminated book known as a *bestiary* was very popular. In it were illustrations of animals, both real and imaginary, and they were described in terms of the human traits they exhibited. Bestiaries also popularized such imaginary creatures as the unicorn and the phoenix. Much of the symbolism explained in this section of the book can be traced back to these medieval bestiaries. Much of our language refers to the characteristics of animals and insects. This language finds its way into our dreamscapes. One woman told me about a dream in which a slug was crawling up her chest. She could not make sense of the dream slug until she started to play with linguistic connections. She came up with "sluggish," which was just how her digestive system was at the time. Once she understood the symbolic significance of the creature, she made some beneficial changes to her diet and has not dreamed of slugs since.

The illustrated Celtic manuscript known as *The Book of Kells* portrays mythical beasts as well as the everyday creatures that feature in this section of *The Dream Bible*. As you explore the nature of these beasts, consider their beauty as well as their indifference to humans and ask yourself, "What part of me does this creature represent? Why has this creature come into my dream now and what is its message to me?"

Cat THE CAT FAMILY,

which includes lions, tigers, panthers, cheetahs, and leopards, as well as domesticated cats, is traditionally linked to the feminine, intuitive side of ourselves. Cats were worshiped in Ancient Egypt because they kept the perilous rodents under control. The cat goddess, Bastet, shown as having the head of a cat and the body of a woman, was the goddess of love and fertility. Cats were mummified and buried with their owners or in specially designated cemeteries.

The Greeks associated Bastet with the goddess Artemis, who, in medieval times, was known as queen of the witches, providing an association with darkness, night, and sinister things. In Norse mythology, cats were linked to weather and said to control winds. Cats were transformed into witches to ride through the stormy night sky. Dreaming of cats can be a warning that someone is being treacherous toward you.

CONNECTIONS

○ *Does your dream cat represent your "dark" side?*

○ *Are you feeling lucky?*

○ *Do you need to pay attention to your intuition?*

All Creatures Great and Small

Dog

DOGS ARE "MAN'S BEST FRIEND" and were the first domesticated animal. Descended from wolves, certain breeds are worked as guards, as guides for the blind, and as drug-sniffers, and are valued for their loyalty and companionship.

The Ancient Egyptians saw dogs as messengers between the living and the dead. Anubis, the black jackal (sometimes mistaken for a dog), was the Egyptian god of the dead and inventor of embalming. It is this "black dog" that may have given rise to the association with depression. Winston Churchill suffered from bouts of depression that he called his "black dog."

Dogs frequently appear in dreams. A woman told me of a series of dreams in which snarling and slavering dogs bit her arm. Then some months later she was savaged by a boxer dog and was badly injured. Now she never has dreams about dogs biting her. The dreams revealed her fears and, she said, prepared her for the attack, which, once it was over, freed her from her terrifying dreams.

CONNECTION

If you dream of being guided or led by a dog, perhaps you are experiencing difficulty finding your way out of a situation.

Cow IN THE FAMOUS BIBLICAL STORY where he is asked to interpret the Pharaoh's dream of the seven fat cows, Joseph says that they represent seven years of plenty in the land of Egypt. Fat, healthy cattle can easily be seen as being positive symbols. Joseph interprets the seven lean cows as representing seven years of famine, enabling Pharaoh to plan ahead and build up the nation's food reserves.

Cows are associated with moon goddesses, many of whom are depicted with the horns of a cow on their head. They are also a symbol of motherhood, because they provide milk and nourishment and were one of the first animals to be domesticated. A milk cow was a great asset to barter in times before money was used. Now we use the term *a cash cow* to mean something that brings us plenty.

CONNECTIONS

๏ *Does your dream of a cow mean that you are giving a lot to others at present?*

๏ *Are you being "milked" or used in some way?*

Bull

STRENGTH, STUBBORNNESS, AND POWER combine in the nature of a bull. The bull is associated with the zodiac sign of Taurus and with Thor, the Norse god of thunder. A bull's bellow is equated with thunder. In Assyrian mythology, the bull's horns represented the crescent moon.

The threat of real bulls in the "bull-infested" country this dreamer lived in triggered an unexpected response:

I dreamed a bull was chasing me; he ran after me and was just about to kill me when, crouching down, I lifted up my feet with my hands and soared up into the air. I was really pleased to have discovered this.

The dreamer does manage to escape and feels empowered by her ability to soar above the threat.

CONNECTIONS

- *If your dream is of someone acting like a "bull in a china shop," rushing about, knocking everything awry, it could be a warning to slow down and to take more care.*
- *If you dream of hitting the "bull's-eye" it means that you will reach the target you are aiming for.*
- *If you are a bully in your dream, perhaps you're trying to impose your will on others. If you are being bullied, you may need to stand up to someone who is trying to force you to do things their way.*

Ox AN OX IS A CASTRATED BULL, sometimes called a steer, and is used as a domestic beast of burden. In this tamed state, oxen are much easier to handle than bulls and work for long periods without protest. The ox is also linked with sacrifice in some traditions, since it has sacrificed its virility to work without complaint for its master.

Saint Luke, author of one of the four Christian Gospels, is depicted as an ox in the seventh-century Celtic manuscript known as *The Book of Kells*. The ox symbolized steady hard work.

The ox has a special place in Chinese astrology; it is the second sign of the Chinese zodiac and people born under the sign are seen as reliable and considerate.

At times in their history, oxen have been protected by law because the idea of eating the meat of an animal that worked so hard was thought to be shameful.

CONNECTIONS
- *Are you engaged in a task that demands patient commitment?*
- *Can you recognize the strength of the ox in yourself?*

Stag

SINCE ITS ANTLERS ARE LIKE BRANCHES, the stag is associated with the Tree of Life (see page 217). It symbolizes the cycles of regeneration and growth because of the way its antlers are shed and renewed. Horned animals, especially stags, are linked with male sexuality. Horns are often used in aphrodisiacs, to ensure potency.

North American shamans often wear stags' horns as a symbol of making or seeking connection between earth and heaven. In this tradition, stags are believed to be messengers of the gods.

In the Middle Ages, the stag was associated with a solitary, pure life. Saint Hubert converted to Christianity after seeing a stag with a crucifix between its antlers. The white stag was the personal emblem of King Richard II of England.

The stag was of particular importance to the Celts. It was associated with the god Cerunnos, lord of the animals. He wore antlers and was the god of fertility, regeneration, and hunting. He is also known as the god of wealth.

CONNECTIONS

◉ *Are you in a process of renewal or do you need to be?*

◉ *Is it time for you to branch out, to make new connections?*

Horse

HORSES WERE SYMBOLS OF WEALTH AND POWER TO THE ANCIENT CELTS and the white horse carved into the chalk on a hillside at Uffington, in Oxfordshire in England, is a mark of how important they were. Sacred to the goddess Rhiannon, horses express the power of primal energy. They are also related to sexuality. The stud and the stallion represent male strength and fertility, as illustrated by this dream:

I was riding a beautiful horse over empty land and then the horse suddenly turned into my boyfriend.

Pegasus was the winged horse of Greek legend and Zeus was reputed to use the horse to carry thunderbolts.

CONNECTIONS

- *Is your dream horse wild or tamed? What does this represent about your behavior?*
- *If you are the rider, can you control the horse and rein in its power?*

Donkey

PROVERBIALLY STUBBORN, STUPID, AND OVERSEXED, donkeys are nonetheless admired because of the cross shape on their back. This cross is said to have appeared after the donkey carried Jesus into Jerusalem on Palm Sunday and was a sign the donkey had been blessed.

Donkeys and mules (a mule is a cross between a donkey and a horse) carry heavy loads without complaint. They symbolize patient acceptance of their lot. Donkeys are used as beasts of burden, so "donkey work" describes drudgery or menial work.

In one of the legends of King Midas, he grew the ears of an ass after presuming to tell the god Apollo that he was a better judge of music than Apollo was. Apollo said that Midas wasn't worthy of the ears of a human and gave him donkey ears instead, and Midas died of shame.

CONNECTIONS

⊚ *Do you feel overburdened?*

⊚ *A donkey dream could indicate some kind of intransigence on your part. Are you refusing to give way on an issue?*

⊚ *Eeyore,* of Winnie-the-Pooh *fame, is a cartoon donkey known for his depressed nature. Are you sluggish or depressed in any way?*

Elephant

ALTHOUGH WILD, THE ELEPHANT CAN BE TAMED. Its strength and dependability are legendary, as is its long memory. Elephants symbolize peace, faithfulness, and happiness. In Indian mythology, an elephant was believed to hold up the heavens, and today you can find carvings of elephants at the foot of the pillars that hold up temple roofs.

Elephants were symbols of powerful sexuality in Ancient India. The Indian elephant god Ganesh impregnated Maya the Virgin Goddess, who gave birth to Buddha. The god Shiva sometimes took on the form of an elephant. Elephant ivory is considered powerful magic and an aphrodisiac in many countries.

I was driving around in a car, very fast. As I was tearing around the place it turned into a jungle and then an elephant started rushing toward me. I flashed my lights and honked my horn, but the elephant still kept rushing toward me. Right at the last minute the elephant turned away from me and ran off.

In this dream, the elephant represents a powerful animal drive that could destroy the dreamer. At the very last minute the elephant turns aside and the dreamer is safe. She needs to consider what part of her life is like a jungle and puts her in danger. As she is in the driver's seat in the dream she will be in control of what happens if she takes decisive action.

CONNECTIONS

◉ *Do you need elephantine strength to carry out your mission?*

◉ *Is there a memory you are holding on to that you need to let go of?*

Hippopotamus

THIS ANIMAL'S NAME ORIGINATES IN THE GREEK WORDS *hippos*, meaning "horse," and *potamos*, meaning "river." This "river horse" was also thought of as a goddess form in the water.

In Ancient Egypt, the male hippopotamus was regarded as a nuisance, since it trampled or ate crops, and hunts were organized to kill it. Hippopotamuses came to symbolize the overthrow of evil and were included in temple paintings. Today, their reputation as aggressive, territorial animals still holds true.

The female hippopotamus represents the Egyptian Great Mother, Amenti, the "bringer forth of the water," goddess of childbirth. She was associated with the *ankh* or key of life. Amenti was a favored household goddess. Many blue glass carvings of hippopotamuses have been found in burial chambers, and these are believed to represent the regenerative power of the River Nile, as well as rebirth.

Hippopotamuses are gregarious animals who wallow in the mud and appear to have a relaxing, unburdened life. If you dream of a group of them, it may represent the desire to get together with friends, away from your daily concerns.

CONNECTIONS

◎ *Does your dream hippopotamus represent concerns about fertility and childbirth?*

Fox IN THE MIDDLE AGES, the fox was the symbol of the devil. In Europe, Reynard is the trickster fox, like the Native American trickster coyote. Foxes are respected for their intelligence and cunning. Reynard appeared to be an ordinary fox, apart from his miraculous godlike escapades and his ability to speak in a human voice, as many magical dream animals can.

Foxes are hunted for their pelts and as a "sport" in England, where it is combined with ritual dressing up. The determination of the female fox, the vixen, to escape and to lead the hunters away from her warren in order to protect her cubs gives her the reputation of a devoted mother.

The fox is stealthy and cunning in its attacks on hen houses in rural areas. However, as more and more foxes, like coyotes, are found in urban areas scavenging for food it is possible that foxes will become more dependent on humans. The fox's instinct for survival that has led to its great adaptability may ultimately damage its ability to survive in the wild.

In Scandinavia, the *aurora borealis*, or northern lights, is sometimes called "the light of the fox."

CONNECTIONS

- *Do you need to be "as wily as a fox" at present?*
- *Does your dream fox need protection and, if so, what can this be linked with in your life?*

Wolf

FIERCE AND PREDATORY, the wolf symbolizes animal survival. Wolves are often depicted as companions of the gods of the dead. For the Romans and Egyptians, wolves represented valor and were frequently depicted as guardians.

In fairy stories and myths, the wolf is usually a negative force that devours its victims. However, according to Roman mythology, it was a she-wolf who nurtured Romulus and his twin brother Remus. They grew up to found the city of Rome.

Wolves are also very social animals, relying on a complex system of roles and status within the pack. Members will lick the mouths of leaders and engage in ritualized play-fighting to reinforce power hierarchies.

In Celtic myths, the wolf is said to swallow the sun, the Sky Father, at night so that the moon can shine. The wolves' eerie howling at the moon reinforces this lunar connection. In Christianity, the wolf represents evil, cruelty, and stealthiness, but it is also the emblem of Saint Francis of Assisi, who is believed to have tamed the wolf of Gubbio which was terrorizing the population of the town. Domesticated wolves evolved into tame dogs, man's greatest friend.

Sheep

IN SOME PLACES, sheep are considered stupid and mindless because of their docility. As domesticated animals, they provide food and wool and make up a large part of the economy in places such as New Zealand.

In some countries, a black sheep is a lucky omen, but is more usually someone who causes sorrow or shame in a family. The black sheep stands out from the rest of the flock. Who or what does your black sheep represent?

The lamb is the symbol of purity and truth and is easily deceived. A lamb may be the sacrificial Easter lamb that goes to its death quietly, "like a lamb to the slaughter," without any resistance. In the New Testament, Christ is called the Lamb of God.

Caring for animals on deserted mountain pastures means that shepherds are or were often isolated for long periods of time, so they became self-sufficient. Shepherds symbolize a simple, natural way of life.

CONNECTIONS

- *"To separate the sheep from the goats" means to pick out any member of a group that is superior to the rest.*
- *"Sheepish" means to look embarrassed or abashed, especially as a result of doing something wrong, or to look foolish.*

Goat

THE GOAT HAS A PLACE in both pagan and Christian traditions. In Israel, there was an atonement ritual at Yom Kippur that involved the sins of the tribes being symbolically heaped onto the "scapegoat," which was ceremonially driven out. We still use the term *scapegoat* to mean an innocent person who has been made to take the blame for the deeds of others.

Goats are associated with rampant sexuality and lechery. Feeling "horny" is synonymous with sexual desire and the word "horn" is sometimes used in reference to the penis. This dreamer felt threatened by the goats in her dream:

I was in a field with some goats. One had huge horns and I was scared he was going to ram me. I woke up before he attacked me.

Goats are also connected with wisdom. Moses and Alexander the Great are sometimes shown wearing horns as a sign of wisdom. Shamans, wise medicine men, are often depicted with horns.

The Roman god Pan was half-man and half-goat. He was closely associated with the natural world and is the strongest pagan connection with the goat.

The name of the mythical monster the *Chimera* means "she-goat."

Rat RATS ARE CREATURES OF THE DARK, and in ancient mythology they were symbols of the night. Bright-eyed and intelligent, they are also destructive eaters and carriers of plague and Weil's disease. They symbolize death, decay, disease, and dirt. There is a British superstition that if rats nibble the furniture, it is a sign of death.

It is said that rats have precognition. For example, they know when to leave a ship before it goes down. In the Hindu tradition, rats are viewed as prudent animals, and the god Ganesh, he who vanquishes all obstacles, is said to ride on the back of a rat.

A nightmare from childhood, which I still have when I am ill, involves rats that are enormous. They are around me and make an intimidating noise, squeaking at me.

For this dreamer the rats are a source of terror because of their size and the noise that they make. They represent something that comes out of the dark, the unknown.

CONNECTIONS

- *"Does your dream of being attacked by rats relate to feeling under attack by friends or colleagues?*
- *Your dream rat may symbolize a "rat"—a friend who has deserted you, or betrayed your trust.*

Mouse

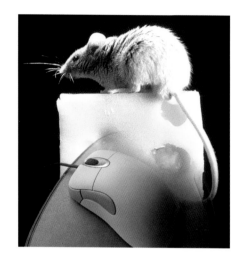

MICE MAY REPRESENT QUIET INDUSTRY, which we see in the harvest mice, or may represent vermin, as when a building is infested with mice that eat food meant for human consumption. Clearly, the setting of the dream is important; if the mice are in the wrong territory it indicates that something is out of place. A dream mouse may even represent your computer "mouse" and a connection with the workplace.

In medieval Europe, people believed that the souls of the dead were carried away in the mouth of a mouse and so mice became soul symbols. Some fairy stories say that at the time of death the soul runs out of the mouth in the form of a mouse.

CONNECTIONS

◎ *Dreaming that you are a mouse could mean that you feel dull and undistinguished, and prefer to keep yourself in the background.*

◎ *Does your dream mouse reveal a lack of confidence? Do you feel small and insignificant?*

Hare

THE HARE OR RABBIT IS A MAJOR SYMBOL OF THE MOON—many cultures see a hare, rather than a man, in the moon. Used widely as a symbol of sacrifice, in Christianity the hare or rabbit is associated with Easter. There is a legend that a hare breeder has only to tell a hare to kill itself and it will do so, thus showing that the hare is capable of self-sacrifice. Hares were sacred to the Anglo-Saxon goddess Eostre and gave rise to the *Easter egg*. The pagan spring festival included the idea that the Moon Hare would lay eggs for good children to eat, although now they are usually made of chocolate. The Moon Hare is still with us today, in the form of the Easter Bunny.

The hare is an archetype—the recurrence of the hare symbol in world mythology cannot be explained in terms of coincidence. The hare was considered by some to be unlucky because of superstitious views that hares were witches' familiars or transformed witches. In some parts of Britain, sailors would refuse to board their ship if a hare crossed their path as they were on their way to the sea.

In March, hares traditionally rush about in their mating season, so we have the saying "mad as a March hare" and talk of "hare-brained schemes."

CONNECTIONS

◎ *Are you making sacrifices at the moment?*

◎ *Are you thinking clearly, or are you becoming involved in unreliable ventures?*

Pig

PIGS WERE CONSIDERED HOLY IN THE GERMANIC AND CELTIC CULTURES. The Celtic god Dagda had a magical pig that could be killed and eaten each day, and the next day it would come alive once more and be eaten again. In this way no one would ever be hungry. The Scandinavians also believed in the supernatural pig or boar, and the custom of eating a roast pig with an apple in its mouth at Christmas originated in the Norse Yule pig sacrifice when a pig was offered to the gods at the turn of the year.

Although pigs are very clean animals, they are often kept in conditions that have led to their reputation for dirtiness. The word "pig" is sometimes used to describe a dirty, greedy, or bad-mannered person. In the Jewish and Muslim traditions, the pig was an animal set apart or "unclean," which meant it could not be eaten.

The saying "pigs might fly" expresses the idea that something will never happen.

CONNECTIONS

- *Are you faced with a seemingly impossible venture?*
- *A "piggy bank" is a place to put money and save for the future.*
  Is your dream pig linked to savings?

Bear

SYMBOLIC OF INSTINCTIVE ANIMAL POWER AND INDEPENDENCE, the bear can be dark and threatening. In Scandinavian languages the word for "god of thunder" and "bear" is the same. There are many superstitions about bears. Some believed that sleeping on a bearskin cures backache, others that the fur of a bear is a talisman against blindness. In the tradition of the Native American Sioux tribe, medicine men dressed as bears because they believed that bears brought healing.

In other traditions, a bearskin coat was supposed to give warriors the strength and courage of a she-bear, who is merciless in defense of her cubs. The bear goddess Artio protected forests and bears and was the patroness of hunting.

Since bears hibernate in winter and reappear in spring, they are symbolic of death and rebirth. The black bear is an animal spirit symbolizing courage and introspection. In the Native American tradition, the bear represents receptive female energy. To go into her cave is to heal the dark places within yourself, to attune to the energies of the Great Mother and to receive her nourishment. In other words, to go into the bear's cave is to go within, and to own what you know.

CONNECTIONS

- *Does your bear dream mean you need to take on the power of the bear?*
- *Can you "bear up"—keep your spirits raised—or can you enlist help to do so?*

Monkey GENERALLY, MONKEYS

AND APES represent the baser instincts of human beings and the unconscious. However, the positive side of this is that the unconscious often surprises us with sudden insight and intuitive flashes of inspiration. This is recognized in China, where the monkey is thought to have the power to grant good health and happiness. In Hong Kong, there is an annual Monkey King festival, in which fire-walking celebrates the protection given by the Monkey King to a Chinese pilgrim.

Monkeys were highly valued in Ancient Egypt, because of their close resemblance to human beings and because of their intelligence. They were embalmed and buried with great care.

They are revered in India, where the Hindu monkey-god is known as Hanuman.

CONNECTIONS

◉ *Does your dream monkey reveal a wilder side of you?*

◉ *The Three Mystic Monkeys cover their eyes, ears, and mouth, showing that they "see no evil, hear no evil, and speak no evil." Do you need to keep your own counsel?*

Lion MAJESTIC RULER OF THE ANIMAL KINGDOM, the lion symbolizes strength and the sun because of his golden color. After he killed the fearsome Nemean lion with his bare hands, Hercules wore its pelt as a sign of his strength. In myths across the world, lions are both strong and wise, and royal dynasties frequently use the lion as a symbol of their greatness.

Many religious traditions include lion images. As a sphinx, the goddess Hathor is depicted with a lion's head and is sometimes shown riding a lion. The lion head surrounded by rays was a sun symbol of Mithraic sun worship. The Lion Throne or *simhasana* is sacred to Buddhists. Sikhs who were prepared to die for the faith were baptised with holy water and were given the name *Singh* meaning "lion."

The name of the city of *Singapore* translates as "city of the lion."

Many healing amulets were carved in the shape of a lion. In the story of Saint Jerome and the lion, the saint takes a thorn from the lion's paw and the lion then becomes his faithful companion. At the heart of this story lies the idea of the power of compassion over strength.

Bat IN THE CHRISTIAN TRADITION, the bat is known as the "bird of the devil." Satan is depicted with bats' wings. In Buddhism, the bat represents "darkened understanding." There are many superstitions about bats. For example, if bats enter a house or flap against a window, it is taken as an omen of death.

In some Native American traditions, bats are seen as rain-bringers and so are considered good omens.

In China, they symbolize wealth, good fortune, and long life. According to Chinese folklore, five bats appearing together represent the five traditional blessings of health, wealth, long life, peace, and happiness.

A bat is a creature of the dark that uses a system of navigation called echolocation, similar to sonar, in which sound signals are emitted and the echo received. This means that bats don't need good vision. How does a dream involving bats relate to your life at present? Is one or more of your senses enhanced because of the impairment of one of your other senses? Have you developed a new sensitivity to what is going on around you?

CONNECTIONS

- *If you dream of bats, perhaps you are being "as blind as a bat," unable or unwilling to see what course of action you should be taking.*
- *Perhaps it means that you are "batty"—an unthinking eccentric who pays little or no attention to the norms of society.*

Frog   AS AN AMPHIBIAN, the frog is at home on land or in water, and symbolizes a union of the elements earth and water. It also represents resurrection because it rises from the water and disappears in the winter, only to reappear when the spring comes. The frog is also linked to fertility, perhaps because it produces so much spawn. The presence of frogs indicates the health of a given environment because their skins are permeable to pollutants.

There is an Australian myth in which a frog swallowed all the water in the world and caused a great drought. This was extremely serious because it meant the earth might die. The only way to rectify the situation was to make the frog laugh, which an eel did, but the force of the water pouring through his wide mouth flooded the world. This is another example of the flood in creation myths.

In China, a frog in a well depicts a person of limited vision and a narrow outlook.

CONNECTIONS

◎ *If you dream of being frogmarched it could be because you are being forced to go somewhere or do something against your will.*

◎ *A dream of the Frog Prince—the enchanted prince who took the form of a frog and could return to his original self only after a kiss from a maiden—symbolizes the process of transformation.*

Crocodile IN ANCIENT EGYPT CROCODILES WERE REVERED.

Depicted with an open mouth, they were portrayed as going against the current, which symbolizes freedom from the limitations of the mortal world, and of finding life through death. This may explain why thousands of mummified crocodile bodies have been found in archaeological sites in Egypt. Since the crocodile can live on land and in water, it represents the dual nature of man.

The crocodile-headed god Sebek in his positive form represented reason, because the crocodile can see clearly even when its eyes are veiled by a covering membrane. In his negative form, Sebek represented brutality, evil, and treachery. Like the alligator, the crocodile is linked to stealthy, sudden aggression. Crocodiles are also connected with strength and hidden power.

Ancient Egyptians believed that crocodiles were the guardians of the underworld, which in dreams may represent the unconscious, so to dream of a crocodile may indicate that you are on the threshold of new awareness about your subconscious drives.

CONNECTION

In one myth the crocodile was said to have swallowed the moon and then shed insincere tears. So, "crocodile tears" are shed by people who are merely pretending to care. A dream of a crocodile could mean you are being deceived by your friends.

Snake

SNAKES ARE ANCIENT SYMBOLS of physical and spiritual healing. Asclepius, the Greek god of healing, is represented with a snake and this gave rise to the *caduceus*, the staff around which two snakes are intertwined. This symbol is still used to represent medicine all around the world.

As snakes shed their skins, they symbolize renewal and regeneration. In the Bible (Psalm 58), adders are said to be deaf. On the principle that like cures like, adder's milk was used as a treatment for deafness and earaches. Adult female adders swallow their young when there is danger, then vomit them up once the threat has gone.

In the *Talmud*, snakes represent richness and wealth, and to kill one in a dream means to lose all your riches.

The serpent tempted Eve to eat from the Tree of Knowledge of Good and Evil, which led to Adam and Eve being expelled from the Garden of Eden. Their innocence was lost and for the first time they knew shame and guilt. The snake symbolizes the consequences of disobedience.

Sometimes we see eagles with serpents in their talons. This represents the power of the spiritual over the base, evil power of the serpent, the archetypal conflict between good and evil. Sexual energy is associated with snakes.

CONNECTION

Consider wordplay—is your "adder" linked with adding something to your life?

Turtle

LIKE THE TORTOISE, THE TURTLE HAS AN ARMORED SHELL into which it can withdraw. The turtle is tough on the outside and tender inside. The turtle's shape led to cosmic links in the Far East—the rounded shell represented heaven, while the flat underside represents the earth. The turtle always symbolized the solidity of earth rather than any transcendent aspect.

The turtle is amphibious and long-lived and is associated with wisdom. Its slow, unperturbed pace represents a steady approach to life and natural evolution. Fidelity and loyalty are attributes of the turtle, which is faithful to its mate.

In the Hindu religion, one incarnation of Vishnu is Kurma, the turtle who carried the world on its back.

In ancient China, Taoists used turtle shells to foretell the future. By placing a red-hot object on the shell, cracks were made and these were read by the oracle seer. The Taoists later developed the *I Ching* as a divinatory system.

For, lo, the winter is past, the rain is over and gone.
The flowers appear on the Earth; the time of the
Singing of birds is come, and the voice of
The turtle is heard in our land.

SONG OF SOLOMON (2.11–12)

CONNECTION

○ *Do you need to develop*
a protective shell around
yourself?

Tortoise

IN THE EAST, a universal view was that the earth was supported on the back of a tortoise. The tortoise symbolized eternal life. In Hindu myths, the creator of all creatures is sometimes referred to as "Old Tortoise Man," while in Chinese mythology, P'an-ku, the first being who burst from the cosmic egg, was accompanied by a dragon, a unicorn, a phoenix, and a tortoise.

In Greek mythology, the first lyre was made from the shell of a tortoise. The god Hermes cleaned out the shell, made holes in the rim, and fixed seven strings of cowgut across it. He also made the first plectrum, or pick.

In the fable *The Tortoise and the Hare*, it is the slow tortoise who wins the race because of his determination and concentration—unlike the hare, he was not overconfident and won in the end.

CONNECTION
Does your dream tortoise indicate that you need to progress in a slow and steady way, instead of rushing ahead?

Beetle IN BRITAIN, THERE USED TO BE A FOLK REMEDY for childhood
coughs that involved catching a beetle and hanging it around the neck of the child.
It was believed that as the beetle decayed so did the cough.

Step on a black beetle, it will rain.
Pick it up and bury it,
The sun will shine again.

ENGLISH SAYING

The scarab, also known as the dung beetle, was venerated
in Egypt. The scarab is the symbol of the sun, the
creation of matter, and of resurrection. It symbolizes
immortality, divine wisdom, and the productive powers
of nature. The scarab seal was made in the shape of
the sacred scarab and the underside was carved with
inscriptions and used to seal or sign documents.
Amulets in the shape of scarabs were worn as good luck
charms and placed in the tombs to ensure eternal life.

In the African Congo the scarab is a lunar symbol and
represents eternal renewal.

CONNECTIONS

◉ *The term "to beetle about" means to scurry or hurry about. In some*
dreams, swarms of beetles cover the dreamer, who wakes up trying
to brush them off. This may represent a large number of small matters
which are bothering you.

◉ *Since beetles bite, it may be that something is biting at you to get*
your attention.

Bee IN MEDIEVAL TIMES, bees were considered intelligent and mysterious. They were known as "the birds of God." Church candles were made of beeswax, and honey is the symbol of God's grace in the Bible.

In earlier centuries, as a way of thanking bees for their hard work, people in England included them in family events and decorated beehives at times of celebration. When a death occurred in the family, the beehive was draped in a black cloth. People thought if they did not tell the bees about the death, the swarm would leave and no longer make honey for the family.

Muhammad was said to have allowed bees to enter paradise because they represented souls.

The industrious nature of bees in making honey is often linked to creating wealth. Like ants, bees demonstrate the power of oneness, all working for the common good. In many British cities, bees are included in decorations in commercial buildings as a sign of industry and success.

CONNECTIONS

- *Are you making a "beeline"—the shortest distance between points—for something you want? Are you going straight for it without looking at other possibilities?*
- *Do your dream bees reflect your hard work?*
- *Do you have a "bee in your bonnet"—an idea that bothers you, but that others may not be concerned about?*
- *Being stung could mean that you're concerned about being hurt.*

Butterfly

Once upon a time, I, Chuang-Tzu, dreamed I was a butterfly fluttering hither and thither. I was aware of only following my fancy as a butterfly and unconscious of my human individuality. Suddenly I awoke and lay there, myself again. Now I do not know whether I was then a man dreaming I was a butterfly, or whether I am now a butterfly dreaming I am a man.

CHUANG-TZU, FOURTH-CENTURY CHINESE PHILOSOPHER

WHICH IS THE REALITY, DREAMING OR WAKING? They are both intrinsic, essential parts of our nature.

In China, a butterfly represents joy and sexual pleasure in marriage, and a jade butterfly is an emblem of love. It is regarded as auspicious for a Chinese bridegroom to give his bride such a token on their wedding day.

The Greek word *psyche* means both "soul" and "butterfly," arising from the idea that the soul took on the form of a butterfly as it searched for a new incarnation. The Celts thought "fly-souls" or butterfly-souls flew around in search of a new mother.

The delicate butterfly is the culmination of the process of transformation from caterpillar larva to pupa to its final state as a butterfly. The butterfly symbolizes death and rebirth, since in the dormant pupa stage it seems dead, then reemerges in a new form.

CONNECTION

◉ *A dream of a butterfly may mean you are in a period of transition. Change is taking place.*

Scorpion

SCORPIONS BELONG TO THE ARACHNID FAMILY and so are related to spiders. Traditionally, scorpions are known for the fatal "sting in the tail" that they use if provoked or cornered, but some have poison glands in their jaws and in their tails. In daylight, they hide under stones and come out at night to hunt and attack their prey.

Scorpions are traditionally associated with death. Native Central and South Americans believe that Mother Scorpion receives the souls of the dead in her home at the end of the Milky Way. The astrological sign of the scorpion, Scorpio, is associated with the underworld, death, and dark secrets. The scorpion also has connections with tenacity, sexuality, and fertility.

In the desert areas of Iran, scorpions are caught and put into jars of olive oil. Later, when the olive oil has absorbed the scorpions' healing juices, it is strained and used to put on cuts and wounds to speed up the healing process.

CONNECTIONS

◑ *Does your dream scorpion represent a sting that you are about to inflict?*

◑ *Have you been stung by someone?*

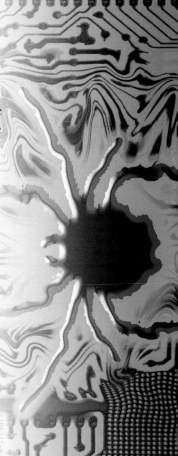

Spider

THE SPIDER IS AN ARCHETYPE of the Great Mother, in her aspect of the weaver of destiny. Spiders often appear in dreams when we need to make a major decision about personal destiny, when the threads of our lives need to be renewed or relocated.

Stories about spiders always recognize the sharp intelligence of the creature. In the creation myth from Native American Cherokee tribes, a spider retrieves the sun from the bottom of a hollow. He catches it in a net and pulls it up, so it can take its place in the sky to light the world. The clever spider kept a little bit of the sun in his web so people could have fire. Spiders are protected by the Native American Navajo tribes, and spiders' webs are rubbed onto the arms of baby girls to insure they will grow to be tireless weavers.

Small spiders, known as money spiders or money spinners, represent new wealth.

Spiders' webs have been traditional ingredients in witches' cauldrons to make spells. In some traditions, cobwebs were put over wounds to staunch the flow of blood. The healing aspect of webs has now been recognized in Western medicine, where they are being used to help in skin grafts.

CONNECTION

◎ *Associations with the World Wide Web mean that a dream of a spider may indicate global communication.*

Bright Birds

BRIGHTLY COLORED BIRDs, such as kingfishers, parakeets, birds of paradise, peacocks, and hummingbirds spread radiance with their glorious colors. They symbolize warmth and cheerfulness.

The hummingbird gets its name from the sound its rapidly beating wings make when it hovers in front of a flower. The hummingbird uses its long tongue to reach nectar, or catch small insects. These birds need to eat their own body weight in nectar every day, because they use so much energy in flight.

Hummingbirds are also highly attracted to the color red, and are the only birds able to fly backward. Is this characteristic applicable to your life now? Are you on a roll and can't stop, in case you fall? Do you want to go back on anything?

When Aztec warriors died, it was believed that they spent four years with the sun god, before returning to earth as hummingbirds.

CONNECTION

If you dream of these birds, think about their native country or places where you've seen them.

Dark Birds

DARK–COLORED BIRDS ARE OFTEN, though not always, associated with death and unhappiness. Ravens, rooks, crows, and vultures are carrion birds that scavenge and eat dead creatures, so they are associated with death. The screeching of crows was said to foretell a death.

The black carrion crow, known as "the bird of battlefields," was one guise of the Celtic goddess Morrigan. She was the goddess of death and war as well as of sexuality and fertility.

In Scandinavian mythology, raven feathers were worn by the Valkyries (warrior maidens) as they chose slain warriors and, also in Scandinavian literature, the dead on battlefields were called "feeders of ravens."

The Crow Mother, revered by the Native American Hopi and Auni tribes, was considered the mother of all *kachinas* (rain spirits) and is also a manifestation of the Black Madonna.

> *I have dreamed my death. The Black Bird of Death*
> *seized me in his talons and carried me to the House of Dust,*
> *the palace of Erkalla, Queen of the Dark.*

ENKIDU IN THE EPIC OF GILGAMESH

CONNECTION

"Crow's feet" is a term used for the fine lines that appear around people's eyes as they get older. Are you worried about getting older?

Migratory Birds

THERE ARE MANY KINDS OF
MIGRATORY BIRDS that travel between different habitats at specific times of the year.
Usually they travel as a group, as do geese, who fly in a V-shape so that each
following goose can rest on the air current created by those in front and so fly long
distances without stopping.

One way in which the Druids practiced divination—seeing into the future—was
to watch the patterns of birds in flight. Greeks and Romans watched the flights
of swallows to forecast the weather.

The swallow was a bird that was sacred to the goddesses Isis and Venus. It is the
symbol of spring and of unending time. It is seen as a good omen to have swallows
build a nest in the eaves of your house. The swallow is also called the "switch-chick"
because of its forked tail.

The Egyptian goddess Hathor was called the "Nile Goose, mother of the Golden
Egg." The goose was sacred to the Celts and so was not eaten.

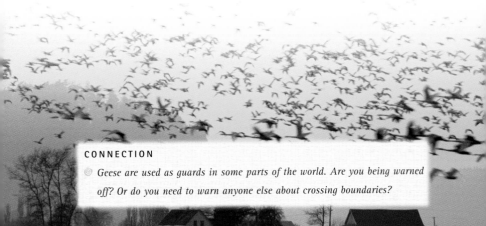

CONNECTION

*Geese are used as guards in some parts of the world. Are you being warned
off? Or do you need to warn anyone else about crossing boundaries?*

Rooster

THE ROOSTER, OR COCK, IS THE MALE BIRD THAT IS LINKED TO THE SUN AND THE SUN GODS, except in Scandinavian and Celtic mythology. The rooster represents masculinity and courage. It is associated with vigilance, which is why it is often used on weather vanes, turning in all directions to watch symbolically for any danger that may arrive. The rooster awakens all at dawn with its loud crow.

In Buddhism, the rooster symbolizes carnal passion and pride. It is also the symbol of France, with similar associations. A cartoon rooster was used as the symbol for the World Cup, the international soccer championship, when France hosted it in 1998. For the Chinese, the rooster symbolizes valor and faithfulness. The red rooster protects against fire, while the white rooster protects against ghosts. A rooster with a hen in a garden symbolizes the joys of rural life. In some Chinese initiation rituals, a white rooster is killed to signify the end of the old life and the birth of the new, pure life.

In the Hebrew tradition, the rooster and hen represent the bridal couple and symbolize male protection, since the rooster will fight to the death to protect his hens. In Japanese Shinto symbolism, a rooster stands on a drum to summon people to prayer. In Mithraism, an ancient Persian religion, the rooster is sacred to Mithras, the sun god (see page 374).

To describe someone as "cocky" means that they are full of challenging, male energy. *Cock* is also a slang term for "the penis" (see page 61).

Dove

A DOVE SYMBOLIZES PEACE, since it was the dove that brought the olive branch back to Noah's Ark after the flood. Doves are symbols of simplicity, gentleness, dependability, and affection.

Like all winged creatures, the dove represents inspiration and spirituality. In some Eastern European countries it is believed that souls fly in the form of doves.

After Jesus Christ was baptized, the Holy Spirit descended in the form of a dove. The release of doves at the end of the opening ceremony of the Olympic Games symbolizes the spirit of the games.

Doves are linked with the Greek goddess of love, Aphrodite. In Greek mythology, it was her doves that brought ambrosia to the god Zeus, which kept him immortal.

"Billing and cooing" is an English expression for lovers' exchanges, and arose from the mating rituals of doves. Doves are also known for their loyalty and fidelity to their mates and are true homing birds, able to find their way back across vast distances. During the two world wars, doves and pigeons carried messages over hundreds of miles when other forms of communication were impossible.

CONNECTIONS

- *Do you need more dovelike calm in your life at present?*
- *Do you need to offer someone the olive branch of peace?*

Peacock

THE IRIDESCENT COLORS AND ELABORATE PLUMES OF THE MALE PEACOCK insure that it has a place in many traditions. In China, the peacock is attributed to the goddess Kwan-yin and the peacock feather was awarded as a sign of imperial honor. In Christianity, the bird symbolizes resurrection and immortality because it can renew its feathers, and the "hundred eyes" of the feathers represent the all-seeing Church. To Hindus, the peacock is an emblem of Sarasvati, goddess of wisdom, music, and poetry. In Hindu mythology, the patterns on the wings of a peacock, which resemble eyes, are taken to represent the stars in their constellations.

The peacock is a sun symbol and is found in tree and sun worship. It symbolizes love, long life, and immortality. In modern times, the peacock has come to represent pride and vanity, since it appears to show off its tail with great ceremony.

In *The Book of Kells*, the peacock symbolizes the incorruptibility of Christ.

The Peacock Throne was the symbol of Mughal power in India and that of the Shahs in Iran.

The peacock becomes restless before rain and is therefore associated with storms.

CONNECTION

Does your dream reveal feelings of pride about a recent achievement?

Cuckoo and Robin THE CALL OF THE

CUCKOO is a sign of the arrival of spring, so the cuckoo is connected to fresh starts. The cuckoo's habit of laying its eggs in other birds' nests became associated with

"cuckolding," and the Romans used to call an adulterer the Latin equivalent of "cuckoo."

"Cuckoo's nest" in folklore refers to a woman's genitals. The word *cuckoo* is also used to describe someone who is crazy.

Robins, with their bright red breasts, are associated in England with winter and Christmas. In the United States, the robin is traditionally a sign of spring. Legend has it that the robin got its red breast because, as it tried to pull out thorns from Christ's crown, a thorn stuck in its chest and the blood stained its breast red for ever afterward. In the nursery rhyme "Who Killed Cock Robin?" the bird was killed with an arrow, a form of sacrifice used to kill pagan heroes.

Folklore in Cambridgeshire in England included the belief that if a robin came into the house it was a sign of a death in the family.

I dreamed I was walking in the snow when I suddenly turned into a robin.

The dreamer was concerned about the approach of Christmas and the chores. Her transformation into a robin releases her from all her human responsibilities.

CONNECTION

Does your dream cuckoo represent someone who is trying to push you out of your rightful place?

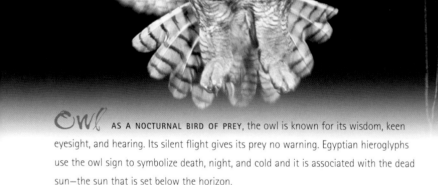

Owl **AS A NOCTURNAL BIRD OF PREY,** the owl is known for its wisdom, keen eyesight, and hearing. Its silent flight gives its prey no warning. Egyptian hieroglyphs use the owl sign to symbolize death, night, and cold and it is associated with the dead sun—the sun that is set below the horizon.

An owl's cry is linked, superstitiously, to death or a disastrous event; it is a harbinger of death. In *Macbeth*, Shakespeare calls the owl the "fatal bell man," as described by Lady Macbeth before the murder of Duncan. In the play *Julius Caesar*, the omens of disaster include a "bird of night." In China the owl is carved on funeral urns. The "little owl" was the symbol of wisdom to Ancient Greeks and was the bird of the goddess Athena.

CONNECTION

Does your dream owl bring wisdom and fresh insight?

Eagle

BIRDS OF PREY, SUCH AS EAGLES AND FALCONS, have keen vision, powerful beaks, and sharp talons that make them formidable hunters. The golden eagle can spot a rabbit from a distance of about a mile (about two kilometers). Many birds of prey have enormous wingspans. Because they fly so high and so effortlessly, these birds are associated with inspiration, the air, and authority. They also represent the spiritual elements within us. The bald eagle is the national bird of the United States.

In Christianity, the eagle is the symbol of the fourth evangelist, John. Eagles are carved on church lecterns and baptismal fonts because they symbolize renewal. According to legend, the bird renewed its youth by flying near the sun and then plunging into water. The eagle also symbolizes Christ's ascension into heaven and the spiritual path of humanity, as well as triumph over external struggles.

Ancient Egyptian myths said that hawks could fly to the sun and return without injury, so the sun gods are often shown with eagles or hawks. They represent the heavens, power, and authority. The god Horus was depicted as a falcon-headed man and the god Sebek-Ra is the hawk-headed crocodile.

CONNECTIONS

◎ If you dreamed of an eagle, are you finally finding the courage to aim high and fulfill your dreams?

◎ If you dream of a bird of prey, consider what aspect of yourself is "preyed upon." Or could it mean that you are hunting for something?

Vulture

THE VULTURE FEEDS ON CARRION, which is positive for the cycle of life, clearing the environment of slowly decaying animals. As a scavenger, the vulture clears away unwanted remains. However, as it hovers around waiting for death, it represents unfeeling opportunism.

In Ancient Egypt, the vulture was the symbol of upper Egypt. Traditionally, vultures were seen as being female, while eagles were seen as being male. The vulture symbolized maternal care and protection. The mother goddess Isis assumed the form of a vulture while other goddesses wore vulture headdresses.

In Greco-Roman mythology the vulture was sacred to Apollo. The Parsees, the adherents of the Zoroastrian religion, mainly found in western India, place their dead in specially built towers known as the towers of silence, so that vultures can eat the remains. They believe that this will insure the rebirth of the dead person.

Among Tibetan Buddhists vultures are regarded as extremely auspicious, because they eat the remains of animals that have died, thus reducing the risk of disease.

Metaphorically, when we describe a person as a "vulture," we mean he preys on others, usually people who are helpless. Often, pimps are described as vultures since they are greedy and ruthless.

CONNECTIONS

- *Do you feel that someone is hovering around, waiting for you to make a mistake?*
- *Is someone preying on you?*

Swan

GRACEFUL AND BEAUTIFUL, the swan is a symbol of sacred purity. It connects earth, air, and water because it can move in each element. In the Irish story *The Children of Lir*, the jealous queen transforms her stepchildren into swans. They retain the power of speech and musical ability and people come to sit and listen to them in their new home on the lake.

Cygnus is the name given to the Northern Cross constellation. The Greeks said it represented the god Zeus, disguised as a swan on his way to one of his many liaisons, in this case with Leda, whom Zeus raped. Leda later gave birth to a baby girl, who was to become the most beautiful woman in the world, Helen of Troy.

The Inuit Dunne-Za of Canada have a creation myth in which a swan turns into a hero who can create life.

A woman brought to an emergency room after an accident had a dream of swans that turned into angels who tended her when she was ill. This dream reassured her that she would recover.

CONNECTIONS

- *In your dream, are you or someone else "swanning about"—looking beautiful but imperious?*
- *Are you singing your "swan song," that is, giving a farewell appearance or pronouncement?*

Seabirds

ALL SEABIRDS SYMBOLIZE TRAVEL and vast seas and skies. They are connected to the heavens and divinity, as well as to fortitude, since they cover so many miles in their flight. Terns, gulls, and cormorants are among the many seabirds that appear in dreams.

The albatross is able to make long flights over distant oceans because of its great wingspan. This allows it to glide but makes it hard to take off. It is known for its endurance. If seen out at sea, it is an omen of bad weather and stormy conditions. The albatross is said to embody the soul of a dead sailor. *The Rime of the Ancient Mariner* is a poem by Samuel Taylor Coleridge in which a sailor kills an albatross and is then forced to wander the seas forever as a punishment. It represents the sanctity of the bird and the heavy burden that was thought to result from killing it.

Legend in British coastal areas has it that seagulls are the souls of drowned sailors and fishermen.

> ### CONNECTIONS
> ● *Does your dream of free-flying seabirds indicate a desire to take off and get away from it all?*

Stork IN SOME TRADITIONS,

DREAMING OF A STORK foretells the birth of a child, or means that the female dreamer will become pregnant. In Holland, where storks build their nests on roof tops, it was believed that the woman of the house beneath would have many children, and easy births. The stork is often depicted carrying a bundle, in which a new baby is wrapped, which is dropped at the house of the new parent. When children ask where babies come from, they are sometimes told that the stork brings them.

The word *stork* derives from Greek *storge*, meaning "mother love" or "great affection."

The stork is a fishing bird, so is also associated with water and creativity. It is a bird of good omen, symbolizing the coming of spring and new life.

In classical mythology, storks were believed to fly to the isle of the blessed,

CONNECTION
Are you expecting a new addition to your family?

where they died and transformed into humans. The stork symbolizes faithfulness to family, devotion to children, and care of the elderly. It is also linked to the "clyster," or syringe, used in enemas or vaginal douches, as the stork flushes itself out as part of its cleaning ritual.

All Creatures Great and Small

Pelican

OFTEN DEPICTED FEEDING HER YOUNG with blood from her own breast, the pelican represents nurturing power, as well as sacrifice and charity. The pelican is also symbolically linked to Christ and blood sacrifices, since he gave his blood to save humankind, just as the pelican appears to pluck her own breast and draw blood in order to save her offspring. Dante wrote of "Christ, our Pelican."

The pelican has a habit that makes use of the large bag under its bill. When the parent bird is about to feed its chicks, it macerates, or mashes up, small fish in this pouch, then, pressing the pouch against its breast, transfers the now bloody mixture into the mouths of the young birds. People who see this conclude that the pelican is feeding its young with its own blood.

CONNECTIONS

◎ *Does the dream pelican represent your care for others, particularly children?*

◎ *Do you feel that you are making too many sacrifices?*

Fish

THE FISH IS THE MOTIF FOR ETERNAL LIFE, mainly following the story of Jonah in the Old Testament. Having been swallowed by a great fish and kept in its stomach for three days, he was deposited alive on the shore. This parallels the entombment of Christ after his Crucifixion and symbolizes death and rebirth.

Fish are the symbol of Christianity because Christ told the apostles that they would be "fishers of men." The Greek word for *fish*, *icthus*, is an acronym for Jesus Christ, Son of God.

The Irish hero Finn mac Cumhaill touched a salmon which had eaten hazelnuts from a tree belonging to the goddess Boinn, and he immediately received limitless knowledge and wisdom. Salmon, which battle their way upstream in the river where they were born in order to spawn, represent strength and determination.

Half-woman, half-fish, the mermaid moves on the liminal land between shore and sea. In many myths she lures sailors into the deep waters of emotion, creating a storm in their lives.

CONNECTION

Fish are linked to sexuality, so if a fishy creature appears in your dreams, consider any emotional or sexual matters affecting you.

Shark

THE SHARK NEVER FULLY SLEEPS. It closes down one half of its brain for a short period of rest and operates using the other half, then the process is reversed. This means that it is ever vigilant in its predatory patrol of the seas. As a predator, it is feared because of the ferocious nature of its attacks and it will eat anything. The shark is also a kind of living fossil because its ancestors swam in our seas more than one hundred million years ago.

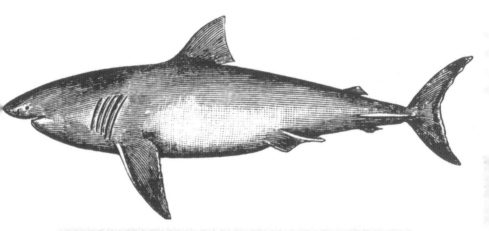

CONNECTIONS

- *The term "loan shark" describes a person who lends money at exorbitant rates of interest.*
- *Shark bell—In Australia, this bell is rung to warn swimmers and surfers of the presence of sharks.*
- *Does your dream shark represent wariness and potential threat?*
- *Are you worrying that someone is trying to "rip you off"?*

Dolphin

THE ORIGIN OF THE WORD DOLPHIN is the Greek word *delphinus*, which means "womb" (see page 59). On Greek funeral urns, dolphins symbolized the soul passing to another world and being born again. In the Celtic tradition, dolphins were associated with well-worship and the power of the waters.

The power, speed, beauty, grace, intelligence, and sociability of dolphins have endeared them to people. As they accompany boats, leaping and playing in front of the bows, their social nature is evident. Present-day dolphins are praised for their ability to help those in physical or emotional distress, and "swimming with dolphins" is hailed as a healing process. There are many tales of people being guided to safety by dolphins after an accident at sea and abundant reports of dolphins keeping swimmers afloat after they have run into difficulties in the ocean.

Two dolphins facing in oppostite directions represent the duality of nature. If you dream of this, it may indicate your need to accept that you are not one-dimensional and that the "negative" part of your character contributes to your wholeness as a human being.

CONNECTION

Is your dream dolphin helping you to survive in choppy seas?

Whale

WHALES ARE AMONG THE LARGEST LIVING MAMMALS ON EARTH. In dreams the large size of whales may be linked to feelings of being dwarfed or overwhelmed. The vast expanse of oceans that are home to whales represent the realm of the emotions.

The belly of the whale symbolizes both death and rebirth. This has come about because the big fish that swallowed Jonah in the Old Testament story (see page 296) was frequently referred to as a whale in popular lore. According to legend, the whale was one of only ten animals believed by Muslims to be allowed into the kingdom of heaven. The novel *Moby Dick* by Herman Melville tells the tale of a great struggle between Captain Ahab and a giant white whale. On one level, the story represents man's pride and the desire to control nature, even if it means death.

The whale has been a staple food for the Inuit tribe for generations. They also use whale oil to fuel lamps and to make candles. However, in some areas, because of industrial whaling, some species have become endangered.

CONNECTIONS

- *Does your dream of whales have any connection with "wailing"?*
- *Does your dream whale indicate concern about ecological issues?*

THE DESIRE AND ABILITY to create are hardwired into the human brain. Creativity is shown in cave paintings, in carvings that have been excavated, and in present-day artwork and practical designs that have changed the way we live. Look around you, wherever you are, and you can probably see electric lights and shades, a telephone, a desk, a chair, a cushion, or maybe a pitcher and cup. Whatever the object,

whether it is a bowl made at a pottery class or a laptop computer made a thousand miles away, it represents the ability of the human race to build and create.

In urban areas in particular, evidence of our technical world surrounds us. In our dreams our innate creativity gets to work and transforms objects to symbolize something of significance to our lives. Dreams use objects to deliver a message we can understand. Your dreams of objects made by humans help you as you explore the symbolism they have for you.

made
by Humans

Made by Humans

I dreamed I was making love with an unknown man on a traffic island in a busy part of the city. The odd thing was that the island was actually a huge blackberry and apple pie, out of which a slice had been cut. We were "performing" in the gap, and afterward, being hungry, we ate part of the traffic island pie in full view of everyone.

Whether this dream represents exhibitionism or not, it is a wonderful example of meeting all the needs of a healthy appetite. The traffic island symbolizes a place apart from the hectic world; it is a resting place, a stop between the roads, and in her dream the dreamer makes use of this "gap" to indulge her appetites for sex and eating.

Your dreams give you pleasure and information about your needs. Listen to

them and learn their rich language, and you will deepen not only your understanding of yourself, but also of the complex world in which you live.

Ella Freeman Sharpe, a British psychoanalyst, wrote in her book *Dream Analysis* about how the contents of dreams reveal physical and mental activity. One of her patients, who had been unwell for some months, had a dream in which she looked at her wristwatch but the dial was completely covered with strips of paper and she could not see what time it was. Some time afterward the woman had to take time off work after a period of insomnia and deep distress. The wristwatch symbolized a need to "watch out" and an inability to manage time. She didn't know what time of day it was; she lost touch with the rhythm of life and suffered a major breakdown. Later, as she recovered, she had another dream of a watch that she could read clearly.

RIGHT *In dreams your view and experience of the world may change completely.*

HOUSES IN DREAMS PROVIDE
METAPHORS for the human body.
Consider the following elements
as symbols:

Roof and Attic —The top of the
house and the attic rooms
represent the head, mind, brain,
and the intellectual and cognitive aspects of the self. If you find yourself in a room
at the top of a building, ask yourself what it is that you have to give some thought to.

Kitchen—The kitchen represents nourishment, the heart of the home, the place of the
goddess of the hearth, Hestia. It may also represent digestion. Consider the relevance
of the expressions "too many cooks spoil the soup," "if you can't take the heat, get out
of the kitchen," and "cooking up a storm."

Basement—This is where the foundations are. The basement is below ground and
symbolizes the subconscious, that which is below conscious knowledge and
awareness. "Base" may indicate primal urges or instincts, or "basic" needs. Is "base"
meant as something low and unworthy? Is there something low or animalistic about
the dream that connects you to the "basement?" *Abasement* means "humbling" or
"belittling." Has this happened to you or are you doing it to someone else?

Corridors—Corridors and halls represent transition, passageways leading to different
doorways or opportunities. The "corridors of power" may symbolize government.

Wiring—Wiring may represent the nervous system or veins and arteries—anything that
transports some form of energy.

Bedroom—The bedroom represents sexuality, reproduction, the theater of dreams,
and meditation.

School

THIS IS A PLACE WHERE WE LEARN. It may be linked back to earlier childhood experiences, or may refer to study and the need for further educational development in the present. If your dream relates to earlier unpleasant experiences while you were at school, it could reflect a situation where you feel you have little control and are at the mercy of the judgments of others.

When I first went to boarding school I had this recurring dream. I was walking with my mother, father, and brother when we became separated by a river. They were on one side of the river, smiling, and I was on my own on the other side, feeling miserable.

Although the school does not feature directly, the basis of the dream is the separation that took place when the girl was sent away to school. Her younger brother stayed at home with her parents. Even though she is now grown-up, this young woman finds that the dream recurs when she is feeling lonely or isolated.

Some groups believe that during sleep the soul travels to a school on a spiritual plane and the dream classroom is interpreted as the setting of spiritual learning.

Hotel IN A HOTEL WE FIND TEMPORARY ACCOMMODATION; it is a meeting place and a place of transition. The impermanence and anonymity of hotels may reflect a desire for change, to go from one point to another without anyone else knowing you or interfering with your plans. A hotel is also a place where we are looked after, taken care of, and can be free of domestic responsibility.

The word *hotel* derives from the Latin word for "hospice" or "hospital." If you dream of a hotel, you may be in need of a change of scene, one where you can rest and be pampered in a luxurious setting.

Hostels, like hotels, provide accommodation, but usually they are more basic and cheaper. Largely used by backpackers and people on a limited income, they represent journeys of exploration, meeting, and mingling. They also indicate that the dreamer is prepared to "rough it"—does that have any significance for you now?

CONNECTION

Does your dream hotel remind you of one you stayed in before? If so, think about what happened there and how you felt. Can you work out what significance it has to your life now?

Made by Humans

Church

A CHURCH, LIKE A TEMPLE OR MOSQUE, is a place of worship where you gather together with others who share your faith. It is associated with rules, strict codes of behavior, and religious practice, which may comfort or constrict, according to your experiences. When you dream of a church, if it is not one you attend, or if you have no religious beliefs, think about what the church symbolizes for you. Does it represent elaborate rituals that are out of date, and, if so, is this a reflection of another area of your life?

The church is associated with transcendence and the sacred. It is a sanctified place where people can find safety and protection. Does your dream offer you the opportunity for safekeeping?

The size and type of church indicate different levels both of simplicity and wealth, as well as formality. An abbey or cathedral spells out grandeur, whereas a chapel or simple unadorned Methodist church or Quaker meeting house symbolizes simplicity and lack of ceremony.

Ella Freeman Sharpe described the dream of one of her patients, who dreamed of Iona Cathedral. This is a wonderful pun for "'I own a cathedral." The woman was concerned about her wealth at the time.

CONNECTION

◎ *Does your church dream connect to a need to explore spirituality or to take it to a deeper level?*

Terminals AIRPORTS, RAILROAD STATIONS, AND BUS STATIONS

are all arrival and departure points. They can represent actual places known to the
dreamer and signify real journeys that have been or are about to be undertaken.
If this isn't the case, then consider the symbolic meaning. Are you departing from
a relationship or old friendships? Are you going to new destinations in your spiritual
or emotional life?

Since terminals are public places, they represent the dreamer's place in the world.
If you are treated well in the dream or in life, terminals may reflect a sense of positive
self-worth, but if you are ignored or
treated badly, they may indicate feelings
of inadequacy or rejection.

Problems at terminals include loss
of tickets or luggage, missing the plane
or bus connections, inability to
understand the language, or not having
the right currency. These are typical
frustration or anxiety dreams, so you
could think about a waking frustration
that is bothering you.

CONNECTIONS

○ *Terminals are places of transit. Do you feel that you are in transition*
right now?

○ *If you dream of a terminal, it may indicate anxieties about your health*
or that of someone close to you, or fear of death.

Hospital

Made by Humans

I realize that illness is to health what dreams are to waking life—the reminder of what is forgotten, the bigger picture working toward resolution.

KAT DUFF: THE ALCHEMY OF ILLNESS

DREAMS OFTEN REFLECT a dreamer's anxiety, although this may not be apparent in waking life. One English woman could not make sense of her dream about going to a theater to take part in a play. She was unhappy because they would not let her act. When we explored the dream, she realized that the "theater" referred to the operating room she was going to for minor surgery. Her dreams expressed her concern that she would have no control over what happened to her, that "no one would let her act."

A female patient undergoing chemotherapy treatment at a major cancer hospital had many distressing dreams, especially since she had been, prior to the cancer, a fit person in her prime at thirty-four. She told me about one dream that had horrified her in which she was crawling on all fours vomiting feces. The dream symbolized the need to get rid of the "shit" that is contaminating her body, both the cancer and the toxic "shit" of her chemotherapy. The treatment reduced her to an incapacitated state, where she had bodily functions but was too ill to do anything else.

Castle

CASTLES ARE ASSOCIATED WITH GRANDEUR, STRENGTH, AND PROTECTION. These fortified buildings had an inner area called a "keep" to protect the people, who would withdraw to the safety of the castle when attacked by enemies. If you dream of a keep, it may indicate a desire to withdraw to a protected place where you feel safer and more secure.

Castles are the stuff of fairy stories, too. Sleeping Beauty was asleep in a castle surrounded by thorny thickets through which her hero had to break to rescue her. Do you have any romantic dreams about being carried off to a castle or being rescued from one?

The castellated walls of castles often have a walkway on the inside where you can look out while still being protected. If you dream of being in that vantage point, it may symbolize a need for protection while you get a clearer view of a situation or a need for greater insight into what "your enemy" is doing.

CONNECTIONS

- *"Castles in the air" are hopes or daydreams that are unlikely to come true.*
- *"A man's home is his castle"—Does your dream castle represent your home?*

$\mathcal{D}oor$ DOORS GIVE US ENTRY TO PLACES and allow us to shut others out. They are the portals through which we enter new spaces and therefore, symbolically, where we embark on new experiences. In your dreams where doors feature, think about whether they are open or closed, flimsy or strongly made, whether they have keys or locks, and which side you are on, the inside or outside.

Carole found her dreams really frustrating:

I'm trying to find some privacy but all the doors are ajar, I can't shut them and there's no quiet place for me.

Her waking life at the time was equally frustrating as she felt she had no privacy.

Doors represent openings and closings in your life. They are also the threshold, a place that marks the transition point from inside to outside and vice versa. The Roman god Janus marked the threshold; with two faces he could look outward and inward at the same time. Now, thresholds are guarded by security staff, caretakers, bouncers, or intercoms. When the threshold is clearly marked, we can choose to continue or turn back.

Doors are also euphemisms for the vagina, the "front door," and the anus, the "back door."

Doors were traditionally left open when someone was about to die so that the spirit of the deceased could pass through into the air.

I was in a pale pink dress. I kept trying to find doors that weren't there. It was like being hunted.

This dreamer felt trapped in a situation from which there was no escape.

Stairs WHEN YOU DREAM OF STAIRS, think about whether you are going up or going down. If you are going up, it could mean that you are achieving success or becoming more aware in your mind. If you are going down, it could reflect lack of success or a need to get back to a foundation, to ground yourself.

Freud theorized that the act of going up and down stairs was symbolic of the act of sexual intercourse.

Stairs of any kind may relate to spiritual matters, to becoming less secular and more sacred. In Christianity, the ascension is the event when Jesus Christ went from earth to heaven.

I am in an elevator and it isn't going to stop but will crash straight through the ceiling. It always stops and the space where I get through is very tight; I feel I will suffocate.

Elevators could symbolize some kind of uprising, being supported and praised, or being belittled and lowered in status. The progression, or lack of it, may refer to your life or career at the moment.

CONNECTION
Does your dream of going downstairs reflect feelings of lack of confidence or a setback you have had?

CONNECTIONS

◎ *"To hit the roof" means to become enraged. Are there feelings of anger around for you at the moment?*

◎ *"To have a slate missing" means to be a little stupid, not completely there. Are you missing the point of something?*

Roof THE ROOF represents that which covers us. It keeps out the elements and if we climb on a roof we get the highest view (see also page 304). Consider the state of your dream roof—is it in good condition, weatherproof, and complete, or is it in need of repair? If it is the last, do you need to pay some attention to your brain or think something through, rather than relying on your gut feeling or your heart? A leaking roof may represent unconscious awareness that is slowly making its knowledge available to you.

In architecture, particularly in temples and churches, the roof is important because it symbolizes the dome of heaven.

Window

WINDOWS GIVE PROTECTION FROM THE ELEMENTS while letting light in and enabling vision between the inside and outside of a building or vehicle. Windows can be open or closed and can be covered with curtains or blinds to give privacy. If you dream of windows, think about where they are situated and the building they are in. Windows in a house may relate to a domestic situation, whereas those in a skyscraper may indicate work or official connections.

Windowpanes are made of glass, which can be transparent, giving a clear view, or opaque where the view is obscured. Can you relate this to your view of a situation at the moment? Also, pane may indicate "pain," so consider whether you are troubled by an issue and whether you need to be more clearsighted about it.

Looking in through a window symbolizes insight, although it may also indicate feelings of being kept out in the cold while others enjoy the light and warmth inside. Looking out of a window may represent your outlook, how you feel about your life. Eyes are sometimes called "the windows of the soul."

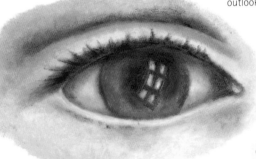

CONNECTIONS

- *Are you feeling "pained" about something?*
- *Do you need more light in your life?*

Walls

WALLS USUALLY REPRESENT BOUNDARIES. They contain what is within and keep out both people and the elements. When they are well maintained, they give protection and privacy. However, when they are damaged, they can be breached and anyone or anything can get through.

The Western Wall, or the Wailing Wall, in Jerusalem is the most sacred site for Jews all over the world. It is the remaining wall of their holy Temple. Here Jews recite prayers or write them on slips of paper that they then press into the cracks between the stones. It is called the Wailing Wall because of the lamentations of the Jews over the destruction of their Temple in 70 C.E.

A wall may symbolize an obstacle or barrier in your life. A "wall of silence" similarly prevents progress in communication, particularly if some kind of investigation is under way.

There is a saying "walls have ears"—in other words, secrets may be overheard and passed on. Is this related to information you have that has been passed on inappropriately?

CONNECTIONS

- *Have you hit a brick wall and feel you can no longer make progress?*
- *Do you feel as if you have been banging your head against a brick wall, getting nowhere?*

Labyrinth and Maze

THE PATHWAYS, TUNNELS, OR CHAMBERS that make up a labyrinth always lead to the center. Some say that labyrinths were walked as a substitute for a pilgrimage and were used as an aid to meditation. In earlier times, monks and nuns went to the center, which was sometimes called Jerusalem, on their knees as an act of penance for their sins.

In Greek mythology, Daedelus built a labyrinth on the island of Crete in which he imprisoned the Minotaur, who had the body of a man and the head of a bull. It fed on human flesh and eventually Theseus was sent into the labyrinth to kill it. In the story, Ariadne spun a golden thread to help Theseus find his way out.

A maze is a symbol of confusion because there are many misleading openings and wrong turns. A maze may symbolize being lost, perhaps having lost the "thread" or lost the plot. The word *maze* comes from an Old English word meaning "baffled."

CONNECTIONS

◎ *When you dream of a labyrinth or maze, think about whether you are stuck in a situation from which you feel there is no way out.*

◎ *Do you feel "amazed" about a current event in your life?*

◎ *Do you want to get to the heart or center of a matter that is bothering you?*

Bridge

A BRIDGE MAY BE A CROSSING PLACE over a river or road and may symbolize an emotional or spiritual transition point.

In the Zoroastrian religion, the way to the afterlife is over a bridge. Everyone is judged at death. If good deeds outweigh bad ones, the soul can cross to heaven; if bad deeds outweigh the good, then the bridge becomes as narrow as the blade of a sword and the soul slips down to hell.

We also use the term *bridge* for people who act as a link. A negotiator or arbitrator may be a "bridge" between parties who disagree, while a counselor or therapist may be the link to understanding yourself and your situation, joining or reconciling different aspects of you.

CONNECTIONS

- *"To burn your bridges" means to sever your connections with others in a self-limiting way.*
- *"To cross a bridge when you come to it" means to deal with difficulties when they arise rather than worrying about them beforehand.*

Chapter Nine

Furniture

THE TYPE OF FURNITURE IN YOUR DREAM reflects the culture in which you live and your tastes, which might be minimalist or ostentatious, as well as the major uses of the furniture. Much depends on the setting. Furniture in a hotel is quite different from that in a den or a massage parlor, although there may be overlaps. When interpreting your dream, consider any pieces of furniture that play a prominent part or hold your interest for some reason.

Chair—Something to rest in, or, on the other hand, something that is sat upon. Are you being suppressed in some way? Are your ideas being "sat upon" or dismissed?

Table—A place to share food, where we literally and symbolically "break bread." A table is also a term for an arrangement of information, e.g., a table of contents.

Sofa—A sofa or couch is where we sit with others. When it is called a *couch*, it may relate to the way we "couch" information, present it in a way that is more acceptable. Do you need to give some facts in an indirect way, rather than giving them baldly?

The furniture in your dream house gives you clues to the meaning of your dream. Cupboards and closets are containers; they hold things that can be concealed. When secrets are kept, a dream cupboard may be closed, thus symbolizing that the secret is locked away. When the secret is revealed, the cupboard may be open. This symbolism of the cupboard/closet is reflected in the saying "to come out of the closet," or declare your homosexuality.

CONNECTION

If you have excess furniture in your dream room it may symbolize an overcrowded lifestyle.

Key

A KEY SYMBOLIZES THE ANSWER TO A QUESTION or gives a way to unlock something that is locked. The locked object could be a house, a box, a safe or, symbolically, anything that is closed off. For example, the key to someone's heart may represent something that enables love to blossom.

The keyhole may also provide the opportunity to gaze into a private space. Keyholes allow you to view what is otherwise concealed, and you yourself can also be spied on. If this happens in a dream, ask yourself if your privacy is being invaded or whether you are prying into other people's affairs.

My husband was trying to open the door but as he put his key in, it bent. I used mine to open the door. I told him he'd have to get a new key cut if he wanted to come in.

The dreamer's husband died some time prior to this dream and the bent key shows that he can no longer enter the home they shared. The dreamer said, "He's in a different place now so his key won't work."

CONNECTION

A rusty key may indicate talents that you have neglected.

Ladder

A LADDER IN YOUR DREAM MAY RELATE TO WORK IN YOUR HOME, such as painting or changing a light bulb, but if you cannot make a practical connection think about the purpose of your dream ladder. How is it being used? Like stairs and elevators, ladders relate to ascending or descending and so may be concerned with progress or the lack of it.

A window cleaner uses a ladder to clean windowpanes, which may symbolize clarification, getting a clearer view. Do you need to clarify your situation? Do you need a higher view or an expert opinion?

Mythically, ladders connect earth and heaven, and the rungs represent different stages on a spiritual journey. It is recorded in the Old Testament that Jacob dreamed of a ladder connecting earth to heaven on which a procession of angels ascended and descended. From the top of the ladder, God told Jacob that his offspring would spread throughout the world.

"Climbing the ladder" indicates a promotion at work or in a social situation. Walking under a ladder is supposed to be unlucky.

Tent

GENERALLY, A TENT IS AN IMPERMANENT STRUCTURE, a movable dwelling place associated with camping and outdoor pursuits. Does this indicate a vacation you have just finished or are planning? Would you like to get back to nature, get closer to the ground by sleeping outdoors under the cover of a tent?

Yurts are tents made of felt that originated in Mongolia, where nomads use them to live in. They are still handmade from wool and provide warmth and beauty in an inhospitable landscape.

Arabic tented cities are exotic and beautifully constructed. The insides of the tents are highly decorated with fabrics and woven carpets. They are traditionally associated with the Bedouins, a nomadic tribe of people who travel from place to place to graze their animals.

CONNECTIONS

- *Do you feel weighed down by the routine of your life? Would you like to try the life of a nomad for a change?*
- *If you are in a tent in your dream, could this link to "intent"? Do you have some intentions that you are not paying attention to?*

Luggage

When I am due to go away on vacation or to a special occasion, like a wedding, I dream I am always going at the last minute and throw things into a suitcase, then miss the plane. Or my luggage goes missing or I can't get dressed in time and I miss the occasion.

This type of frustration dream reflects the pressure to get organized in a busy life. The penalties for missing planes lead us to worry more and our dreams reflect our anxiety. What else could it be? Perhaps too many objects call for our attention? A need to simplify? A need to prioritize so as not be "everywoman" or "everyman"?

Luggage or baggage may symbolize not only what we need for our vacation or trip away from home, but also "unfinished business," unresolved emotional issues that hold us back. When people talk about their "emotional baggage," they usually mean that they feel held back by negative patterns and unable to move forward in their emotional lives.

CONNECTIONS

If you dream of losing your luggage, is that good or bad for you? Does it offer you an opportunity to start afresh and create your identity anew?

If your dream luggage is very elegant and all items match, does it represent a need to make a good impression wherever you are?

Made by Humans

Wheel

THE WHEEL INDICATES TRAVEL, although it can also symbolize the cycle of life. A wheel can also indicate progress, although much depends on the nature of the wheel—for instance, a steering wheel may indicate the opportunity to control your direction, while a water wheel may represent harnessing the power of natural elements. A potter's wheel symbolizes creativity and the transformation of earth into useful and beautiful objects. The "wheel of fortune" represents luck or chance.

The teachings of the Buddha are often symbolized by a wheel. In his first sermon at Benares, the Buddha said that he was setting in motion the *wheel of dharma*, which is the Buddhist system of thought, meditation, and spiritual exercises based on the teachings of Buddha.

The Indian flag carries the image of a wheel, representing earthly rule and kingship.

CONNECTIONS

- *Are you making progress or going around in circles?*
- *A dream of a wheel of fortune may indicate over-reliance on chance or luck.*

Purse

THINGS LIKE WALLETS, PURSES, OR HANDBAGS represent identity. In them you carry your passport, credit cards, driver's license, personal objects such as photos, house keys, membership cards and so on. All these items give clues about who you are and the kind of interests you have.

If you dream of a very expensive designer bag you may feel a need to have a more glamorous image. The name on the bag symbolizes wealth and social position, as well as the need to display your status in public.

A worn purse may symbolize feelings of being worn out, battered around the edges, and shabby. Do you need to freshen up your identity, to give yourself a polish so that you look and feel brighter? If your dream purse is in need of repair, ask

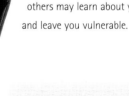

yourself what it is you might lose if you don't make some repairs or some changes.

Your purse may symbolize your private thoughts and desires, which are away from public view. If you lose your bag, others may learn about you and leave you vulnerable.

CONNECTION

◉ *Is your dream wallet full or empty? Does this relate to your current financial situation?*

Made by Humans

Mirror AS A SYMBOL OF THE MIND, the mirror indicates the act of reflection, of looking at the truth of who you are, or seeing yourself in a different way or in a new light. According to superstition, breaking a mirror means that seven years of bad luck will follow.

In medieval times, mirrors symbolized the transience of worldly pleasures.

I had this awful dream—one of those where I feel I am awake in the dream. I am looking into a big mirror box, but by looking in the mirror I could see a girl being murdered. It was like watching a cinema screen. But the girl looked like I imagine my daughter will look when she is twenty. I stopped myself from dreaming any more.

A mirror allows us some distance, and in the dream above the dreamer faces something she could not bear to see directly. In it she witnesses her worst nightmare, the death of her daughter. The dream expresses hidden fears for her daughter's safety.

CONNECTIONS

Do you need to reflect on something that is bothering you?

If you looked at yourself in your dream mirror, were you happy with your reflection or do you need to make changes?

Lighting

ILLUMINATION IS VITAL to both personal and spiritual development. It symbolizes intuition, an inner guiding light. If you dream of lights, consider their shape. Are they like candles flaring upward, or are they contained like a light bulb? Is the light like the flaming flares travelers carried, similar to the torch used at the Olympic Games? Or is it more like a flickering candle, wavering when it is almost extinguished? What does this represent in your life right now?

Light often symbolizes guidance. Do you feel that you need a mentor or guru? Before a significant change in outlook or lifestyle, dreamers often talk about having had dreams in which the light is brighter and more intense and in which a voice has given guidance.

CONNECTION

◎ *Does your dream of carrying a flare mean you have a "flair" for something, a talent you are not using? Or does it indicate that you are about to "flare up," have an angry outburst?*

Made by Humans

Photographs

PHOTOGRAPHS CAPTURE MOMENTS in time. They reflect your history and your relationships, so if you dream of a photograph, the person or place it shows will have particular significance for you.

In your dream, if you are looking at photographs of people who have died, it may indicate that they have some information or wise words for you. Think about their qualities or words of advice they gave in the past, and consider how those might be of use to you now. If you are looking at photographs of yourself when you were younger, reflect on what life was like for you at that time. Is there some unfinished business you need to work on, or did you have qualities then that you need to reintroduce to your life now?

In some cultures, it is believed that the camera captures the soul of the person photographed.

It used to be said that the camera never lies. However, with digital photography and enhanced computer technology, people can be removed from photographs and others inserted in their place. If this happens in a dream, ask yourself why this might be, or what it is about a particular person you don't like.

CONNECTION

Do you feel a need to capture a special event in your life?

Book

BOOKS CONTAIN KNOWLEDGE, they educate, entertain, and communicate, telling us of times long gone or yet to be. In stories, we read of faraway places and mysterious events. In the book *The House of Doctor Dee*, the story of an alchemist, by Peter Ackroyd, Doctor Dee has a series of dreams about books that culminate in the fifth dream in which he says, "I look down on myself, and find myself with letters and words all upon me, and I know that I have been turned into a book ..." His search for knowledge consumes him. Or is he "an open book" or a source of great knowledge, feeling scholarly and important?

A notebook contains any amount of information, ideas, and reminders. As a container, it may symbolize items you need to note or to bear in mind. If you are looking through a notebook in a dream, consider the contents—do they represent emotions you need to keep track of? Do the notes call your attention to issues you avoid during waking hours? A notebook is there to help you manage and record details. How important are the notes to you? If in a dream you discover a notebook that has been hidden away in a desk drawer or box, it may signify information that is finally being brought into the open in waking life.

Musical Instruments

WHETHER IT IS A PIANO, a guitar, a violin, or a drum, a musical instrument represents communication and artistry. If you play an instrument, your dream of it probably means you are continuing to work on your technique as you sleep or are rehearsing to enhance your skill. If you don't play an instrument in waking life, then think about what the instrument means to you.

Music symbolizes emotion and soul and can affect us profoundly. The nature of the music in your dream and the quality of the instruments and their tone will give you information to help interpret your dream. Strident, out-of-tune instruments may indicate discord and lack of harmony in yourself or your relationships. Is your dream drum an African drum, a snare drum, or an Irish bodhran? The type and origin of the drum indicates a focus you could use in working out the dream. If you dream of someone playing the blues on a honky-tonk piano, it may relate to feeling blue or being low in spirits.

Sir Paul McCartney, when he was part of The Beatles, woke up one morning with a tune running through his mind. It seemed so familiar that he thought he had heard it somewhere. He played it to his friends and asked them what it was called, but no one recognized it. Then he realized he had dreamed up the tune, which later became the award-winning song *Yesterday*.

Television

TELEVISIONS REPRESENT COMMUNICATION and inform and entertain us. Thanks to instant satellite communication, we can know what is happening on the other side of the globe while it is still happening. Your dreams will sometimes be triggered by what you have watched on television. If you dream of watching television, consider what it is you are watching and your reaction to it. If you are remote and detached from what is happening, it may signify feelings of indifference to a topic. Soap operas tell us about other people's fictional lives, which reflect the concerns of the community in which the drama is set. If you dream of one of these television series, it may be because you identify with one of the characters or that the story line echoes experiences in your own life.

If you dream of appearing on television, you might be seeking a higher profile or wider exposure. What you are doing or saying and how you feel during the appearance will give you clues about the nature of your desire.

CONNECTIONS

◉ *Is there a drama being acted out in your life in which you feel you are the observer?*

◉ *Is there something you want to broadcast to the whole world?*

Computer

WE USE COMPUTERS AT WORK AND AT HOME, and we communicate via e-mail and Internet chatrooms. This instant communication may appear in our dreams, and often reflects our personal use of computers.

Computers give us the opportunity to play games, so if you dream of this, consider whether the dream games are relaxing, fun, stimulating, or competitive. What is the outcome—lose, draw, or win? Games often reflect a situation in waking life, so consider what the dream game represents for you now. "The game is over" may refer to being found out, indicating that a pretence must come to an end.

CONNECTION
◎ *If you dream of problems with your computer could this reflect anxiety about communication or technological changes?*

Numbers

NUMBERS PLAY AN IMPORTANT ROLE IN MYTHS, legends, and fairy tales and these ancient connections, which Carl Jung called "root symbols," are expressed in dreams. Numbers represent time, days, weeks, years, and important numbers for the dreamer; they may represent age, the number of your house, the number of children you have and their birth order. When you dream of a number, first consider what connections you can make to the dream number.

Consider repetitions. Do you have a lot of dreams of doubles (twos)? The Celts believed that twins had supernatural powers.

Even numbers have traditionally been regarded as feminine, while odd numbers have masculine characteristics. The art of numerology represents the language of numbers. One may represent both a number and "oneself," so if you dream of the number one, does it symbolize you, the dreamer? Two may represent you and your partner or a twosome that you are involved with. "Three's a crowd" means there is an intruder, one more than is necessary.

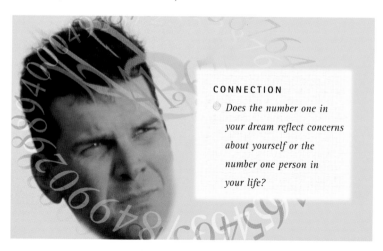

CONNECTION

Does the number one in your dream reflect concerns about yourself or the number one person in your life?

Toys

TOYS COME IN ALL VARIETIES—from handmade wooden trains to state-of-the-art computer-driven toy cars. The type of toy, its age, and its connection to your life will reveal its significance to you.

Dolls represent playthings of childhood over which a child has domination. "Baby doll" describes a doll that is literally a replica of a baby, but it is also used to describe a woman dressing and behaving as a cute, compliant sexual object. The type of doll in a dream gives good clues about the meaning. A Barbie doll, a Ken doll (Barbie's male equivalent), or GI Joe symbolize different characteristics, while an anatomically correct doll in your dream may be linked to the investigation of child sexual abuse. The characteristics of the doll and what is happening to it help to reveal its meaning. Dolls covered in beads were used as fetish figures by the African Xhosa tribe.

A ball can symbolize the sun or the moon, and ball games are connected to solar and lunar festivals. "To play ball" means to join in, do the right thing. Balls, symbolizing testicles, can be associated with strength or courage, as in "He's got no balls," meaning he is afraid. In ancient mythological tales, gods would show their power by hurling globes across the skies—perhaps this is somehow linked to the idolization of world-class soccer players.

CONNECTION

Does your dream of toys indicate that you need to make more time in your life for play?

Food WHEN YOU DREAM OF FOOD, it may be because you are hungry or are compensating for lack of food because you are on a diet. Different types of food have distinct associations.

Bread is the staff of life and is a staple food known to all societies. "Use your loaf" is a saying that means you need to use your brain and think about the situation, and what you need to do. Loaves rise, so do you need to rise to a challenge or rise above something to disentangle your emotions or get an overview? Where bread is being placed in an oven and rising, it is linked to conception and pregnancy. This may be the conception of a child or the development of a new way of living. To have "a bun in the oven" means to be pregnant, while "half-baked" means incomplete or undeveloped.

Cake is a celebratory food that is often used in rituals or rites of passage—think of birthday cake, wedding cake, cake used in offerings to gods or spirits of the dead. Is your symbol linked to "having your cake and eating it too"? In other words, are you being a bit selfish or thoughtless? A "cake walk" describes a task that is easy, and this may translate literally in your dream to walking on or around a cake. Is something you were worrying about actually easy to deal with? Too easy?

If you dream of salt in a medical setting, for example, in a doctor's office, it may be that salt is influencing your physical condition in some way. "Salt of the earth" describes a humble, unpretentious person. Salt is also used as a preservative.

CONNECTION

If you dream of salt being spread on an icy road, it could mean that you're looking for an easier route to the solution to a problem.

Alcohol ALCOHOL CAN BE LIFE-ENHANCING OR DESTRUCTIVE.

Not only is it a cornerstone of many cultural traditions, it also features prominently in religious rituals. For example, when Christians of most traditions take communion during religious ceremonies, wine symbolizes the blood of Jesus Christ, sacrificed for his people.

Alcohol can enhance life in celebrations or in cardiovascular health. Some medical experts recommend a glass of wine a day. Or it can be destructive, impairing judgment, mobility, reaction time, and vision, to disastrous ends; drunk driving, for example, is a top killer in some countries. Alcoholism, a disease of addiction to alcohol, can destroy relationships and careers, ruining the lives of those affected by it.

Look at the context of your dream. Are you worried about drinking in your dream, concerned you might be addicted to it, or is it adding to the social pleasure of the event? How does the dream relate to your waking attitude toward alcohol? Some people find that alcohol loosens them up and lets them speak the truth. Is this the symbolic meaning of your dream?

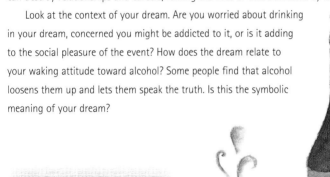

CONNECTION

If wine plays an important part in your dream, it could be that you need to be aware of a tendency to "whine" in your waking life.

Weapon CLUBS ARE SYMBOLS OF AGGRESSION AND

POWER. The Celtic god Dagda, the Cerne Abbas giant in England, carries a club to show his power as the god of life and death. For Celts, beautifully decorated weapons were their most precious possessions and they would be buried with them and carried into the afterlife.

Knives can be used as weapons, but they also have peaceful, practical uses, such as cutting branches or preparing food.

If you dream of a knife, consider how it is being used. If you are a Sikh, then the *kirpan*, or dagger, will have religious connections for you.

There is a superstition that to give a knife as a present would "cut the friendship" and that if you stir something with a knife you "stir up strife."

King Arthur's sword, Excalibur, was invested with the power to prevent loss of blood during battle. A sword is also used to invest a knighthood in Britain, which is done by the monarch touching the shoulder of the recipient with a sword.

CONNECTIONS

- If you dream of weapons, are you in warrior mode?
- Do you feel under physical attack? Consider who is wielding the weapon and who or what is the target.

Money

MONEY ALLOWS US TO PURCHASE WHAT WE NEED—we exchange it for goods. If you are buying something in your dream, think about how much you spent and whether you were happy with the transaction. Dreams in which you are overspending may reflect concerns about your bank balance.

If the money in your dream is metal rather than paper or plastic, think about which metal it is. Gold has high value; silver symbolizes intuitive or psychic powers; copper relates to healing, which is why many older people wear copper bracelets to ease rheumatism.

Coins with holes in them or that are misshapen are regarded as lucky. *Coin of the realm* means the legal currency. If you dream of coins, are you "coining it in," making lots of money?

A bank is a depository where money is collected and recirculated. This may symbolize the gathering and circulation of energy or the circulatory system of the body. A bank is a symbol of reliability and the saying "you can bank on it" reflects this.

CONNECTION

◎ *Does your bank dream reflect the dependable side of your character?*

Calendar

A CALENDAR REPRESENTS THE PASSAGE OF TIME, the change of the seasons and the days of the year. If you dream of a calendar, it may be that an important date is coming up, perhaps a birthday or an anniversary. If you see a calendar in your dream, does it show you a date that is significant for you? What does it say about the passing of time and how you are passing your life?

There have been many different types of calendar throughout history, including the Julian Calendar, the Gregorian Calendar, or the New Style, which is used in Britain, and the Islamic Calendar, which dates from July 16, 622, the day of Hegira, the start of the Muslim era.

The *Hilal*, the crescent moon and star, is the symbol of Islam. The moon is a reminder that the Islamic year is ruled by a lunar calendar and the star reminds us that Allah, as the Qur'an states, created stars to guide people to their destination.

CONNECTION

Is your dream reminding you of an anniversary or special event you have overlooked?

Ship or Boat

Made by Humans

SHIPS AND BOATS SIGNIFY JOURNEYS and may be a metaphor for the voyage of life. Where there is danger that the vessel might sink, it could indicate a crisis the dreamer is facing. If you "ship out," you leave your present place or position for new territory, so there may be changes ahead.

The Ark was the ship that Noah built, which ensured survival after the devastating flood. The Ark may represent rebirth, protection, or safety.

Oars symbolize a journey across water or, in terms of the psyche, a journey across the unconscious. As oars dip into the water they break through the surface, representing penetration into the emotional aspects of our being. If only one oar is present, then the "boat" may go around in circles or be unable to move forward. It may mean that you need a partner to complete the pair.

CONNECTIONS

◉ "To abandon ship" is to save yourself when hope of salvaging the present situation has gone. If you dream that you are abandoning ship it may mean that you need to learn when to let go and move on.

◉ "When my ship comes in" refers to the time when you get your just rewards for earlier investment.

Canal

CANALS PROVIDE A NETWORK OF TRANSPORTATION in many areas of the world. They contain restricted amounts of water, and since water may represent emotions, a dream of a canal may indicate feelings of emotional constriction. It may also represent a very conventional approach to life or spirituality.

Canal boats, or barges, are specially built for traveling on canals, either to carry freight or to live on. In England, they are usually painted in bright colors. If you dream of these barges it may reflect a cheerful mood or jaunty attitude. Canal boats are also rented out for vacations, so your dream barge may represent a need to go for a break on a slow moving boat, to prevent you rushing around so much.

I was walking along the side of a canal with my mother and sister and when we came to the bend we saw the canal was on fire. At this point we all flew over it.

The dreamer overcomes the obstacle of fire by "taking off" (see opposite).

CONNECTION

◎ *Does your dream of a canal boat represent a need to feel more contained or defined?*

Made by Humans

Airplane

AIRPLANES ALLOW US TO TRAVEL GREAT DISTANCES across the world. They may symbolize the need to "take off," to initiate new ventures and to get away from it all, to leave the old life behind and begin anew.

I'm in a plane. It is about to crash. I can see darkness outside the window. I know I'm going to die and I'm afraid. Then I don't know what happens, only that I'm alive afterward.

This dream indicates the dreamer's fear that she is about to face a disaster that will overwhelm her. In fact, she does survive but the dream comes as a warning that she has to work out what the "darkness" is and come down to earth and face reality, rather than taking flight to escape a situation.

A parachute in a dream often symbolizes the need for safety precautions as you leap into a new situation. A parachute slows a fall and softens a landing, so it may indicate the need to slow down to prevent bad results. "Plane" may be a pun on "plain," something or someone unadorned or unattractive. Does this reflect feelings you have about your appearance?

CONNECTION

◎ *A dream of flying in an airplane may symbolize a need to get a higher view so you can get a broader perspective on things.*

Vehicle

VEHICLES MAY BE SHARED with other members of the public or may be for private use. If you dream of a bus, it may reflect the public you, whereas a car usually indicates the private you. All vehicles represent movement and progress, although this may be hampered in some way. Consider the state of the vehicle, any unusual qualities it has, and how well it performs.

I was sitting in a convertible outside a night club I used to go to. It was the morning after an all-night party and my friends climbed onto the car and it started flying over the city with me at the wheel.

If you dream of a car, it is always useful to think about who is in "the driver's seat"—it often represents the person who is in control of a situation or relationship. Vehicles that are moving represent action and desire for progress, and the speed and quality of the journey are good indicators of how well you are doing.

Dreams can also bring warnings:

About two weeks before our beloved son was tragically killed in a road accident, he said to me, "Mom, I had such a clear dream last night. I was riding my motorcycle and something crashed into me, and I don't remember anything else. Do you think my dream was a warning?"

Made by Humans

Road ROADS OFTEN SYMBOLIZE THE LIFE PATH. Driving along a road and making progress indicates success in achieving your goals, getting to your destination. The following dream, set in a place associated with spirituality, reassured the dreamer that she was on the right path:

In my dream I noticed a mound, like Glastonbury Tor, with a spiral path to the summit. People were everywhere on the path and the mound was reddish brown and burnt looking. Where I was to walk was untrodden, green, and fresh.

Sometimes, instead of a road in your dreams, you will have a highway. This may represent your path in life, a "high" way, the top way. Crossroads in dreams are a common symbol for decision making and may indicate a change of direction. They can relate to a "cross to bear," a burden, or anger, as in being cross and irritated. Until 1823 English law insisted that anyone who had committed suicide be buried in the highway, usually at the crossroads. In earlier times, people executed as witches and criminals were also buried there, because the cross, the sign of Christ, was believed to prevent them from haunting the area.

CONNECTION

Do you feel that you are at a crossroads in your life at present?

Clothing

CLOTHING REPRESENTS THE OUTER PERSONA of the dreamer, the façade you show to others. Clothes are the protective layer that keeps you warm and they are also a way of expressing which group or groups you belong to. A uniform, such as that of a sailor, police officer, surgeon, or flight attendant, carries an association to that profession. If you dream of a soldier, it may indicate feelings of having to battle on, or the need for a peace-keeping force. New clothes represent new beginnings and a fresh start. If you are repairing clothes, you may want to make amends or mend some damage to your image. Dirty clothes signify feelings of being sullied or stained in some way and indicate a need to clean up or "come clean." If you look dirty in your dream, it may reflect concern about how others perceive you.

If you are in a public place in your underwear, it could indicate exhibitionism or vulnerability—much depends on how you feel in the dream. If you are trying to cover up your nakedness, are you trying to cover up an issue in your waking life?

CONNECTION

◎ *If you are wearing a uniform in your dream, does it link with a need for more rules and greater self-discipline?*

Gloves

WOOLLEN AND LEATHER GLOVES and mittens protect the hands from the cold and their material, color, and design also indicate something about the personality of the wearer.

Dreams of waterproof gloves often relate to dirty work that must be done, as well as to washing, cleaning, and general housework. Oven mitts are used to remove hot items from the oven or stove. Gardening gloves may reflect an interest in plants, while boxing gloves are connected to boxing or fighting outside the ring. Evening gown gloves cover the forearm to the elbow and are usually made of silk or satin-like material. Latex gloves are worn by surgeons and other medical practitioners, as well as laboratory scientists.

Highly decorative gold burial gloves have been found in Inca remains. The dead person could continue on his journey in the underworld with his hands well protected.

CONNECTION

A gauntlet is a glove that is thrown down as a challenge and was used to initiate a challenge to a duel. If you dream that you are "throwing down the gauntlet," perhaps you feel the need to challenge someone about something?

Hat

HATS ARE BOTH DECORATIVE AND USEFUL. In dreams, hats may relate to what is worn on the head but may also symbolize your mental outlook or attitude. If you change hats in your dream, it may indicate different thoughts or opinions. This could be a change of consciousness. It could also indicate a change of roles, just as different uniforms do.

The type of hat you wear in a dream represents qualities you may need. For instance, if you dream of wearing a bowler hat it may be linked to formality and the City of London, while a baseball cap may represent casual relaxation or sport, or symbolize the United States.

Before it was associated with bridal wear, a veil was a sign of humility, accepting darkness and a spiritual guide who would take you through the mysterious, perhaps on a journey of self-awareness. A veil can also be a type of mask, protecting the wearer from recognition. Turbans may be seen as a type of hat and may symbolize religious affiliation. Sikh men wear turbans to cover their uncut hair.

The fringe on Native American clothes and head coverings symbolizes falling rain, a vital resource in desert lands.

CONNECTION

Does your dream hat represent a longed-for status or occupation?

Jewelry

PERSONAL DECORATION in the form of brooches, necklaces, and bracelets has always been associated with status. Archaeologists have found jewelry in sites as far apart as Egypt and Ireland, Peru and France.

Pearls symbolize the tears of the moon goddess or sadness, but they are also traditionally a classic, elegant choice of adornment in Western society. What you feel about the pearls in your dream is the best indicator for your personal interpretation. A string of pearls may symbolize conformity, while "pearls of wisdom thrown before swine" may indicate a useless action.

Bracelets and bangles may signify adornment. However, if you dream of the *kara*, the steel bangle that Sikhs wear as a symbol of their faith, it may have spiritual significance.

A ring in a dream may symbolize a need for wholeness and continuity, since the circle is a profound symbol of these in all cultures.

CONNECTION

◉ *Does your dream ring relate*
to attachment or marriage?

Cosmetics

THE USE OF COSMETICS TO ENHANCE appearance and bodily aroma is long established. In Ancient Egypt, cosmetics were kept in ornamental glass jars in the shape of fish. There are many paintings from Ancient Egypt showing people applying cosmetics, so that we can see that concern about image has been around for a long time. Both men and women used cosmetics in their daily routines and these included oils, perfumes, and eye paints. Cosmetics were also included in funerary equipment entombed with the dead.

Blusher may indicate that you feel embarrassed, turning red over an indiscretion. If you dream that you are using cosmetics or hair color to enhance or change your appearance, think about what you would like to alter in the way you look.

CONNECTIONS

◉ *Do you feel you need to add to what you already have?*
◉ *What are you trying to change at a superficial level?*
   Can you go deeper to find the "real" you?

Made by Humans

Amulet 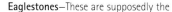 AMULETS COME
IN MANY FORMS, from a trinket or shell
to a precious gemstone. Whatever the
form the amulet or charm takes, its
purpose is to protect its owner from
the threat of evil.

Celtic amulets included spiral
stones with prehistoric carvings on
them. These are known as *glyphs* and
many have been found on sacred sites.

Eaglestones—These are supposedly the
finest amulets for use in pregnancy and childbirth. Also known as *aetites*, eaglestones
are hollow stones, usually brown and egg-shaped, in which sand or small stones are
found. Legendarily found in eagles' nests, it was believed that without them an eagle
could not have any young. Eaglestones were believed to prevent miscarriage and to
aid delivery.

Charms—Originating from the Latin *carmen*, "a chant," the word *charm* reveals that
charms or remedies were spoken aloud, probably as a repetitive incantation. However,
charms can also be objects, such as a lucky charm or mascot. Certain objects are
considered healing charms. For instance, stones with holes in them were said to help
anyone who had sore eyes.

CONNECTION

*If you dream that you have been given an amulet, think about
what you may need protection from.*

Anchor TO A SAILOR AN ANCHOR IS THE SYMBOL OF HOME. The

anchor symbolizes connection, stability, and being held firm in the choppy seas of life.
The Egyptian word *ankh*, a symbol for life, may have given us the word *anchor*. When
a ship is "at anchor" it can ride out a storm. The sheet anchor is the largest anchor and
is used only in difficult seas; to lose it may bring catastrophic consequences. The word
sheet is a corruption of the old Dutch word *shote*, which meant "thrown out." In
Ancient Greek and Roman times, the ship's sheet anchor was regarded as sacred and
was named after a god. Symbolically, a sheet anchor represents your last hope, your
last refuge.

To "weigh anchor" is to set sail, to begin your journey.

Saint Nicholas of Bari was martyred by being bound to an anchor and thrown out
to sea. He is the patron saint of sailors.

CONNECTIONS

*⬤ Do you feel tossed about
by emotions and events
at present?*

*⬤ Does your dream anchor
indicate a need for
stability?*

Bell

BELLS ARE USED IN CHURCHES to mark times for prayer and to summon people to services or to mark a wedding or funeral; thus, bells are linked to information and rituals. The angelus bell rings out three times a day to remind Catholics to pray. The name comes from the Latin phrase *angelus domini nuntiavit Mariae*, "the angel of the Lord brought tidings to Mary." Bells may indicate new tidings for the dreamer.

If your dream bell is a doorbell, used by visitors to your home, it may reflect thoughts about someone coming to see you or a desire for company.

At New Year, bells "ring out the old and ring in the new," and so symbolize the ending of one aspect of life and the beginning of another.

In Buddhism, the bell represents emptiness or wisdom. If something is as "sound as a bell," it means it is in perfect condition. Is this how you feel at present?

In many mountainous areas of Europe, bells are put around the necks of mountain goats and cattle so that their owners will know where to find them. Domestic cats are sometimes "belled" so that birds have a chance to escape before the cat pounces. "To bell the cat" means to undertake a dangerous mission.

CONNECTION

Is there news ringing out for you or news you are about to give?

Scythe

THE SCYTHE IS AN IMPLEMENT WITH A CURVED BLADE used for cutting down crops. However, it is the scythe's association with death that most people are familiar with. The Grim Reaper is the man of death who comes to take people from life, and in illustrations he always carries a scythe. He "reaps" people when their season is over by cutting them down.

If you dream of a scythe, it may relate to fears of death or a feeling that you are "cut off" in some way. Such dreams can help you identify what is coming to an end for you, a stage of life that you are leaving behind or attachments you need to break in order to move forward.

In medieval plays the Grim Reaper wore a skeleton suit and a mask, or "grim," and carried an hourglass to convey the message that time was running out. The Grim Reaper reminded the audience of their mortality and that they needed to consider their soul and piety because death might strike at any moment.

CONNECTION
Are you feeling isolated or cut off from others?

Made by Humans

Coffin

A COFFIN IN A DREAM may be triggered by the death of someone you know. A coffin is a container for a corpse, which is then buried or cremated, so coffins are connected to finality and a submerging or disposing of that which has ceased to function. This may not always be a person but could symbolize ideas or values that no longer have a useful purpose.

As a child I dreamed my parents were dead. I had them stuffed and put in upright coffins at each side of the door.

Many children face the fear of death in their dreams, and in this dream, the young dreamer keeps the attachment, keeps her parents present in her life after their deaths in a way that reminds us of Egyptian mummies. They guard the threshold, still offering her protection.

A pall is a large white cloth used to cover the coffin when it comes into church for the final service. It serves as a reminder of the Christian baptismal garment.

If the coffin in the dream is placed in a grave, it could indicate that you are feeling grave, serious, or concerned about a matter. Are you involved in a solemn situation? Do you have to make a decision that has grave (that is, serious or profound) implications? To tread on a grave is regarded as unlucky, as is picking flowers that grow on a grave.

10

PEOPLE WHO INTERPRET DREAMS have been around as long as there have been dreamers: Shamans in Siberia, temple diviners in Ancient Greece, Babylonian *baru* priests, medicine men and women in Africa and America, and wise women everywhere. On every continent, these dream interpreters have found that spirituality plays a profound role in our dream life. When we dream, we glimpse the potential of all we can be, emotionally and spiritually. Without the censoring side of ourselves to interfere, we are open to new possibilities, fresh insights, and spiritual connections. Our creativity is expanded to amazing dimensions and we can integrate our inner and outer lives.

Some dreams feel especially significant. They are those "big" dreams that stay with you, the dreams Jung described as "numinous," or sacred. These potentially transformational dreams connect us to something more, something greater than ourselves. Such dreams can become the richest gems in your heart and soul. Sometimes, spiritual symbols involve the appearance of an illuminated figure, a radiant being—an angelic form or a robed figure, for example. These figures typically give guidance or reveal truths to the dreamer. In many religious traditions, including Christianity, Islam, and Buddhism, dreams reaffirm the tenets of faith.

Spiritual Connections

Spiritual Connections

*When I attain this highest perfect wisdom,
I will deliver all sentient beings into the eternal
peace of nirvana.*

THE WORDS OF THE BUDDHA IN THE OLDEST PRINTED BOOK IN THE WORLD, THE DIAMOND SUTRA

It was because of a dream that the Emperor Ming Ti (100 C.E.) sent representatives to central Asia to bring back sacred Buddhist texts to China. His dream told him that it was through these texts that he could deepen his spirituality.

Buddhists were generally encouraged to record their dreams and to be alert to visitations by spirits bringing messages. They also believed in precognitive dreams, as well as in dreams that could be considered to resolve spiritual problems.

In many cultures, such as the Inuit tribes of Canada, who have lived as hunter-gatherers for generations, dreaming is seen as a way to cross the boundary between this world and other worlds. The dreamer journeys to far vistas as his body sleeps in the safety of his home. He crosses between the world of humans and animals, making contact with the prey he hopes to catch, and he moves between the boundaries of time, into the past and toward the future. As the writer Hugh Brody says in his book *The Other Side of Eden*, "Along with other forms of insight and intuition, hunters use dreams to help them decide where to hunt, when to go there, and what to hunt."

The Old Testament has many stories, such as Pharaoh's dream of the cows (see page 252), that illustrate the importance accorded to dreams in the Ancient Egyptian and Hebrew traditions.

The religious aspect of dreaming of gods and devils, of the afterlife, and of dreaming for spiritual guidance is just as relevant for us in the twenty-first century as it was for our earliest ancestors. Whether you have a religious practice or not, your dreams can bring you closer to the web that binds humanity together so that you can appreciate the spiritual, inspirational dimension of life.

BELOW *Spiritual dreams are found in all cultures throughout the world.*

Christian Connections

IN THE BIBLE, as with other religious texts, we find many references to dreams.

When I say, My bed shall comfort me, my couch shall ease my complaint;
then thou scarest me with dreams, and terrifiest me
through visions: so that my soul choosest
strangling, and death rather than my life.

JOB 7

Like Job, we might not like what confronts
us in dreams, but they can return again
and again until we make the connection
that helps us move on.

After Jesus died, the twelve disciples
were talking about how best to spread
the word of God when suddenly the room
was filled with "a rushing mighty wind and
cloven tongues of fire." The disciples were filled
with the Holy Spirit, which enabled them to speak in
other languages so that they could spread the word of God
everywhere. In dreams, this sense of being filled with an overwhelming sense of spirit
can bring about transformations to the dreamer, who may then change his or her
waking life. The dove is the traditional sign of the Holy Spirit, so if you dream of
a dove, consider the symbolic meaning the bird brings (see page 286).

I am with you always
Even unto the end of the world

JESUS'S PROMISE IN THE GOSPEL OF MATTHEW (MATT. 28:20)

Hindu Connections

HINDUS BELIEVE IN **ONE GOD** who can be understood and worshiped in many different forms. An early Hindu text, the *Brahmavaivarta Purana*, is a guide to the interpretation of dreams. For example, it says "If a Brahmana takes somebody in a chariot and shows him different strata of heaven in a dream, the seer gets enhanced life and wealth." In this interpretation, the "seer" is the dreamer.

Ganesh, the elephant-headed Hindu god, is the god of new beginnings and is invoked at the beginning of all religious ceremonies (other than funerals) in order to insure fruitful worship. Ganesh is universally known as the Lord of Obstacles and the Giver of Success. If you dream of Ganesh or of elephants (see page 258), it may reassure you of success in an undertaking.

The cross is highly symbolic in many cultures. Its four arms are found in the Christian cross of crucifixion and in the ancient Hindu sacred swastika, which was the symbol of good luck and prosperity until it was taken over as the emblem of the Nazi Party in Germany in the 1930s.

A flowing river is a living symbol for Hindus, since it represents the cycle from the source of the river to the sea and back again to the source. At the traditional pilgrimage site of Varanasi, the Hindus bathe in the Ganges River as a demonstration of their religious devotion. If you have a dream of bathing in a river it may be linked to the need for a form of ritual purification.

Muslim Connections

LIKE THE FOUNDER OF OTHER RELIGIONS,
Muhammad was inspired to make his spiritual
mission after having a dream, which also revealed
to him several sections of the *Qur'an*. A medieval
Persian text says that a dream of the Prophet
Muhammad indicates that the dreamer will have
a long and blessed life.

The Arabic dream book *ad-Dinawari* includes
a vast array of dreams that reflect the cultural,
religious, and social life of medieval Islam in tenth-
century Baghdad.

Minaret means "place of fire or light" and has
its origins in watchtowers spread across vast
landscapes. It is the place that is used to call
Muslims to prayer and is a symbol of devotion and
obedience. In a dream, a minaret may symbolize
news of a spiritual nature or an upsurge in interest
in your spiritual development.

For devout Muslims, fasting during the month
of Ramadan is a religious duty for everyone over
the age of twelve years. During this period, Muslims
who fast may well experience an increase in dreams
about food as a means of compensation. Anyone
who is on a restricted diet, either because of
fasting, dieting, or preparation for an operation
may also experience more dreams about food.

Jewish Connections

JUDAISM IS THE OLDEST MONOTHEISTIC RELIGION. Abraham was the first Jew and the grandfather of Jacob. One night Jacob dreamed that he saw angels climbing a ladder to heaven and heard God promising that he and his family would own the land on which they slept. Years later, Jacob met a stranger who revealed himself as an angel of God. The angel told Jacob that he should change his name to *Israel*, which means "one who strives with God." The twelve tribes of Israel are said to have descended from Jacob's twelve sons and fulfilled the promise made in Jacob's dream.

The *Talmud* (code of Jewish law) has over two hundred references to dreams and states that "an uninterpreted dream is like an unopened letter," in other words, dreams bring us important messages and are a form of communication that needs to be thought about and elaborated until the message is clear. However, the *Talmud* does emphasize the difficulties associated with dream interpretation, because "just as there is no wheat without straw, so there is no dream without worthless things." This is an admonition to dream interpreters to take extreme care when analyzing a dream so that they can separate the significant, revelatory parts of the dream from the distorted or trivial aspects.

Buddhist Connections

BUDDHA SHAKYAMUNI HAD A SERIES OF FIVE DREAMS that led him on the path to enlightenment, and dreams are still held in high regard by Buddhists.

The Ganges valley is particularly important to Buddhists, since the Buddha (whose private name was Siddhartha Gautama) was born there, enlightened there, preached his first sermon there and died there. To dream of a river may indicate spiritual resources that are there if you wish to find them.

During the reign of Ashoka in India (c. 265–238 B.C.E.), the teachings of the Buddha were represented in symbols. Images were carved into doorways and included the following:

The wheel of law or teaching was an eight-spoke wheel symbolizing the Eightfold Path to enlightenment. It was a symbol of earthly rule.

The lotus symbolized the possibility of enlightenment from ignorance. It has its roots in mud but its blossoms are pure and white on the surface of still water.

The empty throne symbolized the Buddha as a spiritual leader and his royal nature before his enlightenment.

The footprint symbolized the Buddha's presence in his teaching.

The four highest states in Buddhism are compassion, lovingkindness, sympathetic joy, and equanimity. If you are behaving in a thoughtless way, a dream of being cruel to animals may remind you of your duty to behave with care toward all sentient beings, as well as toward yourself.

Pagan Connections THE CELTS DID NOT

LIVE AS A SINGLE NATION, and so their varied traditions and gods appear in dreams in many forms. The Celts sought harmony with nature, had highly developed artistic

skills, and rewarded loyalty and bravery in their fierce fighters. As in many pagan societies, the sun played an important part in the beliefs of the Celts. In his novel *That They Might Face The Rising Sun*, John McGahern describes how the importance of the sun lived on in Celtic beliefs after Christianity had been imposed in Ireland. The "pedantic priests" would try to get the people to bury their dead facing the church as a sign that they bowed to the Church's authority, but the Irish insisted on burying their dead "facing the rising sun" to acknowledge the greater power of nature.

Cernunnos, the "Horned One," was the Celtic god of animals and was a major figure in legend and folklore. Cernunnos was an early sun god. Dreams of horned creatures or of sacrifice may be connected to earlier pagan traditions that have been transformed into present-day festivals such as May Day and Halloween. Many pagan ceremonies involved sacrifice to appease gods. The "Wicker Man" is one example. The ceremony was used in Celtic times and captives were burned inside the wooden structure. If you dream of being trapped and burned as part of a ritualized punishment it could mean that you feel in need of purification.

God **GOD IS THE DIVINE FATHER.** Many religious traditions acknowledge an all-powerful God, including the Christian, Jewish, and Muslim traditions. God is often represented as a wise and powerful old man—an example is the depiction of God by Michelangelo in the Sistine Chapel in Rome. However, the idea of knowing God or defining him, other than that he is infinite and eternal, is beyond human understanding.

The Lamb of God is a powerful symbol of redemption in Christianity. The Lamb of God represents being saved from the sins of the world to enjoy the kingdom of heaven. Many other symbols of rebirth and regeneration come in animal form, as described in Chapter Eight. If you dream of a divine presence, consider what guidance or teachings are being given to you.

The influence of religious teaching can have a powerful effect on dream content. One dreamer told me of a number of dreams in which Christ sat by her bed and talked to her. The dreams came when she was under the influence of a pious teacher.

I have several dreams of being in really violent situations—war, civil unrest, gangsters—and have been shot and killed but I am still alive. At the moment of death I would frantically pray to God for forgiveness of my sins.

Devil

THE DEVIL SYMBOLIZES ANY EVIL FORCE and comes in many guises, from a masked monster to an imp. He has many names including Satan, Beelzebub, Lucifer, and "The Prince of Darkness."

The Christian philosopher Macrobius wrote *The Commentary on the Dream of Scipio* in the fourth century C.E. It was an enormously influential book and became the most important dream book in medieval Europe. Macrobius detailed a hierarchy of dream lore that described the ascending order of spiritual dreams. The lower spheres of dreaming were controlled by demons he called *incubi* and *succubi*.

An *incubus* was a male demon and was believed to have sexual intercourse with women as they slept, while the *succubus*, the female demon, sexually molested her male victims. Today, many dreamers describe terrifying dreams of an evil creature that sits on their chests with a sexually predatory intent. This may be caused by some of the many images of devils and evil, otherworldly creatures that are familiar through paintings, such as those by Goya, Bosch, and Bruegel, and horror stories and movies such as *Dracula*.

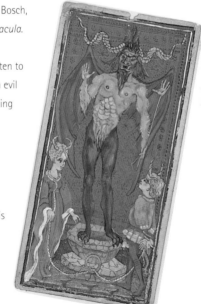

The devil in dreams may represent difficulties and limitations, negative thinking, fear, and the refusal to listen to our own intuition and inner wisdom. If you dream of an evil presence, think about what is troubling you in your waking life, what you are afraid of, or whose power feels overwhelming.

I am in a fun fair and everywhere is red and there's an awful smell and there is the devil laughing in my face.

Red is the color of danger and passion and, for this dreamer, there is danger in a public place meant for enjoyment. The foul smell indicates decay or toxicity.

Soul

The dream is a hidden door to the innermost recesses of the soul.

CARL JUNG

HINDUS BELIEVE THAT EACH INDIVIDUAL HAS AN ETERNAL SOUL, *atman*, which can be born many, many times in different forms or incarnations. It is the law of *karma*, the moral law of the universe, that decides how many times a soul can be born and in how many forms.

For the Ancient Egyptians, *ba* was the human soul, depicted as a bird or a bird with a human body. Ba symbolized the idea that after death the soul could fly off like a bird and join the ancestors. For this purpose, small passageways connected tombs to the outside world so that souls could come and go in the life after death.

At times, we feel beset by problems and feel we have lost our way. The Spanish mystic Saint John of the Cross described this as "the dark night of the soul." Our dreams reveal this troublesome passage and also let us know that the light of the dawn follows the darkness, if we have faith, in God, in ourselves, and in others.

Out-of-body experiences may be encountered in the dream state:

In my dream I left my body and traveled to another place. I met others who, like me, had no body, yet we could communicate. It was a beautiful feeling.

Saint GENERALLY, SAINTS ARE GOOD PEOPLE who have served God and helped others; they may represent those qualities in your life. However, if a named saint appears in your dreams, consider the particular virtues of the saint:

Saint Francis of Assisi was close to nature and animals. Birds were said to come and hear him preach.

Saint Benedict founded the Benedictine order of monks, who were devoted to an austere life of study, prayer, and also manual work.

Saint Catherine opposed Roman persecution and was martyred by being strapped to a spiked wheel and tortured to death.

Saint Bernadette's visions of the Virgin Mary led to the foundation of the pilgrimage site of Lourdes in France, where thousands of people go for healing.

Saint Sebastian was martyred by being

bound to tree and shot at with arrows. He is the patron saint of archers.

Saint George is reputed to have killed a dragon, symbolizing the triumph of Christianity over evil. He is the patron saint of England.

Centuries ago, the pope had a dream that he was unable to ignore. It happened following a visit from Francis of Assisi, who had asked his permission to set up his own religious order. The pope had refused, but had then had a dream in which he saw a desperate figure holding up a collapsing church building. Realizing that his dream building represented the institution of the Church, he summoned Francis and gave him permission to establish the Franciscan order.

Ministers of Religion

ONE OF THE MAIN JOBS OF A MINISTER OF RELIGION is to mediate between people and God. He represents the Church and God. In the Christian tradition, the priest administers the sacraments, such as baptism and marriage. A sacrament is defined as "an outward and visible sign of an inward and spiritual grace." In dreams, you may meet priests who perform baptisms and marriage ceremonies in which you are involved. Consider these in relation to your own state of spirituality or grace.

Monks are associated with religious orders and if a monk is in your dream think about times in your life you have seen monks and what they represent for you. This dreamer associated monks with vows of chastity and benevolence, so she was surprised when she dreamed of a monk with a deathly face and a menacing manner leaning over her when she was in bed. She said, "Not long after I learned that my husband was seeing another woman." His face was deathly white when he broke the news, and she remembered the dream immediately.

I am tied to a stake and a black monk with a white-hot poker burns me. He says, "This is burning out the evil in you 100 percent." I rise up from my body and look down on it, then I wake up.

Religious figures may represent the repressive side of orthodoxy, which was seen in the horrors of the Inquisition, when thousands perished because of zealous power. This dream recaptures the horror of misguided bigotry.

Madonna Figure MARY, THE MOTHER OF CHRIST,

was venerated above all saints during the Middle Ages. The Cult of the Virgin echoed earlier religions in which the Earth Mother dominated pagan worship. The first month of summer, May, became a month dedicated to Mary. Most of the events surrounding the birth of Christ involve dreams: Joseph was told of Mary's pregnancy in a dream; later he was warned in a dream that he and Mary should flee to Egypt to avoid Herod's soldiers.

In many Christian traditions, icons of Mary, often depicting her with her infant son Jesus, are kept on display. The Black Madonna of Walsingham in England is a major site of pilgrimage.

In the tarot (a system of divination using specially designed cards), the card bearing the image of the High Priestess represents intuitive awareness and symbolizes the wise woman, love without sexual desire, and the virgin archetype. She seeks knowledge and learning and represents study and spiritual enlightenment, psychological development and wisdom. She harnesses the power of the occult for positive purposes. A dream of the High Priestess, or of the Madonna, symbolizes the power of the feminine to bring about change in your life.

Spiritual Connections

Angel

ANGELS ACT AS INTERMEDIARIES; they bring divine messages to earth. The word *angel* comes from the Greek *angelos*, meaning "messenger."

Angels are also called "beings of Light." They symbolize spiritual connections, and a guardian angel is believed to offer protection.

In Islam, it is believed that everyone is attended by two angels, known as *kiramu*, every minute of their lives. One records all thought and actions that are good; the other records all that is bad. The angel Jibril, or Gabriel, revealed the teachings of Allah to Muhammad, which were brought together in the Qur'an. The Muslim angel of death is called *Azrael*, and death is known as "the wings of Azrael."

A bas-relief of a six-winged angel dating from 1000 B.C.E in an art gallery in Baltimore, Maryland, tells us that angels have been part of our iconography for a long time. Angels are found principally in religions based on revelations, such as Judaism, Christianity, and Islam.

There are not only God's angels, but also the "fallen angels" who have rebelled against God and become demonic. The devil is the fallen angel Lucifer.

"The more materialistic Science becomes, the more angels I shall paint." The Pre-Raphaelite painter, Sir Edward Burne-Jones, used this as the subtitle for his exhibition, *Victorian Artist-Dreamer*. He described his work as "a dream, a noble dream."

CONNECTIONS

◎ *When you dream of angels, do you feel touched by a divine presence?*

◎ *Is the angel bringing a message of inspiration?*

Guides and Gurus

GUIDES AND GURUS are helpers on life's journey. They may appear in dreams, as you can see in the following dream of a woman who was exploring the Buddhist path:

I am in a castle running down a spiral stone staircase. I escape the danger behind me. Brightly lit, in a field, I find an old man. He sits surrounded by scientific equipment in a circle of light from an arc lamp overhead. He can advise me on which way to go; he cannot come with me but he can advise me.

The archetypal wise old man who appears in this dream reassured her that she was on the right spiritual path and that she could continue with her exploration.

Guru means "one who brings enlightenment, dispels darkness and is a spiritual teacher."

Guru Nanak founded Sikhism in the sixteenth century C.E. and laid down the five symbols of faith. These may appear in dreams as signs to remind the dreamer of the faith. They are: *kesh*, uncut hair; *kanga*, a comb; *kara*, a steel bangle; *kirpan*, a dagger; and *kaccha*, short trousers.

CONNECTIONS

Do you need guidance in your life?

Does your dream guide offer advice or wise counsel that you could use effectively in your waking life?

Gods

GODS ARRIVE IN DREAMS IN ALL FORMS AND FROM ALL SPIRITUAL TRADITIONS. As you work on your dream interpretation, consider the recognized connections you find below, but always reflect on your personal thoughts and feelings to elaborate the meaning of your dream.

Thor, a Norse god, pounded the sky with his hammer (Mjollnir), causing thunder, according to legend. Thor's hammer was as important to a pagan Viking as a cross was to a Christian.

Zeus was the father of the gods in Greek mythology, and was known to the Romans as Jupiter.

Apollo was the sun god, the god of healing, and the god of prophecy to the Ancient Greeks and Romans.

Mars was the Roman god of war.

Mercury was the Roman messenger god.

Cupid was the Roman god of love.

Pluto was the Roman god of the underworld, signifying sexuality, power, death, transformation, and rebirth.

Dagda, the father-figure god in Celtic mythology, was the protector of his people and the symbol of strength and sexual appetite.

Shiva and **Vishnu** are Hindu gods engaged in an eternal dance of creation and destruction.

Osiris was the Egyptian god of the Underworld, and husband of Isis, the mother goddess.

We are all influenced by our cultures and traditions and so the gods that we are most familiar with are likely to appear in our dreams. Whenever a god appears in your dreams, think about his special characteristics and what they might symbolize in your life at present.

Goddesses

GODDESSES REPRESENT MANY ASPECTS OF **HUMANITY,** from nurturing goodness to devouring destruction. Where a goddess figure appears in your dream, think about what qualities she represents in your life or what she brings that you lack. A goddess figure may also represent the mother figure from which all life began, which is why many of the most ancient religions were cults of the goddess.

Sibyl was a legendary seer of pagan times. She represents the intuitive abilities of women to see beyond the superficial. To dream of her may indicate that you recognize more than what is on the surface; that your "insight" is well developed.

Athena was the patron goddess of Athens, as her name indicates. Her symbol was the owl, for wisdom, and her color was yellow. In Homer's *Odyssey*, he tells of a dream in which Athena appears to Penelope to ease her sorrow and reassure her that Odysseus would soon return to her. Such dreams keep up our spirits when we are in the depths of despair.

Mama was the Babylonian goddess of dreams, also known as Makhir.

In Egyptian hieroglyphics, the *ankh* means both "life" and "hand mirror" and originates in images of the mother goddess, Isis. The ankh became known as the symbol of sexual union and the immortality of the gods. The loop of the ankh, usually painted red, represented female life blood, while the white cross below the loop represented the phallus. The ankh promises the gift of eternal life.

Mithras

THE ZOROASTRIAN RELIGION, founded by the Persian prophet, Zarathustra, in the seventh century B.C.E., is based on the worship of the sun. Mithra or Mithras was the highest of divinities to the Ancient Persians and the ruler of the universe. The word *mithra* means "friend," and Mithras befriends people in this life and protects them from evil spirits after death.

I dreamed a voice was telling me I should learn about Mithras. I couldn't understand what the word meant, so in the dream I was shown how to spell it. Immediately when I woke up I wrote it down.

The person who had this dream had no conscious knowledge of this spiritual tradition, but felt compelled to set about exploring its significance for her life because the dream felt so powerful.

Usually, the word *abracadabra* was set out in a triangle, and this was one of the names given to Mithras. This magical incantation, originally from the Hebrew *abreq ad habra*, translates as "hurl your thunderbolt even unto death." Lots of special words are used in rituals and have magical incantation properties. The Roman festival *The Birthday of the Unconquered Sun* honored the god Mithras and other sun gods and was held at the time we now celebrate as Christmas. This festival was also linked to bulls, who were revered for their strength. The ritual sacrifice of bulls, in which initiates bathed in bull's blood, was believed to give the baptized person eternal life.

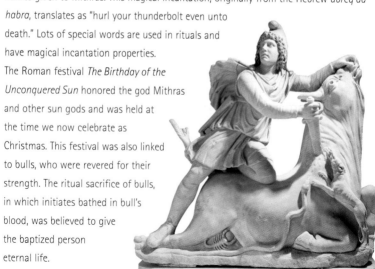

Rituals

A RITUAL IS A CEREMONY that marks significant life events such as birth, marriage, and death, and though they vary from country to country there is a great deal of overlap.

In Japan, Shinto rituals play a significant part particularly in relation to entering shrines. Worshipers go through a *torii*, which is an archway that separates the outside world from the sacred inner sanctum. Next they wash their hands and rinse their mouths in a trough of running water. Such purification rituals are found in many other religions and frequently appear in dreams where washing in some form takes place.

There are many rituals that come at the time of a person's death. In China, paper models of desirable objects or paper pictures of such things as cars, money, and food are burnt to symbolize their being available to the deceased in the afterlife.

I dreamed of long black worms. This older woman wanted me to look after them and respect them; otherwise, they would attack me. When they die I have to eat them; it's part of a ritual.

This dream describes an unpleasant ritual that is connected to the idea of the cycle of life. After death, a buried body is consumed by worms, yet in the dream it is the dreamer who must eat the dead worms. The reversal described in this dream can help us realize that we share life and death with all creatures.

Baptism

AS A SYMBOL OF PURIFICATION OR INITIATION, baptism is a fundamental rite in Christian religions. The pouring of water symbolizes the washing away of sin or impurity. Immersion in water represents a return to the original state prior to birth, followed by a new beginning as the person reemerges from under the water. When you dream of being submerged in water or being under a waterfall, it may represent some kind of rebirth or new beginning.

In dreams, baptism may be symbolized by washing away dirt or trying to clean yourself or another person.

"Baptism by fire," or dreams of being caught up in flames, may indicate purification, the burning away of what is no longer needed. These dreams represent an ordeal that must be undergone before the dreamer can move to the next level of his or her spiritual development.

CONNECTIONS

- *Does your dream of baptism indicate that you are about to embark on a new project or make a significant change in your life?*
- *Could your dream of baptism link to feeling guilty about some misdeed for which you want to be forgiven?*

Blessing A BLESSING IS GIVEN to

bring divine protection or help. A blessing may also represent approval, as when we say something like "Her father gave his blessing to the marriage," so to dream of a blessing is very favorable.

On the annual Children's Day in Japan, parents bring their children to shrines to receive a blessing for their future.

Dreams sometimes feel like blessings because they bring comfort and a deep sense of connection with life. Ella Freeman Sharpe, in her book *Dream Analysis*, wrote of this final dream of an eighty-one-year-old woman. She died three days after she had dreamed it, filled with hope and a sense of renewal.

I saw all my sicknesses gathered together and as I looked they were no longer sicknesses but roses, and I knew the roses would be planted and that they would grow.

One of my clients told me of a dream she had after the death of her mother. In the dream, she looked from an upstairs window as her mother was welcomed into a car:

Two well-dressed and neatly coiffed ladies got out of the car. I heard remarks like "You are very welcome" and "We welcome you in his name."

The dreamer felt that this represented her mother being taken to heaven by members of the religion to which she belonged.

Candle and Incense

THE FLAME OF THE CANDLE represents fire, which is a universal symbol of purification. Candles represent the light of goodness and spirituality. During the Jewish festival of Hanukkah, eight candles light the menorah, a branched candlestick. In the Christian tradition, candles symbolize the light that Jesus brought to the world and, before saying a prayer, worshippers often light a candle. Candles are used in many religious rituals, including exorcism, where the candle must be kept alight to counter the darkness of evil.

There is a superstitious belief that "corpse candles," also known as "corpse lights," appear near the home of a person about to die. These flickering lights may appear on the route the funeral will take to the churchyard. Of course, glow worms might account for this phenomenon, but what might a dream of these lights mean to you?

Incense is burned in many religious or spiritual ceremonies. In the Chinese Taoist tradition, special tiered burners are made, often in the shape of mountains, because mountains are sacred places. Burning incense shows devotion to the gods.

CONNECTION
Do you need to symbolically light a candle to bring more light into your life?

Divine Light

DIVINE LIGHT ILLUMINATES US SPIRITUALLY, just as the sun gives light to our days. Black indicates an absence of light and typifies the powers of darkness, which are in direct conflict with light. In *Songs of Innocence*, the English poet and visionary William Blake describes black as being "bereaved of light." However, dreams in which a bright light illuminates a dark scene imply the opposite. This radiance may signify a breakthrough in consciousness, a new understanding of your life and your situation.

The halo is a luminous circle, like a crown, that indicates high spiritual development. Haloes are often seen in Christian paintings or icons of saints. They represent supernatural force, energy, or mystical connection with the Creator. The electromagnetic aura that surrounds our bodies may be visible to some people in the form of light radiating from the body.

Saint Lucy is the patron saint of light, and in Sweden her festival at the winter solstice is celebrated by a *lussibruden*, or "Lucy Bride," who wears a crown of candles. This symbolizes the bringing back of light after darkness.

CONNECTION

◉ *A dream in which you encounter some kind of divine light may indicate your need for reassurance of some kind to ease your fears.*

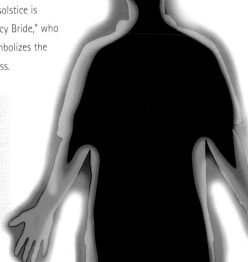

Altar

ALTARS WERE ORIGINALLY PLACES WHERE BLOOD SACRIFICES WERE MADE. We see echoes of the original sacrifices in marriages where the bride-to-be is "led up" up the aisle to the altar and "given away" by her father or another male relative.

Early altars may have been tombs on which offerings were made to god-like ancestors. Christians adapted this practice by placing relics of saints in shallow cavities

cut into the surface of altars. Also, altars were tables where communion, the sharing of food and drink, took place, and this is replicated in the sharing of the Eucharistic sacrifice, the "communion," in Christian church ceremonies.

In many churches and temples you will find votive offerings. These may be silver replicas of hands, arms or other parts of the body. The owner puts them on an altar or shrine as a representation of the part for which healing is desired. Dismembered parts of a body in a dream may signify that special attention is needed for that part or that the dreamer is "cut off" in some way.

CONNECTION

Does your dream of an altar mean you have to "alter" the way you live your life?

Temple

A TEMPLE IS A PLACE devoted to the worship of a god or gods and originates from a Latin word meaning "open or consecrated space," in which an image or symbol of the one who is worshiped is kept.

In Ancient Egypt, the first temples were funeral chapels for kings. The great pyramids were tombs to which chapels were attached so that offerings to the dead king could be made. The Jewish Temple was built in Jerusalem by King Solomon in

950 B.C.E. and housed the Ark of the Covenant, which held the Ten Commandments, the tablets of the Law of the Jewish religion. Your dream of a temple may indicate a need to find a place of safety in which to keep that which you hold precious.

If you dream of a temple it may relate to your religious beliefs, but if this does not seem relevant consider the setting of the temple. Does it link to a particular place that you have visited? Many temples are situated in places of great beauty which, in themselves, inspire us and lift our spirits.

Pilgrimage

THERE ARE MANY WAYS TO EXPRESS SPIRITUAL BELIEF including making or visiting shrines or going on pilgrimages.

A pilgrimage is a journey to grace to fulfill a promise, to ask for help, or to ask for forgiveness. Santiago de Compostela in Spain is a famous site of pilgrimage for Christians and on arrival at the cathedral there, it is customary to say prayers and to make an offering. If you dream of being on a pilgrimage, this may indicate a desire for spiritual development.

The Ganges, the holiest river in India, is said to be the goddess Ganga, "the swift-goer." She has the power to wash away the sins of anyone who bathes in her, which is why many Hindus make a pilgrimage, called *yatra*, to the source of the Ganges in the foothills of the Himalayas.

Pilgrimage plays a central part in Islam. All healthy adult Muslims who can afford to are expected to make the major pilgrimage to Mecca (known as the *hajj*) at least once in their lives.

The Golden Temple at Amritsar is a place of pilgrimage for Sikhs. The apostle Saint James is the patron saint of pilgrims in the Christian tradition and is represented with a scallop shell, a staff, and a gourd bottle. The Tendai Buddhists of Japan shave their heads as a sign that they have renounced worldly vanities when they go on pilgrimage.

CONNECTION

Does your dream of pilgrimage indicate a need to take time out to explore your spiritual path?

Shaman SHAMANISM IS THE OLDEST SPIRITUAL HEALING PRACTICE.

Shamans are usually "wounded healers." They have been hurt physically or emotionally but transform this hurt by undergoing rites of passage, initiation, and meetings with their spirit guides and totem animals. To dream of a shaman is to link with a powerful primal source of energy and spirituality. Shamans are found in many cultures, from the snow wastes of Siberia to the heat of the North American plains. Try to work out the tradition of your dream shaman. What guidance does he or she give?

Native American spiritual tradition is based on ideas of oneness and harmony with the environment and with the self. These traditions of oneness are known as the "Great Mystery" and the origin of all things. Shamanic dreaming is seen as a way of connecting to yourself, both in ordinary dreams and in out-of-body experiences. Dreaming, like many shamanic techniques, allows a form of knowledge that, in effect, processes all other knowledge.

If you dream that a human body is amalgamated with that of another creature, think about the qualities associated with it. A lion head may mean power and strength, whereas the head of a donkey may be linked to stubbornness.

When you dream of being both male and female or changing from one sex to the other, it may indicate the need to integrate both sides of your character and to find balance. In folklore, dressing as the opposite sex is linked to fertility rituals and symbolizes the integration of the masculine and feminine aspects of our natures.

Oracle

AN ORACLE CAN BE A PERSON OR A PLACE where prophecies are made or truths revealed. The word comes from the Latin *orare* and means "to request." In ancient times, there were shrines where people went to ask for help or to receive guidance. The most famous was the Oracle of Apollo at Delphi in Greece, which was originally dedicated to the earth goddess Gaia. Prophetic answers were always given by women because of women's perceived link with the occult.

Today, we can see oracles symbolically as a combination of an advice center, a place of therapy, a fortune teller's booth. To dream of an oracle may indicate that the dreamer feels a need for guidance.

Other forms of oracles may arise in dreams. These might include the *I Ching*, runes, or the *tarot*, which is a system of divination that originally came from Egypt and was named after the god Thoth. The images on tarot cards are highly symbolic and when these images appear in your dream, you could explore their meaning. The star represents bright hope and new directions; reversed, it symbolizes loss and abandonment. The justice card represents truth and loyalty. Reversed, it signifies severe disappointment.

CONNECTION

● *Do you have a request or question that is preoccupying you at present? If so, use the dream incubation technique to help you find a solution or resolution (see page 25).*

Reincarnation

Death is the middle of a long life.

CELTIC SAYING

THE DRUIDS AND THE CELTS believed that the soul survived death and passed on into another body. This belief in immortality made them powerful warriors, because they did not fear death.

In Ancient Egypt, wheat or barley was placed in the hands of the deceased and then watered so that it would sprout at the time of resurrection. The mother goddess, death and rebirth, and the fertility of the earth are all symbolized in wheat. Ancient Egyptians used wheat to represent the god Osiris rising from the dead, and so it symbolized reincarnation. If you have not experienced dreams of reincarnation, it may help to hear from someone who believes she has. Lizzie has had a number of dreams of being dead and rising out of her body. In one she says:

I float easily through the wall and am faced with an incredible sunset on a sea, so beautiful it defies description and I am crying ... More than anything else my dreams incline me to believe in reincarnation. When I was eight or nine I had a series of dreams in which I grew up from a small boy in a Victorian household. In another I dreamed of being hunted through woods in fifteenth-century Germany, as a young witch. When the villagers caught up with me they slashed me with knives in the form of a cross. Later I read that this was one way of depriving a witch of her power.

Heaven

Mutual forgiveness of each vice
Such are the gates of paradise.
WILLIAM BLAKE: A POISON TREE

THERE ARE MANY VERSIONS OF HEAVEN, and in your dreams it may take any form. You know you have dreamed of paradise by the sense of peace and wonder that pervades the dream. Heaven has many different names:

Tir-nan-Og was the land of perpetual youth in Irish mythology; it is the traditional Irish paradise.

Asgard is the home of the gods in Norse legends, and held their most important palace, Valhalla. Valhalla was made by Odin, the most important Norse god. To reach Asgard, you had to walk across a rainbow, the bridge between earth and heaven.

The Garden of Eden was paradise before the Fall, when Adam and Eve were sent out into the world.

Nirvana, the ultimate goal of Buddhists, is the state of perfect knowledge and perfect peace. The Buddha reached the state of nirvana under the tree of enlightenment.

The Other World was where the Celts believed the gods lived in a state of paradise and where men went to prove how heroic they were.

CONNECTIONS

Does your dream of heaven compensate for a period of unhappiness?

If you dream of paradise, can you link it a place you know that makes you feel wonderful? Can you make time to visit it?

Hell

HELL DERIVES from the Teutonic word *hel*, meaning "to conceal" or "to cover." In many religions, hell is seen as a place, beneath the earth, where fires consume those who have sinned. In the Jewish tradition it is called *sheol*, the underworld where the dead go. For the Ancient Greeks their hell, called *gehenna*, was a place of punishment for those who were wicked in life. The Christian concept of hell as a place of torment derives from this.

Hell is a place of great suffering and, in psychological terms, hell is a state of mind in which we feel tortured and abandoned. If you dream of being in hell it may reveal a sense of guilt or anxiety about being punished. You may feel that you have "sinned" or have transgressed some code, let down a friend, hurt someone who relied on you, or even committed a crime. Your dream hell may indicate a guilty conscience.

CONNECTION

◎ *If you see someone else in hell in your dream, would you like to tell that person to "Go to hell" in waking life?*

Sources of Reference

Ackroyd, Peter. *The House of Doctor Dee*. Penguin, 1994.

Artemidorus. *The Interpretation of Dreams*. Translated by Robert J. White. Banton Press, 1991.

Auden, W.H. "Thanksgiving For A Habitat." In *The Oxford Book of Dreams*, edited by Stephen Brook. Oxford Paperbacks, 2002.

Bhattacharyya, Pandit Ramesh Chandra, ed. *Interpretation of Dreams According to the Brahmavaivarta Purana* P.B.Roy. Prabaratk Printing and Halftone, Calcutta, India, 1970.

Blake, William, *A Poison Tree* (poem, 1793).

Brody, Hugh. *The Other Side of Eden*. Faber and Faber, 2000.

Bullen, J.B. "Burne-Jones's Dream Work." In *Modern Painters* (winter 1998): 92–94.

Bosma, Harry. "Sleep and Sleep Disorders." *http://www.xs4all.nl/~hbosma/ healing_dreams/sleep.html*

Bosma, Harry. "Vivid dreams and nightmares." *http://www.xs4all.nl/~hbosma/healing_dreams/ nightmare.html*

Boss, Medard. *The Analysis of Dreams*. Rider & Co., 1957.

Brook, Stephen, ed. *The Oxford Book of Dreams*. Oxford Paperbacks, 2002.

Bulkeley, Kelly. *Spiritual Dreaming: A Cross-cultural and Historical Journey*. Paulist Press, 1962.

Bulkeley, Kelly. *Transforming Dreams*. John Wiley & Sons, 2000.

Carrington, Leonora. *The Stone Door*. St. Martin's Press, 1977.

Campbell, Joseph. *The Hero With A Thousand Faces*. Fontana, 1993.

Circot, J.E. *A Dictionary of Symbols*. Translated by Jack Sage. Routledge & Kegan Paul, 1962

Clarke, Peter B., ed. *The World's Religions: Understanding the Living Faiths*. Reader's Digest Association Ltd, 1993.

Dante, Alighieri. *The Divine Comedy*.

Duff, Kat. *Alchemy of Illness*. Virago, 1994.

Estes, Clarissa Pinkola. *Women Who Run With The Wolves: Myths and stories of the Wild Woman Archetype*. Rider, 1992.

Faraday, Ann. *The Dream Game*. HarperPaperbacks, 1990.

Fletcher, Alan. *The Art of Looking Sideways*. Phaidon Press, 2001.

Freud, Sigmund. *The Interpretation of Dreams*. Edited by James Strachey. Barnes & Noble, 1976.

Gardner, John and John Maier, trans. *Gilgamesh*. Vintage Books, 1984.

Garfield, Patricia. *The Healing Power of Dreams*. Simon & Schuster, 1992.

Gifford, Jane. *The Celtic Wisdom of Trees*. Godsfield Press, 2000.

Goodenough, Simon, *Celtic Mythology*. Tiger Books International, 1997.

Guiley, Rosemary Ellen. *The Encyclopedia of Dreams*. Berkley Books, 1995.

Heller, Joseph. *Something Happened*. Random House, 1974.

Iyer, Pico. *The Global Soul: Jet Lag, Shopping Malls and the Search for Home*. Vintage Press, 2000.

Jung, C.J. *Man and his Symbols*. Aldus Books, 1964.

Krippner, Stanley. Paper to *Association for the Study of Dreams (ASD)* annual conference, Santa Cruz, California, 1999. (Quote, p.6.)

Lambton, Lucinda. *Woman's Hour*, BBC Radio 4, September 23, 2000.

Lewis, James R. *The Dream Encyclopedia*. Visible Ink Press, 1995.

Macrobius. *Commentary on "The Dream of Scipio."* Translated by William Harris Stahl. Columbia University Press, 1952.

Mallon, Brenda. *Dreams, Counseling and Healing*. Gill & MacMillan, 2000.

Mallon, Brenda. *Venus Dreaming: A Guide to Women's Dreams & Nightmares*. Gill & MacMillan, 2001.

Mallon, Brenda. *The Illustrated Guide To Dreams*. Godsfield Press, 2000.

Mallon, Brenda. *Children Dreaming*. Penguin, 1989.

Mallon, Brenda. *Creative Visualization With Color*. Element, 1999.

Mallon, Brenda. *Women Dreaming*. Fontana, 1987.

McGahern, John. *That They May Face The Rising Sun*. Faber and Faber, 2002.

Morgan, Lucien. *Dreams & Symbols*. Tiger Books International, 1996.

Nordenskjold, Otto and Gunnar Andersonn. "Antartica." In *Conflict and Dream*, W.H. Rivers. op.cit., 1905.

O'Flaherty, Wendy Doniger. *Dreams, Illusion and Other Realities*. University of Chicago Press, 1986.

Opie, Iona and Moira Tatem. *A Dictionary of Superstitions*. Oxford University Press, 1989.

Rivers, Capt. W.H.R. *Conflict and Dream*. Kegan Paul, 1923.

Rose, Suzanna. "Psychological trauma: a historical perspective." In *Counseling* (May 1999): 139-42.

Siegel, Bernie S. *Love, Medicine and Miracles*. Arrow Books, 1988.

Sharpe, Ella Freeman. *Dream Analysis*. Hogarth Press,1937.

Stewart, William. *Dictionary of Images and Symbols in Counseling*. Jessica Kingsley Publishers, 1998.

Van de Castle, Robert. *Our Dreaming Mind*. Ballantine Books, 1994.

von Franz, Maria-Louise. *Creation Myths*. Shambhala Publications, 1995.

Walker, Barbara G. *A Woman's Dictionary of Symbols and Sacred Objects*. HarperSanFrancisco, 1988.

Whitman, Walt. "Old War Dream 1985–86." In *The Oxford Book of Dreams*, edited by Stephen Brook. Oxford Paperbacks, 2002.

Winget, C. and E. Kapp. "The Relationship of the Manifest Contents of Dreams to the Duration of Childbirth in Prima Gravidae." In *Psychosomatic Medicine* 34, no. 2 (1972): 313-20.

Wood, Juliet. *The Celtic Book of Living and Dying*. Duncan Baird Publishers, 2000.

Woodman, Marion. *Bone: Dying Into Life*. Penguin, 2000.

Index

Acknowledgments

The author would like to thank the publishers of the books and works listed in the Sources of Reference on pages 388–389, with particular thanks to those publishers from whose works quotes are reproduced.

Picture Credits

Bridgewater Books would like to thank the following for the permission to reproduce copyright material: Corbis pp.9 (Kevin Fleming), 25 (Hans Georg Roth), 28 (Françoise de Mulder), 33 (Philip Harvey), 43 (Mimmo Jodice), 46 (José Luis Pelaez), 57 (Howard Sochurek), 59 (Anna Palma), 60 (Christie's Images), 65 (Steve Thornton), 74 (Peter Turnley), 86 (Robert Essel), 91 (The Purcell Team), 104/105 (Lawrence Manning), 116 (Craig Lovell), 120 (Jon Feingersch), 130 (Rick Gayle Studio Inc.), 144 (Michael S. Yamashita), 150/151 (Françoise de Mulder), 179 (Raymond Gehman), 220 (Robert Maass), 224 (LWA-JDC), 225 (main picture: Martin B. Withers/Frank Lane Picture Agency), 225 (inset: Roger Tidman), 228 (Archivio Iconografico S.A.), 250 (Koopman), 255 (Niall Benuie), 269 (Arvind Garg), 286 (John Heseltine), 301 & 330/331 (Henry Blackham), 305 (Stephanie Maze), 321 (Christie's Images), 322 (JFPI Studios, Inc.), 323 (Gunther Marx), 353 (Sean Sexton Collection), 359 (Ric Ergenbright), 368 (Gail Mooney), 374 (Archivio Iconografico S.A.), 382 (Danny Lehman); Getty pp.21 (Joseph Van Os), 176 (David Woodfall), 184 (Alex Williams), 387 (Claire Hayden); Sarah Howerd pp.44, 61, 71, 158, 262; The Hutchison Picture Library p.13; Johnstons-Press pp.202 (Sussex Express). Tarot card on p.365 reproduced by permission of U.S. Games Systems Inc., Stamford, CT 06902 U.S.A.

*Dreams are the language
of the soul*

MARION WOODMAN